LIFE, EMERGENT

Life, Emergent

THE SOCIAL IN THE AFTERLIVES
OF VIOLENCE

Yasmeen Arif

A Quadrant Book

UNIVERSITY OF MINNESOTA PRESS
Minneapolis · London

Quadrant, a joint initiative of the University of Minnesota Press and the Institute for Advanced Study at the University of Minnesota, provides support for interdisciplinary scholarship within a new, more collaborative model of research and publication.

QUADRANT

Sponsored by the Quadrant Global Cultures group (advisory board: Evelyn Davidheiser, Michael Goldman, Helga Leitner, Margaret Werry) and by the Institute for Global Studies at the University of Minnesota.

Quadrant is generously funded by the Andrew W. Mellon Foundation.
http://quadrant.umn.edu.

Published by the University of Minnesota Press
111 Third Avenue South, Suite 290
Minneapolis, MN 55401-2520
http://www.upress.umn.edu

Printed in the United States of America on acid-free paper

The University of Minnesota is an equal-opportunity educator and employer.

22 21 20 19 18 17 16   10 9 8 7 6 5 4 3 2 1

Library of Congress Cataloging-in-Publication Data
Names: Arif, Yasmeen, author.
Title: Life, emergent : the social in the afterlives of violence / Yasmeen Arif.
Description: Minneapolis : University of Minnesota Press, [2016] | Includes bibliographical references and index.
Identifiers: LCCN 2016008374 (print) | ISBN 978-1-5179-0054-0 (hc) | ISBN 978-1-5179-0055-7 (pb)
Subjects: LCSH: Political violence—Developing countries. | Social conflict—Developing countries. | Civil society—Developing countries. | Citizenship—Developing countries. | Humanity—Developing countries. | Developing countries—Social conditions.
Classification: LCC HN981.V5 A75 2016 (print) | DDC 303.609712/4—dc23
LC record available at https://lccn.loc.gov/2016008374

Contents

Afterlife

VIOLENCE, THE SOCIAL, AND LIFE

For anyone undertaking a genealogical study of the concept of "life" in our culture, one of the first and most instructive observations to be made is that the concept never gets defined as such. And yet, this thing that remains indeterminate gets articulated and divided time and again through a series of caesurae and oppositions that invest it with a strategic function in domains as apparently distant as philosophy, theology, politics and— only later—medicine and biology. That is to say, everything happens as if, in our culture, life were what cannot be defined, yet precisely for this reason must be ceaselessly articulated and divided.

—Giorgio Agamben, *The Open*

FRAMES OF LIFE

The query, what is life? is an arrogant one. With due restraint, this book does pose such a query, but with the following intent: how can the question of damaged life, in all its incessant living and dying, be posed as a query of the social? The possibility of answers is sought in archaeologies of the contemporary, in an assembly of locations of mass violence where such articulations could be found and which calls them *afterlife*— "afterlife" as a metaphor or a metonym that suggests life after damage.

Life, as it lives or dies, in a momentum consonant with damage, inscribes an emerging, dynamic, fluid, ever-changing explosion of relationalities on the cognizable realm called society. These relationalities, like the momentary patterns in a kaleidoscope, despite their ephemeral destiny, still manage to capture the shape of a pattern and inscribe a permanence on the universe of patterns—life in the multiple contexts of vulnerability or potential, defeat or triumph, compromise or fulfillment, articulates a pattern of the social, temporary in its duration, perhaps, but durable in its expression of the social. While the making and unmaking of life unfolds through these relationalities, so does the making of the social. This exploration seeks life in its social embedding and its individuated experience, life that is reclaimed, mediated, or disavowed after mass violence, damage, and suffering. *Life, Emergent* traces the continuation of life and its sustenance after disruptive transformation just as much as it reveals its disintegration and failure. This book thus compiles an aggregate of contexts transformed by violence, frames them in the notion of an afterlife, and suggests that, while these afterlives emerge in the contingency of the moment, they trace the destiny of life and the social.

So intended, the damage and afterlife that I explore here are in the context of a set of events and institutions. In conventional terms, the events are episodes of political violence in Lebanon, India, and Sierra Leone. I do not parenthesize the events together as similar in kind, nor do I attempt to understand a causes-and-consequences paradigm. Rather, I focus, on one hand, on the combinations of formal institutions, mechanisms, and other practices that come to bear on the event of violence in its aftermath. On the other, I explore the lived experiences that underline the affective worlds of social relationalities as well as dimensions of subjects, subjectivities, and subjectifications that emerge in that aftermath. I borrow the idea of subjectification, with some interpretation, from Agamben's association of it with the notion of an apparatus. He understands subjectification as a process that results from a relation, "a fight" even, between living beings and apparatuses; for instance, in his words, "the same individual, the same substance, can be the place of multiple processes of subjectification: the user of cellular phones, the web surfer, the writer of stories, the tango aficionado, the anti-globalization activist, and so on and so forth."[1] In the notion of apparatus that I will employ here, I will imply the assembly of practices and discourses that develop the afterlife paradigm, where subjectification is that position in which a subject can simultaneously be the place of a victim, a survivor, a bureaucratic category, a kin relation, an identity, a legal entity, and so forth. Over all, neither affect nor the formal mechanisms stay separate in the way they inhabit the realms of the social, and I do not understand either as clear and separate categories of analysis. Bringing them together is an ensemble of relations, where, again, affect certainly does not exhaust their interpretive potential, and neither do the formal mechanisms, but together, they guide an understanding of the connections among and between knowledges, discourses, institutions, laws, administrative measures, philosophies, moralities, or experiences. The social remains on the proscenium and, from there, asks and answers the question, how and what is the articulation of life? In another way, what is the nature of (re)constituted life, as it emerges in the (extra)ordinary realms of the social after violent damage?

Shaping this intent of privileging the social is the prior work on social suffering and violence—this book uses that work as a foundation and places itself in that path of concern. My reference is to the body of work that has proposed that suffering is social in its meaning, experience, and representation.[2] The notion that violence and the social compose an inclusive and expanding assemblage of discourses, experiences, representations, or pragmatics, which often get artificially separated in perspectival categories of disciplinary work or in practical bureaucratic and policy concerns, is the ground I build on. From that perspective, when the social is captured through suffering, or equally, when suffering is captured through the social, the possibilities of what constitutes either and how they fuse together in lived worlds lead to a breaking down of dichotomies, not least of which are the relationships between global and local or individual and collective. When these separations are traversed, it is clear that the pursuit of the social is an expansive field that can be circumscribed around the damages caused by violence—in diverse locations or in temporal spans.

Though I ground my work here in the conjunction of social suffering and violence, I do not seek an analytical intervention in either; rather, I take their intersection as an a priori given and proceed to a temporality that suggests an "after" to mass violence. I suggest an evented-ness to episodes of violence, not to mark out temporal limits in time that will parenthesize a beginning and an end of an episode, but rather to point toward those experiences, representations, discourses, and practices that emanate from the transformative effects of that "event" of violence. This consciousness may well surpass the temporal boundaries of the episode, whether into the past or into the future—thus disrupting the idea of a chronology. Construing the "after" of violence as a paradigm, I suggest a methodological approach, an "event–afterlife" paradigm to frame in an analytic but not a diagnostic.[3] It is not the remedies, redresses, and reprisals for violence per se that this paradigm emphasizes, nor does it dwell on its effects on memory, mourning, trauma, healing, or coping alone, although all of these populate the registers of an afterlife. Rather, this approach identifies the preceding as part of an inclusive assemblage that comes into being in the contingencies of life and a social transformed by violence. It is in this transformed and transforming arena that an "afterlife" emerges, where the event certainly remains as an iterative presence, but more so, it grounds the potential of how life, the social, and their interplay will now be constituted.

Though social suffering finds increasing recognition and analytical clarity, the framing of an "afterlife" (whether in its terms of social policy or in the discourses of experience and representation) is yet not too coherent a frame. As an initiating set of ideas that can set the milieu for the arguments made throughout the discussions in this and the following chapters, I turn to the outlines of social recovery so far available through the discourse that anchors social suffering, especially the set of arguments initiated by Veena Das, Arthur Kleinman, and their collaborators.[4] The various instantiations of recovery are often about how "communities 'cope' with—endure, work through, break apart under, transcend—both traumatic violence and other more insidious forms of social suffering."[5] Reiterating the fact that the notions of violence, suffering, coping, and healing are not separate registers but "fibers" that twist one on another, Das et al. mention the following:

> (a) relation between collective and individual memory; (b) creation of alternate public spheres for articulating and recounting experiences silenced by officially sanctioned narratives; (c) retrieval of voice in the face of recalcitrance of tragedy; (d) meaning of healing and return to the everyday.
> ... The project of re-creating "normality" seems to engage the survivors of collective tragedies in, on the one hand, creating a public space in which experience of victim and survivor can not only be represented but also be molded, and, on the other, engaging in repair of relationships in the deep recesses of family, neighborhood and community.[6]

In the contexts that I elaborate in the following—Sierra Leone, India, and Lebanon—each interweaves to extract differing textures in different afterlives. Collective and individual memories and remembrances; public spheres and publics that manifest official and other experiences and narratives; acts of articulation and their founding in voice; the emergence of relationships, some of which repair and reconcile old ones and others that discover new ones—all of these appear in a realm of recovery. The implied tone in these fibers is indeed of coping—an active engagement with a return to "normality" however altered, and a sense of healing—which remains part of the contexts I elaborate. Moving beyond, I do not suggest developing a sense of how social life returns to those conditions prior to the devastation, nor do I suggest an emphasis on how conditions of life achieve a "successful" negotiation with the devastation caused by the violence through arenas of justice, forgiveness, reconciliation, and so forth. Rather, my framing begins by leaving out those interpretations of the social that suggest a clear notion of ethical consequence, a distinct traversing of a specific "real time" of violence and the consequent successes and failures. Instead, it includes the continuation of social life where the duration of violence does not suggest a beginning or an end but rather indicates an ongoing transformation and acknowledgment of devastation and damage. Paying heed to the registers of social recovery, but moving on, the framing proceeds to explore and evaluate the experiences, representations, discourses, and practices that come to bear on that duration of an afterlife.[7]

The questions and issues that are developed in this book, the contexts I have chosen for discussion and the conceptual framework I have applied, indicate a negotiation with a body of ascendant research in the human sciences—humanitarianisms and the family of issues that they connect—such as law, rights, and justice mechanisms; professional humanitarian activity in nongovernmental organizations or community work; state policy and practice; aid, recovery, and rehabilitation operations alongside issues of memory, forgiveness, or compassion, to list a few. Alongside these goals that aim at equitable society, humanitarianisms are also about the interplay of power with ethical responsibility. In aftermaths of mass violence, where humanitarian intent and activity involve salvaging lives and communities, with either emergency or long-term aid, clearly the question of life is central, as is the social world in which those operations are applied. Keeping humanitarian discourse and practice as part of the discursive milieu, the chapters unpack what remains silent or unsaid within or what remains outside and suppressed in those discourses and practices. Like suffering, humanitarian activity aimed at its alleviation can also be approached through clinical separations of disciplinary perspectives, for instance, keeping social or individual affective representations separate from the legal regimes of justice or keeping the political economy of rights separate from its affective economies. Once again, it is in exploring multiple contexts that the messy combination of institutional strategies, social worlds, and individual experiences show overlap and resonance. At the same time, these multiple contexts show that life pursued in the spectrum from sustenance to denial and in forms yet to be found finds expression in realms outside and in addition to what humanitarianisms, in genealogy, theory and practice, have set in current agenda.

To reiterate, afterlife is not just about consequence or effect; it is about vulnerability as much as it is about potential. It intertwines time with space, history with place, futures with location. It implies individual people, citizens, and communities; it involves the contours of a nation or of transnational communities; it could as well implicate local occurrence as it can international regimes of influence. Gathering together these intents, then, I develop two interrelated analytical strands. First, I decipher a notion of how a social can be proposed and framed as suited to the particular conditions of afterlife, and second, I trace a notion of life that can find form and embodiment in that social. In the former, I imply an understanding of *pathos,* and in the latter, I use an application of the idea of *bios*—both are amplified in what follows.

Using these two analytical strands, I explore four different locations/ occasions of afterlife to find how each, differently but with resonance, articulates these proposals of the social and their forms of life. These locations, as mentioned, are the civil wars in Sierra Leone; the Gujarat violence and the Sikh Carnage in India; and, finally, the civil wars in Lebanon. Each enunciates a particular afterlife, and their combined exploration suggests both an empirical and an analytical depth to the themes of life and the social in the contemporary. Moreover, the list of locations is meant to be an exercise not in conventional comparison but rather as singular contexts, each of which resonates with the others but together reach toward the larger query posed here. While the choice and list of locations may conjure up a sense of comparison, I will persist in their inability to be compared with reference to common theoretical parameters; rather, I pursue a sense of how, in fact, the (re)formulation of damaged life and its social requires a processing of possibilities and potentials. I am persuaded that assembling that diversity, though not exhaustive, underlines the necessity to place a query for life (and the social) in a multiplicity precisely because there must be no standardizing analysis of what suffering entails in an afterlife. In effect, it is the mutual unfolding of life and the social in multiple locations of afterlives that shows how differing contexts of violence can enunciate themes that dominate the making of *that* life and in *that* social. As I will elaborate, the epistemological approach here, too, is a reflection of this intention, and through what I call the *event–afterlife paradigm,* I do not seek to secure a uniformity but rather substantiate form with varying content. Overall, this suggests that the life query, in its very nature, has to be explored in both the extant and the potential. The separate instances in this book thus understand the empirical as inherently a statement on the plural.

That plural is also the reflection of an ongoing journey that started with my doctoral work in postwar Lebanon, a part of which appears as a chapter here. More than a decade or so since the time of that fieldwork, I have moved my work on to other contexts of violence with other research agendas. Through that time, the problem that condensed itself through the various concerns and issues of violence was how the idea of life, and the social in which it can be lived, comes to be hurtled into consciousness and experience at the time of its greatest threat. Over the threshold that recognizes a transition from devastation and into a consciousness of what now seems transformed, the inextricably knotted realm of discourses, practices, and experiences appears as that complexity that has bearing on how life can be led. In reading these contexts, I unravel some of these knots to see how it may be possible to decipher responses to the problem of life and the social. I privilege the responses that emerge in a list of themes—as law, justice, community, and identity—one in each location, as outlined in the following.

This introduction, "Afterlife: Violence, the Social, and Life," poses the overall problem in its theoretical precedents and anchors. Chapter 1, "The International Social: Humanity, Crime, and Law in Sierra Leone," bases itself on the civil wars in Sierra Leone, which lasted for more than eleven years, through the 1990s. In that chapter, I follow the establishment and workings of the Special Court of Sierra Leone in Freetown, the first hybrid court of its nature constituted with the mandate of the International Criminal Court. In the work of that court, I explore the convictions made for the first time in international criminal law, under international humanitarian regimes. I read one such new "crime against humanity" that the court codifies—child conscription. Delving into what makes for the meaning of humanity in "crimes against" it, I trace the inscription of formal humanitarian discourse and practice in the making of law. I suggest that an international emotional response to suffering finds its professionalized expression in law when it locates that suffering in the figure of violated childhood—channeling a sense of protected humanity through that figure. The making of international law in this case assembles what I call an *international social*, through which a universalized notion of life, actualized in the shape of a protected child, comes to be.

Chapter 2, "Compassionate Citizenship: Nyayagrah, Gandhi, and Justice in Gujarat," moves to some months of violence during 2002 in the state of Gujarat, West India, that were associated with the burning of train compartments carrying Hindu pilgrims in a town called Godhra. The unleashing of unprecedented violence across the state against Muslims is a well-documented occasion of "communal" violence in recent times in India. However, the afterlife that I visit here is the making of a "justice movement" called Nyayagrah, which is currently gaining some subterranean ground in the state but has not seen any academic reflection. Following Gandhian principles drawn from the anticolonial movement Satyagraha, but reincarnated in current India, Nyayagrah insists on claiming democratic citizenship through the process of legal redress. A collective of empathy manifests the assembly of a social, which is generated from within the locale of suffering. Their articulation of citizen life as an aspiration, imagined through a claim to justice, is the afterlife that I emphasize here. When relating these movements to the concerns discussed in the context of Sierra Leone, some issues appear compelling. In international humanitarian regimes, the matter of who will decide about who can and will be saved is a well-argued critique of power, even when it is worked through law. In Gujarat, when a well-rehearsed justice mechanism like a truth and reconciliation commission cannot be activated, as this is not a transitory regime, the question of how justice can be imagined in the face of state-endorsed hostility becomes significant. Second, and in consequence, when an international social cannot be constituted in the face of national sovereign immunity, local collectives like that of the Nyayagrah movement suggest a sense of egalitarian compassion between the saviors and the saved, which delivers another intonation of how power is deployed in afterlives.

Chapter 3, "Wounding Attachment: Suffering, Surviving, and Community in Delhi," revisits the Sikh Carnage of 1984, when the assassination of the Indian prime minister by her Sikh bodyguards led to a genocidal killing of Sikh men in many locations around India. The capital city of Delhi suffered the worst onslaught, where various Sikh neighborhoods were attacked, men were killed, and property was damaged in horrific proportions. I explore the work of surviving within this community, nearly twenty-five years after the incident, and I juxtapose my ethnography with anthropological work done during the immediate aftermath of the event. Veena Das's work at the time established her groundwork for social suffering, and I follow that ethnographic thread to a widow's colony established soon after the event by state authorities and sustained by community efforts since that time. Alongside this group of survivors, I engage with another Sikh neighborhood in Delhi that was attacked, Bhogal, to understand how community experiences of suffering and survival, when explored from within, find expression. Mapping these experiences over time, I suggest that the work of surviving striates the notion of a homogenous community identity—especially when targeted violence against politicized identities appears to create boundaries around such groups. Not unlike the Gujarat context, the Sikh Carnage is an ongoing narrative of justice denied for those killed or of insufficient or no compensation for other losses. However, unlike the Gujarat situation, I shift the focus here to an understanding of the community negotiating itself rather than the quest for citizenship in a larger national space. Going against the grain of those arguments that suggest that communities, bound together by *ressentiment,* imbue a sense of political solidarity as well as succor to their members, my ethnography traces the lines of separation and those that tenaciously sustain integration.

Chapter 4, "Emotional Geographies: War, Nostalgia, and Identity in Beirut," explores a span of civil violence in Lebanon, and particularly its effects on the city of Beirut. I start with the years of civil strife commonly termed the Lebanese Civil Wars, 1975–89, to a later episode (2006) of fighting between Israel and Lebanon that led to the bombardment of certain Beirut suburbs. The undergirding motif in Beirut that has been compelling not only during the violence itself but also in its afterlife is the deep etching of an emotional spatiality. For a city (and a nation) that, in peacetime, was organized around strictly defined neighborhoods of confessional communities, the onslaught of continuing violence inscribed itself onto these neighborhoods and marked them into territorially bounded places, literally transforming the ideal of a multicultural urban space into a patchwork city of confessional emplacements, which often led to extreme hostilities. The infusion of faith-based identity and experience in the density of a city scarred by violence, the afterlife here considers emotions of lost urban ideals and anxieties of destabilized cosmopolitanisms that are made acute by the memories and anticipations of devastating hostility. Life and the social here are about recognizing physical space as an immutable condition of an afterlife—a condition that prolongs the emplacement of embodied experiences of violence in the social texts of suffering. This chapter, then, emphasizes space along with time and proposes its necessary inclusion in the understanding of life and the social in an afterlife. In that same stroke, it is also able to make some sense of how the national, the communitarian, and the personal come to have an intense relationship with space—making the imagination of the figure of life in an afterlife impossible without its sense of emplacement.

Chapter 5, "Bios, Pathos, and Life Emergent," is a bringing together of the various strands of life and the social that the concerns in each chapter have disentangled and unknotted. Laying them all down together in this chapter allows a concluding, a still incomplete framing of a politics of and in life that the discussions inevitably lead to. This then becomes the answer to the question posed at the very beginning: how does life, explored in the social, address the contemporary environment of "life" theory? As I will elaborate, this intent is posed as an engagement with the current biopolitical rendition of life, with the explicit aim of making the social as much a cadence in the making of life as is the sensing of the biological. Inevitably, this is also a question of politics, and this concluding chapter offers a reflection on the nature of politics that I would like to negotiate with from here, thus laying out what has remained so far hinted at in the discussions. These negotiations are with the work of Roberto Esposito and those philosophical positions he condenses in his notion of an affirmative biopolitics. This chapter also outlines the epistemological paradigm, event–afterlife, that I propose as a method with which to approach the question of afterlife.

Each of the chapters is prefaced with a short descriptive sketch about the events of violence that are being discussed, and these sketches are intended as references to the arguments and not as interventions into the nature of the violence itself. Together, these chapters indicate the potential of parameters that range from the global and international to the national and communitarian, the individual or the collective, the private or the public, the material and the virtual—thus listing an agenda of inquiry into the notion of an afterlife.[8] To reinforce a proposal made in the beginning, while they do not claim an exhaustive list, this multiplicity of contexts is essential in approaching events in their singularity and difference, and yet understand that conceptualizing life and the social is an endeavor toward accretion, not one that aims toward establishing universals that conceal more than they reveal. In that same intent, life and the social as has been conceptualized here may open up the possibility of what we might yet make of the social.

LIFE BEYOND THE BIOPOLITICAL

In one of Foucault's later lectures, he says that in the nineteenth century, sovereignty's right to "take life or let live" underwent a major change, to be replaced by an opposite right—"make live and let die."[9] This slight turn of phrase, but a profound change in meaning in Foucault's words, suggested a turning away of sovereign power—understanding this shift in the contemporary has led to an amplification of Foucauldian biopolitics in the direction of the latter—the "letting die," rather than the former, "making live," suggesting that the biopolitical concern today is mainly about thanatopolitics or the politics of death. I ground this book in a proposition that argues for a transference of meaning in biopolitics from a focus on the "politics of death" alone to a possible "politics of and in life." Drawing from that transference, I further suggest that a politics of and in life, or *Life, Emergent,* has its generative potential in the social, thereby opening the possibility of epistemologies other than those of a strictly biological emphasis on understanding the "meaning" of life.

Stating the problem in another way, I pose a query about a "meaning" of life in an environment altered by mass violence. I seek answers to this query in four different contexts of mass violence, and although they speak of differing politics, peoples, histories, and geographies, a common thread ties them together—they are all durations of mass violence that have provoked transformations in both social and individual life. They are also environments where death predominates and infiltrates both life and its social embedding. Posing a query of life in situations where the sign of death predominates inevitably leads to a thanatopolitical emphasis in ways that "taking life" becomes the leitmotif in the discussion. Instead, if I rephrase the question as to what mass violence does to life as "making live," I retrain my focus on another arrangement of a politics of life. In this focus, the possible answers look for what power or what forces effect a constitution of life, whether survived, lived, forsaken, or denied. I look for those effects in the arena of the social—the social here, then, appears as a double articulation. First, there is a conscious reframing and movement away from the seeming unidimensionality of the biopolitical genre in the evaluation of life—away from those concerns that tend to privilege the interface between biology, species, and power and find their conjecture in a politics of death, a "taking life," a thanatopolitics. Second, this reframing initiates the possibility of posing the social as a dimension that could support a conception of life that traces the parleys of "making live."

"Letting die" and "making live" have been Foucauldian essentials that have shown how human life has been at the center of governmental strategy through the "bipolar diagram of power over life," one pole of which is the "anatamo-politics of the human body" and the second the regulatory "bio-politics of the population."[10] Foucault's expositions convince about how life, which was once at the disposal of the sovereign, is now at the disposal of life itself, or in other words, it is in the name of life that knowledge regimes about body and population together create governmental strategies that manage or dispense human life.[11] Taking a lead from Foucault, Agamben, in his conceptualization of life, argues for a formulation of a life exposed to death, or "bare-life," or life "returned" to its biological state without any politics, as the figure of modern political life. Agamben's leading from where Foucault leaves off takes us to an overwhelming power over death (his *logos* of political modernity is the Nazi concentration camp), where sovereign power is capable of making whole populations, identified biopolitically, dispensable. Making, thus, biopolitics a thanatopolitics, Agamben proposes the Nazi concentration camp as the prototype of modern biopower over death.[12] Unlike Foucault, however, he suggests the return of the sovereign in the shape of power through the principle of law, which is capable of reducing political life into bare life by excluding life from legal protection but, at the same time, legally exposing it to death. In both, it would seem that life in its biological form presupposes what life is and subsequently also moves life toward an encapsulation in a politics of death.[13]

However, there have been critiques as well as postscripts that indicate the excavation of life beyond the biopolitics of death, and it is in that effort that I place my arguments here.[14] Thus, instead of understanding how life is defined in its exposure to death (in its expression through the nexus of biology, species, and power), this orientation is about how life is constituted in the contemporary when it is exposed to *life* as such—as it is legally constituted, economically structured, politically formed, philosophically approached, and so on, but importantly here, as it is socially lived. Hardt and Negri's propositions, for instance, mark one such movement of biopolitics away from a thanatopolitics, and this flags a crucial forking of paths, leading to two contrasting applications of biopolitics or biopower.[15] Hardt and Negri, in some contrast to Agamben, offer an allegedly positive reading of biopower when they suggest a possibility of affirmative biopolitics as the new assertion of life in the commons, in the multitude—a figuration that breaks away from state sovereign power.[16] What emerges for my reading here is an endorsed focus on the "making live" aspect of biopower, in effect, a politics of life that is generated from a power *of* and *in* life rather than a power *over* life.

The negotiation of life after mass violence is such an aspect of power of and in life, where making live rather than letting die ascends—where the power of making live, I emphasize, lies not just in governmental strategies but also in the form of life itself. By suggesting this, I do not want to say that power of and in life is in any way morally more valuable and efficacious but rather that life finds a manifestation even outside governmental power and, in effect, in the social. A double articulation will be necessary here, where life is first recognized as a social value and, second, as a value that is individuated into forms of embodiment and, in that sense, into visceral, biological carriers of life that are sustained in that social. To quickly illustrate with a brief reference to the chapter on Sierra Leone—it is the idea of life encapsulated in childhood that comes to be protected when children in war are protected by international humanitarian law. There is a persuasive communicative and affective power in the notion of "childhood" itself that emerges in the sociality of international moral witnessing of child soldiers. Therein is the power of and in life, founded in the figure called childhood in that afterlife, so as to construe and persuade a form of life. In this case, it is, of course, a codified legality and, in that sense, an affective governmentality that coopts and channels that power. I would add that it is the equal power of and in childhood that makes that form of life one that is sustained and lived in the afterlife of Sierra Leone, which then makes itself available to law. In the chapter on Gujarat, however, the arguments recognize the aspiration to transform identity into citizenship, and in effect, this is an attempt to enter governmentality from the outside, from the social. And in this social, the persuasive power is again of affect in that it is through relationships of egalitarian compassion that the transformative potential of one form of life into another form (or new) life is found. When an afterlife captures and exposes that life as a form, as that of a figure to be sustained (childhood in Sierra Leone or citizenship in Gujarat), there is an assertion of life that can claim an affirmative biopolitics. In this sense, the making live of biopolitics is articulated through an ongoing and perpetual recognition of forms of life that are to be let live or are lived. As I have proposed, and will continue to argue, these recognitions are made analytically persuasive by their affective valence.

How, then, does an inquiry into life from the social rather than only the biological look? In what contours of the social does the question of life become central? Or, in another way, how does the question of making live invoke a sense of the social? Without belaboring the point, this distinction between the social and the biological can hardly be made as an oppositional dualism or even as discrete categories. Their mutuality is inevitable as much as a social life is lived in a biological body—yet my insistence on the social is a reiteration of a social that seems lost in the discursive persuasion of the biopolitical. The turn away does not seek an alternative to biopolitics; rather, it seeks an accretion to the approaches of how life can be addressed in the contemporary. Privileging a politics of making live in the way that I do here is not about a valorized affirmation of life, nor is it a prescription for a valiant politics for life; rather, it is an analytical stance that leans toward how and what life is sustained, lived, and experienced, within and without the state, and thus not only about what and how life is dispensed with through state strategy and power.[17] In that shift of perspective, a politics of life does not mean a neglect of understanding how and what life is let die, that is to say, denied and disavowed in the business of sustaining life.

To retrace a few steps, sociological genealogies have constructed "society" (rather than the "social") as a disciplinary object of study where axiomatic propositions, constructs of form, abstractions of concept, and methodological specificity have indeed informed what society could be. "Structural" concepts such as religion, kinship, politics, and language, or "poststructural" ones, like culture, experience, the everyday, are parts of this repertoire of the sociological–anthropological.[18] While learning from this genealogy, the "life" query leaves a lingering need to take cognizance of how these notions in fact enmesh and entangle, leaving imprints on an empirical plane in ways that slip out of the cognitive sureties of sociological–anthropological concept and measure. In the horizon of the afterlife, whether as legal codifications that universalize a relation or as intimacies of quotidian life that inscribe particularities of practices, these enmeshings and entanglements appear especially relevant. I suggest the recognition of these assemblies as an emerging sphere of relationalities that find form and content in the social lay of an afterlife. These relationalities proliferate in the turbulence of the ordinary and in the banality of the extraordinary, in the techniques of local policy or global discourse, or in the realms of the public and private. More significantly, they emerge in the context and because of the context of an afterlife that draws connectivities between and among people, regions, experiences, institutions, governmentalities, techniques, and policies—all as nodes and positions that seek out and make links that are involved in the task of acknowledging threatened (and often threatening) life. These *social* formations, some of which are sustained, others of which fade or transform, express what I would understand as an instance of how human life comes to be formed in the social. The following two sections, about pathos and bios, respectively, develop these aspirations into conceptual clarity.

PATHOS OR THE AFFECTIVE SOCIAL

Glossing Aristotle's *Poetics* with a bare understanding, it could be said that pathos, which apparently remains underexplained in the Aristotelian theatrical dynamic, is still recognizable as an element of tragic drama—where pity and fear as tragic emotions semantically accompany such words as "suffering," "scene of suffering," "the moving accident," "suffering or calamity," "crises of feeling," or "catastrophe."[19] Past this translation, the ready movement of semantics into a semiotic circumscription seems inevitable. An event is played out in a theatrical staging and is enveloped by a meaning content of emotion (very particular emotions of pity, of suffering, of empathy), which is then played out in the interstices of actors, plots, and relations—the *mise en scène* of pathos. And as Anne Carson says, "violence occurs; through violence we are intimate with some characters onstage in an exorbitant way for a brief time; that's all it is."[20] This *mise en scène* induces an intimacy, a participation, an involvement, that seems to be a response to persuasion, momentarily, perhaps, but lasting in its effect. The power of persuasion in delivering that pathos is the skill onstage. But, in the way of all the world being a stage, where, not too differently, disruptive events of devastating proportions create and legitimate spectacles of emotion, and also where pain, suffering, loss, and grief, alongside sympathy and compassion, produce theaters of passion. Robert Buch portrays an aspect of what I would wish to convey when I suggest the empathetic possibility of pathos:

> Pathos, however, is not only what is at stake, in a quasi-literal fashion, in the exhibition of violence and suffering. It is also what is reflected in the reactions these spectacles elicit from those who behold them....
>
> ...But then, on the other hand, pathos is also the name of compassion. It is the means by which we relate to another's pain and by which the suffering other is recognized and affirmed as human, precisely at the point of radical crisis.[21]

The persuasive power of suffering, its rhetorical force as an aesthetic even, and the response to it of compassion cannot be undermined. No wonder, then, that Allen Feldman calls his essay "Memory Theatres, Virtual Witnessing, and the Trauma Aesthetic," to label such scenes of humane redress in the context of the South African Truth and Reconciliation Commission.

Situating an introduction to the idea of pathos, but without preempting the detail of description that will emerge in each of the locations, I suggest a coming together of affect and social relationality in the transformations incurred by violence, especially the condition of suffering. I understand this coming together as the meeting of realms of affect that are articulated, communicated, and participated in, with the concatenations of suffering on one hand and, on the other, embodied and created subjects, subjectivities, and subjectifications—this meeting, or in other words, these relationalities, takes the force of a pathos. Within these relationalities emerge the ways of acting and being that are guided by the discursive recognition and knowing of the transformations released by the violence. Some of these ways are often made available in professional or bureaucratic categories of administrative technique and policy that seek to identify and order that suffering into recognizable categories that go with mandated redress, for example, declaring whole societies as undergoing posttraumatic stress disorder and therefore requiring therapeutic governance in the shape of mandatory mental health checkups in post-disaster areas. There are other ways that lie outside those categories but still emerge from the coming together of a sociality that engages in the work of living and survival, but in ways that not only sometimes challenge the efficacies of administrative policy but even tear apart the fabric of society. History documents pathos or, more aptly, theaters of passion not just in emotive empathy in the wake of suffering but also pathos that is capable of engendering suffering—it is not difficult to trace in the very "events" I list here repetitions of vengeance, or of offense and defense, repetitive tragedies and ruptures, that imply yet another temporal motif in the afterlife paradigm. Emerging from these conurbations, I suggest, is the social effect of an afterlife, one that channels and is channeled by affect in the silhouettes of pathos.

Clearly an understanding of affect in social processes is central to the notions of social suffering, and I privilege that intervention in tracing the movement of suffering into an afterlife. Affect plays an analytical role in showing how its socialization in conditions of suffering make possible emotional arenas of social connectivity (or even *dis*-connectivity, as will be seen) that underline experience and representation in the afterlife. Often these are emotional terrains that are exchanged between individuals and their social embedding and thus speak of an embodiment of subjectivity and of subjectification. At other levels, these are emotional conditions of constituting collectivities that work as networks of relationships that engender moral activity and strategies of survival. Together, they create a peculiar sense of the social unique to the conditions of an afterlife of violence. Founding the social as such on a ground of emotional relationalities, I find its expression in an assemblage of discourse, experience, and practice; in bodiliness and transpersonal experience; in cultural representation or collective memory; in vectors of the political and emotional, which together reveal a social.

The arguments toward the pathos that I underscore, as the making of the social, are initiated not just by a reading of affect theory, as it is taking form currently, but also with an adequate understanding of pathos in its "authentic" legacy of rhetoric, which claims, communicates, and participates in, as I have said, the concatenations of suffering. Without attempting a thick comment on the idea of rhetoric, I return to Aristotle and take the following words out of his *Rhetoric* to indicate an outline of ideas that appear in the following discussions on pathos (as is their connection through their mutual place in Greek theater). Rhetorical study, Aristotle states, is concerned with the modes of persuasion. He says,

> There are, then, these three means of effecting persuasion. The man who is in command of them must, it is clear, be able (1) to reason logically, (2) to understand human character and goodness in their various forms, and (3) to understand the emotions—that is, to name them and describe them, to know their causes and the way in which they are excited.[22]

I suggest that pathos is a relationality generated by forces of affective persuasion, especially those that emanate in the life-worlds of suffering that are described here. In the empirical substance of the chapters here, this "understanding of emotions" appears in the "reasoned logic" of the pursuit of law, in the "understanding of human character and goodness" in community attachments or in politicized identities. These forces of affect are recognized here as emotion, and I turn to an elaboration of affect as emotion in ways that illuminate what emotions create pathos as a mode of the social.

To begin with, the epic battle between reason and passion that has marked a large swath of continental philosophy (if a chronology has to be marked, then the Enlightenment is the usual milestone) along with other genealogies provides the basis for what is now circulated as affect theory.[23] Affect theory, in a sense, is about making intelligible the troubled and somewhat hidden genealogy of what place realms of feeling, emotion, or sentiment have in human thought and practice.[24] One of affect theory's recent and somewhat controversial versions is *Parables for the Virtual* by the cultural theorist Brian Massumi. Although I cannot say that I find my arguments closely in that discussion, I do draw on the way he builds a distinction between affect and emotion—as he says,

> call the coupling of a unit of quasi corporeality with a unit of passion as affect; an ability to affect and susceptibility to be affected. . . . An emotion or feeling is a recognized affect, an identified intensity as re-injected into stimulus-response paths, into action-reaction circuits of infolding and externalization—in short, into subject-object relations.[25]

The understanding of affect here is as intensity or as an experienced state that is created by external or internal conditions, a state that is physiological, visceral, or corporeal, that is felt but not yet marked with recognition or intention. The coupling of a corporeal state with an intentionality and its crystallization into a recognized expressive state mark the movement from pure neurophysiology to cognition, in a way, from pure, virtual affect to emotion. A further nuance in understanding this distinction can be through a drawing out of a "social" parameter, thus affect as "prepersonal," feeling as personal/biographical and emotion as social expression.[26] This focused sense of emotion as social expression provides the clarity for me in the reading of emotion, for instance, in the humanitarian effect, in terms of recognized social expressions of sympathy, compassion, and empathy.[27] The sense of the social in these pathways of affecting and being affected brings to relief my emphasis on the social as a plane of relationalities, thus returning me to my initial proposition that affective relationalities are a condition of pathos. But I should make clear here that although all of the social is relational, the constituted sphere that is parenthesized is that of the emotional relationalities of sentiment emerging in the transformations of violence. What compiles assemblages of suffering, gives individuals or groups their positionalities, and makes them self-aware is the web of pathos. I would propose that a certain pathos of suffering, its witnessing and its alleviation, is also the indestructible, but quite gossamer (following the web analogy far enough to a poetics of representation here), web that incessantly proliferates ever growing fractals of relations, connections, experiences, and, eventually, strategies, institutions, and mechanisms that constitute the social of the afterlife.

The pathos in these theaters of passion creates specific relationalities that generate assemblies of social relations. They bring into position actors or agents, voices or silences, subjectivities and subjects, narrations and testimonies, witnesses and witnessed, knowledges and powers. For instance, the pathos in articulation finds coherence or incoherence in the efficacy of language, in narrative function, in the eloquence of silence, in the expression of grief or of mourning, in registering realms of memory and remembrance, in the moral economy of vengeance and forgiveness or in formulating hopes and reclaiming rights. At the same time, these are articulations that commit political communities; configure publics and public spheres; effect *ressentiment* and socialize suffering; rearrange relationships in society, family, and community; make populations affectively recognizable; narrate gendered experience all within or beyond given territorialities of locality, nation, or trans-nation. They are sometimes subjective articulations and internalities that slide into realms of the *anti-* or the *a*-social, such as in the realms of suicide and self-annihilation. The pathos of the afterlife, at times, becomes expressive of a sensory domain and material culture as well, in arenas of spatialized living and in emplacements of subjectified living where afterlives of violence are also inscribed into geography (twentieth-century camps come to mind). Or, they proliferate as mediatized representations of packaged suffering (a simple survey of websites of the world's most successful international nongovernmental organizations involved in humanitarian work, such as World Vision, ICRC, Child Care, or even the various United Nations agencies, is enough, replicating down to localized versions of the theme) that suggest "the appeal or dismay of images," as Kleinman and Kleinman have documented.[28] Overall, the affective effect is the insistent genealogy of pathos, without doubt, in humanitarian discourse and practice but also in the unceasing drama of an afterlife.

What seems to emanate from this spectacle of suffering, its pathos, is an inherent intent, almost ubiquitous in its essence, toward a grasping of humanity, a humanity that is dispensed toward its saving. And that humanity, I propose here, comes to the fore when it is engaged in the articulation of life in an afterlife. Robert Buch engages with this question of humanity retrieved in the face of incessant violence, in the last century but surely and all too much into this one as well.[29] I employ that sense here to show how pathos—in its witnessing and in its participation—through the persuasive force of immanent emotion, can have a place in the kind of afterlife that I propose here, one in which a notion of being human can reveal itself and in which a response to life remains occulted. At the end of it, the recourse to the idea of pathos is to dwell on its semantic sphere, actually depend on it, to understand a meaning of human participation that does not just witness and suffer violence but also retains a distance from it to command some control over it. This control has a certain grit, a certain response of life that proliferates (hence the widening of the semantic sphere) and distances itself from the suffering and devastation in violence, by its sheer tenacity of a will to live, however much has been history's ability to crush that value. The pathos that constitutes an afterlife, then, retrieves this value of life through a sense of human response, thus staging a meaning of life itself. This widened semantic sphere includes the acknowledgment and the understanding of how this pathos manages to perpetrate (manipulate the emotions, as it were) life's disavowal or its negation. The reality of pathos leading to the perpetuation of suffering on others, allegedly legitimated by pathos of another event, is often how violence is repeated. The pathos then becomes the emotional dimension of an afterlife of violence, the affective force that imbues the apparatus that directs what is implied in the meaning of life.[30] As I emphasize later in this introduction, in the making live of life, there is a power of and in life, but that does not deny the power over life as well. What becomes important, then, is deciphering the constituents of that pathos in institutions, in practices, in experiences, and in discourses—which make both life and death possible.

In this conceptual framing, then, the social in the afterlife implies affective relationalities generated in pathos. The affective realm of reconstituting life and its implications of pathos can very well measure the discursive and pragmatic distance between the self and the social, relocating the affected/affective self, as it were, simultaneously in the depths of personal experience as much as it emplaces it in relational groups. This is where we are led on to decipher the subjects, subjectivities, and subjectifications that affect and emotion find embodiment in corporeal and ideational forms. Marking the social of the afterlife as realms of affect or relationalities of emotion flags the significant transferring of the biological implications of classifying populations to the affective recognition and classification of social formations (qua populations), thus moving from the biopolitical to the social. It is from here, from these embodiments, then, that it becomes possible to carve out the place of life from the realm of an afterlife and to call it bios, sculpting as it were the two legs of pathos and bios, or social and life, on which the apparatus of an afterlife will stand. Continuing this explanation, the following section outlines the idea of bios.

BIOS OR THE AFFECTIVE FORMS OF LIFE

The "life" query ("bare life," "life itself," or biopolitics and biopower) is undoubtable in current theory and debate; equally undoubtable is its formulation in the biocentric. This biocentricity in understanding life seems to exempt any further exploration—it would seem that this unequivocality of life explains all that is possible in the realm of living, or in that same take, all that is impossible. However, Roberto Esposito's philosophical and semantic revisitation of biopolitics underlines, among other things, an affirmative biopolitics and does not endorse the overexposed reading of biopolitics as one of thanatopolitics, and this is a trajectory that I rely on in my following arguments.[31] I draw from Esposito's genre the important idea that Foucault may not have intended his understanding of biopolitics as a determined explanation that can only be amplified in a politics of death. Rather, the apparatus of power and knowledge does make possible the opening of those other vectors of life that can yet remain outside of a thanatopolitics—one such vector of life is what I attempt to elucidate here.

In laying out the stones with which the path to bios can be paved, the one about how life is mixed up with its biological determinants and how a politics *of* life then proceeds has to be an especially visible one. One way of looking at it is that the politics of life is associated with a biological predominance—as in Nikolas Rose's "life itself," which finds form in the highly medicalized and biotechnologized environment through which living comes to be engineered and governed.[32] I have already mentioned Agamben's excavation of "bare life," life whose removal from politics returns it to its (*a*)politicized biology, where it becomes life that can be disposed, in essence, by law. These analytical orientations toward understanding life and its biopolitics accept the first principle of division between *zoē* and bios, where *zoē* is the basic, simple sense of biological life, shared by all living beings, and bios is forms of life—qualified, constructed, political, or otherwise, and formed as human life. It is the latter that I retain as the initial signification of bios in my arguments here, and I propose a specific understanding of bios as that form of life that is qualified and constructed by the pathos of an afterlife, one that emerges in the life-worlds after violence. Insomuch that political violence can itself be framed within a biopolitical paradigm, the apparatus of violence can be understood as one that has power *over* life (especially in readings like that of Agamben), one that leads to a politics of death or a thanatopolitics. However, my intention is to read the apparatus of pathos as that which moves away from the thanatopolitical apparatus/*dispositif,* developing, rather, an affirmative biopolitics—not in the sense of redemptive politics but rather as the play of life extant—as the power of and in life.

Recognizing and saving vulnerable life, as the lowest denominator of humanitarian operations, is inevitably a play of that affirmative biopolitics—a political (and, now, managerial) decision to recognize (or *mis*-recognize) populations and collectives that are threatened, a decision that is made from within the apparatus/*dispositif* of policies, strategies, techniques, and intents of humanitarianisms. Needless to say, it will be entrenched in geopolitics. Notwithstanding, posing the problem of bios in an afterlife seems to urge the question, can there be forms of life, any nuance of its living or failing, where the biocentric alone cannot sufficiently hold sway, especially in the habitus of the social that the afterlife generates? How can this kind of extrabiological life be traced—in its becoming perhaps, or in the shadows that it shapes from life edifices built earlier? In another way, why does the question of life outside the biological as that which is crucial need even be posed in the problem of the afterlife?

Gil Anidjar, in a humorous but supremely potent gesture, poses the much too unutterable problem of "the meaning of life" and its currently determinate biocentric answer in the following way: "Life is old (always biological, it awaited its modern discovery as such), yet life is new (it is a novel, emergent object). Either way, life is biological. . . . However, has it always been that?" His compelling answer is about the "sacralization" of a certain aspect of the larger, undefinable sphere of something that may be life into a sign of the biological. As he says,

> Always political, this sacralization constitutes one thread or moment in a bioethical surge that has not only made this or that life sacred but has identified life (and its others), lifted and isolated it, elevated it above all. . . . More

than a religion and less than a universal, its moment remains uninterrogated as a potential and privileged realm of answers regarding the meaning or meanings given to life.[33]

Anidjar reads Giorgio Agamben's *Homo Sacer* as an embedded historiography but not an explained notion of life, which, before it was to be biological (and thus biopolitical) had first to be made sacred or had to be first separated from the profane. And in this crafting of a genealogy, he suggests, is the greatest obfuscation in the lineage of how we know what life is. Life became sacred, but we know little about how and why, at least in Agamben's tracings. Leading up to what he will call the biotheological formulation of life, Anidjar then ushers in Christianity as a vector that takes us to Hannah Arendt's *The Human Condition*.

Arendt's arguments about the triumph of natural life and of the *animal laborans* that marked the emergence of the *homo-laborans* in modernity (we are agreed by now that "life" is indeed a "modern" notion, following Foucault and the bibliography here) also marked an individualization of life, a relationship with nature and work that subsumed the political, that subverted the body politic for individualized life. It was not political action that mattered but the sustenance of life above all else, above the world. Human life on earth as the beginning of immortal life or even transcendental life becomes the sole concern and the highest good— and this was, if we are to follow this argument correctly, the doing of Western Christianity. Arendt thus writes of "the undisputable fact that only when the immortality of individual life became the central creed of Western mankind, that is only with the rise of Christianity, did life on earth also became the highest good of man."[34] The movement from here to the biopolitical is thus Anidjar's encapsulation of the theological in the biological—the "biotheological" conception of life. To cross the bridge from this to my arguments here, there is an inevitable glance at the turbulence that one is crossing, the turbulence captured when Anidjar says that the philosophy of "sacred" biopolitics needs to recognize its place in colonialism and mark the need for a decolonization or analytical and descriptive unraveling of Christianity.[35] This leads me to an incomplete acknowledgment here of the decolonizing need addressed at the universe of organized humanitarian work, as it operates today in its practices and policies, and also to locate how sacralized, immortal, transcendent life (not just life in Christianity) plays out in the social as much as the pursuit of it, the making and unmaking of it, plays out in the afterlife. But those are other projects that I only initialize here.[36] What I will retain from this argument is the elevation of life to a highest good, a bioethical value, the supreme value that I parenthesize as a value achieved through *belief*—as will be explained in the following pages.

Life as the highest good serves as the metasignifier under which all desires of lived life crystallize in the social, or in the individuated bodily (biological) carriers, as its signifieds. What remains to be discovered is the work of time and how history makes possible the chain of signifiers, the endless metonyms of technique and desire that will substantiate life into its forms. To quickly anchor this in the context of the afterlife, what metonyms of suffering and its alleviation (humanitarian sentiment), what metonyms of justice (human rights; compensations; rehabilitations and reconstructions; institutions of justice, forgiveness, and reconciliation), or what techniques of science, technology, and rationality (medical aid, pharmaceutical research, disaster and pandemic management), what futures and what pasts, can be signified by the sign of life so that its pursuits remain in honest loyalty to its valued ideal? What nature or forms of life will these metonyms become signs of? If the fusion of the biological empirical, that is to say, biopolitics in its embodied forms, *with* the elevated metasignifier affectively construed in the social will illustrate how life is to be known, loved, lived, governed, and made political around the globe, how do we understand that movement?

In developing an answer, which will take the shape of bios as life extant or life emergent in the afterlife, I foreground Roberto Esposito's notion of individuation.[37] Timothy Campbell expresses this succinctly when he explains Esposito's notion of life as bios:

> An ontology of the individual or the subject becomes less a concern than the process of individuation associated with the appearance of life, be it individual or collective. Attempts to immunize life against death give way to strategies that seek to promote new forms of individuation. The emphasis on individuation (and not the individual) allows Esposito to argue that the individual is the subject that produces itself through individuation, which is

to say that the individual "is not definable outside of the political relationship with those that share the vital experience."

. . . Rather than limiting bios to the immunization of life, Esposito imagines an affirmative bios that privileges those conditions in which life as manifested across different forms is equipped for individuation. There will be no life that isn't born anew and hence that isn't inscribed in the horizon of bios. Thus Esposito repositions bios as the living common to all beings that allows for individuation to take place, not through the notion of a common body . . . but rather through a bios that is inscribed in the flesh of the world.[38]

I rely on this precious distance that Campbell reads in the difference that Esposito finds, first between the individual and individuation and second between an individuation that augurs a *thanato*-politics and one that can potentially signal an affirmative one—to allow me to grasp the latter as the crucible for the forms of life I position here, with Esposito, as bios.[39] Reading through these propositions, I attach to them the sense of pathos as the social way of recognizing living or life as a value common to all, especially when it is at its most vulnerable or in the moment of its destruction. I am persuaded that it is indeed a "vital experience" that comes to be thrust into a reckoning of commonality and into a politics. While suffering can be socially created, I add to it the conviction that "life" appears in it stark reality of commonness when, at its moment of greatest threat, nothing else remains to be shared but the cognizance of life. I consider this cognition as a belief, which finds conceptual fruition in the following way.

When I seek to privilege a sociality, or the social, as the epistemology for life, I draw from the notion of belief as a concept that Gilles Deleuze credits to David Hume—the contribution of belief in the place of knowledge, or knowledge as legitimate belief that emerges out of the persistent association of ideas. When ice and cold go together consistently, their association produces a legitimate belief, a knowledge. Consider Deleuze's brief illustration in his preface to the English language edition of one his earliest works, *Empiricism and Subjectivity: An Essay on Hume's Theory of Human Nature*:

He created the first logic of relations, showing in it that all relations . . . are external to their terms. As a result, he constituted a multifarious world of experience based upon the principle of the exteriority of relations. We start with atomic parts, but these atomic parts have transitions, passages, "tendencies," which circulate from one to another. These tendencies give rise to habits. Isn't this the answer to the question "what are we?" We are habits, nothing but habits—the habit of saying "I." Perhaps, there is no more striking answer to the problem of self.[40]

Can social relations, external to us, be the conduits of affective experience through which life as something that is common and equally present in all be posed as a legitimate belief, which congeals into knowledge that claims universality? Can this be a knowledge that is possible only because life emerges as a habit in the social—life as a persistent association of sameness that, in its inception, suspends all other differences with others? Can this be learned through the habit of recognizing *life* as common, a recognition that can only emerge from the fact of being in a social world with others? If yes, then when faced with the social relations of violence, when life is at its greatest threat, nothing other than life emerges as the only commonality that we share. I am persuaded that we believe that it is life that we share, and nothing or little else, because of our constant association, or constant habit of knowing, that we all have something called life. That knowledge makes us believe, socially, the existence of life.[41]

Life as belief captures the essence of a metaphor that is found in its virtuality and its simultaneous actuality—where the latter never exhausts the former, but it is the actuality that leads to the impulse to desire, to imagine the virtual. I suggest this as an intuition, an instinct, a belief, and not as a concept, to mark a distance from when life indeed becomes the thrust of conceptualizing—in identity, in politics, in society, in philosophy, in biology and any other realm. Life, then, becomes the metaphor for the virtual archive of meaning of what life is, which is recognized and measured incrementally, the accretion of all that has and will continue to be its forms, whether sustained or transgressed. In making that archive possible, we do not construct the accretive qualities of what life is or is not—we do not decipher the normativity or morality or ethic of life. We, in effect, compile the ways in which life itself is constituted—in childhood, in aging, in death, in disease, in masculinity, in femininity, in gender, in community, in identity, in sexuality, in faith, in technology, and by other means that I cannot list but recognize in their possibility and potentiality. This compilation emerges from the sphere of social relationalities, just as those unnamed will appear in the potential of what relationalities remain to emerge or are yet not recognized. Violated life is a constitution of life, not its transgression. When life is violated, we arrive at the constitution of what it is—it is a basic essence that is intuited without concept but recognized and given meaning as metonymic forms of life. These forms, in the final call, exemplify the metaphoric operation of condensation, where the meaning of life can be extrapolated to all its forms, just as all its forms can revert back to the figure of life.

But the specificity of suffering makes us individuate our experience— we are, for example, the *ethnic targets* of genocide, the *queer recipients* of gendered violence, the *colored* in the racially oppressed, the *Dalits* in caste hegemonies, and we are also those who seek to stand for, be resilient toward, or even retaliate on behalf of those who occupy those forms of life. We share in the group, yet we are the individual carriers, in our biological flesh and blood the signifieds of a process of individuation that recognizes us only through our politicized social relations. In all the venues of suffering, there will be renewed individuation that will emerge from our belief of life as shared but will find form in the specificities of our political and social relations. These bodies in suffering are the *flesh* of the world (their biological and natural forms), and their *social* suffer- ing (the shared experience) makes them amenable to individuations of life as such. This coming together of bios with *zoē,* that is, qualified life with natural life, nurtures a sense of life as bios where it subsumes *zoē.* A politics of and in life sutures their separation, where the politics over life separates them. In the question of life in the afterlife, where an experience and articulation of life's vulnerability come to the fore, the recognition of sustained life as life reborn in guises or, as I have said, in forms of life recognized in individuation becomes crucial in understanding how life as bios need be proposed here.[42]

It is this sense of bios that I add to pathos to undergird the pursuit of life and the social in the afterlife. Understanding them together is also once again an expression of how each, bios and pathos, mutually influ- ences the other. The politics of and in life that emerges in the aftermath of suffering emerges as one that necessarily collectivizes the life-worlds in the aftermath and makes it social, just as much as it makes the social articulate an individuated sense of a form, a guise of life, within that social.[43] This negotiation between individuation and the social, and the affective effect that surrounds it, seems to be the challenge in understanding what life could be contemporarily. The associations that undergird life as belief—the relationalities, the techniques, the technologies, the discourses, that channel and shape that emotional apparatus of the social—I would suggest, mutually define the subjects, subjectivities, and subjectifications, on one hand, and the social, on the other. And this leads us once again to come clear on recognizing the antinomy of affect, which will take us back to Deleuze on Hume in a passage that requires some lengthy reproducing here:

> The principles of association in fact acquire their sense only in relation to passions: not only do affective circumstances guide the association of ideas, but the relations themselves are given a meaning, a direction, an irreversibility, an exclusivity as a result of the passions. In short, what constitutes human nature, what gives the mind a nature or a constancy, is not only the principles of association from which relations derive but also the principles of passion from which "inclinations" follow.
> ... But the passions have the effect of restricting the range of the mind, fixating it on privileged ideas and objects, for the basis of passion is not egotism but partiality, which is much worse. We are passionate in the first place about our parents, about those who are close to us and are like us.... But we should not see Hume's saying that man is by nature partial rather than egotistical as a simple nuance; rather we should see it as a radical change in the practical way the problem of society is posed.... Society is thus seen no longer as a system of contractual limitations but as an institutional invention: an artifice. How can we create institutions that force passions to go beyond their partialities and form moral, judicial, political sentiments (for example, the feeling of justice)?[44]

Life as belief (as knowledge arising from social belief) will have its partialities and will show them in the forms of life, the bios, I have contoured here. And the question will still remain, perhaps more in the realm of philosophical anthropology, which I can meaningfully respond to only at the end of this book rather than the beginning, what affect will go beyond partialities, and what are those artifices that can institutionalize that affect? Justice, to echo the preceding, in the social is once again an antinomy of affect. Leaving those paradoxes aside and returning to the focused context I use here (afterlife) is thus one expression of that mutual making of bios and pathos in the social. The life that comes to be construed, the bios, in that sense, also comes to be colored by what is indeed social about it, or in other words, what is the pathos in that social, which has influenced that life?

To return to an anchoring idea, this taking away of the vector from individualistic (but retaining individuated) biopolitics, the query of life, here takes on other possibilities. Alluding briefly to the chapter on law in the context of Sierra Leone that follows, the pathos that is in operation is that of a global moral community anchored in institutions like that of the International Criminal Court, which enables meanings of humanity by prosecuting crimes against it. The inscription of global humanitarian emotion into the making of international law is one such implication of pathos where social relationalities are extended from an international community to the Special Court in Sierra Leone, assembling in that operation global emotions of sympathy and compassion with localized experiences of suffering and translating them into legal categories of redress. Through this relationality, an *international social,* so to speak, manifests—one that has assembled itself in the pathos of witnessing and alleviating suffering (named and channeled through humanitarian discourse and practice translated into law). Emerging from that assembly, and in this case, through the making of law, is the embodiment of life in that casting of the forms of life that are being reclaimed, protected, or, consequently, condemned (in this case, the child soldiers and their warlords). They are formed in the shape of subjects, embodied and emplaced subjectivities as well as subjectifications, those that make the law or those that are produced by law. Framing the social as such, I am led to the ways in which this way of knowing how life comes to be configured through the assembly of the social also necessarily construes notions of bios. Just as pathos coheres a sense of the social through affective relationalities, bios reigns in the idea of life—together, they aid the reading of life and its social in the afterlife of violence.

The archives of life epistemologies are an immense library, even when it is only the catalog of modern life or its biopolitical substance that is searched. My intent has been to outline a frame that exceeds the biological to encompass what can result from the loosening of the resolute tie between the politics over life and the biological—my proposition lies in a combination of pathos and bios outlined earlier. Social/Pathos and Life/Bios are the double ellipses, the semiotic/semantic spheres that find expression in this book as the *life-social.* To reiterate, there is not much to argue against the biological as reasoning for life, which seems to proliferate in our current times into science (medicine, the life sciences), law (sovereignty, bare life, right to life), and economics (labor, circulation, sustainability), each of which sustains the putative biological principle in understanding the politics inscribed in its articulated arena. The making of life-political is subsumed under these broad categories. What remains subterranean, perhaps, but yet solidly foundational, is the accretion of life as a supreme value (perhaps devoted to the sacrality Anidjar suggests), where the work of the social is the affective recognition of immanent life as value, as belief—the pursuit of which makes an incisive separation of letting die in thanatopolitics from the making live in affirmative biopolitics. The perpetuation of the social requires this force of making live, and no other circumstance makes that more acute than in the afterlife, when life and the social both are threatened sometimes to the point of annihilation. Even bare life—the alleged politically stripped life—is not bare life in the work of time, in the work of knowing. The death of bare life lives, literally, in the pathos of witnessing, of acknowledgment, and most of all, in the archive of suffering. This is the archive that fuels the passions for making live—whatever focus they choose in the spectrum of life made valuable—as rights to the vulnerable, as creations of the human and humane, as laws of protected life, and even as reasons to violate life, to perpetuate the unmaking of life. This archive, in cataloging the various forms it may take, also includes not just saved lives but feasible lives, or in other words, life that can be lived and sustained in and by the social that values, or simply sustains, that feasibility.

Life as a derivative of bios and social relationalities as a derivative of pathos together contour the paradigm of the life-social in the afterlife. As I elaborate in each of the chapters of this volume, I seek out the derivatives of bios and pathos, the traces of life and social—not as empirically separate realms but as analytically useful heuristic devices that make sense in the afterlife. Each chapter highlights the diffusion or fusion of one and the other or both in the assemblage of the emerging afterlives. The emphasis is to show how each attempt at the articulation of life, crafted through bios and pathos, in effect makes for the crystallization of the social. The exploratory field is thus composed by juxtaposing unusual assemblies of events and their corresponding documents and texts so as to develop a multifaceted sensitivity toward deciphering what remains unsaid or separated in the discursive and lived worlds of the afterlife. Clearly it is not going to be an exhaustive exercise but rather one that brings in new lenses on accepted practices or even their critiques. At the same time, it encounters, it redescribes or revisits, empirical fragments to construct conceptualizations that could attend to both social theory and embedded practice. With any of the responses, I do not attempt a moral-philosophical stance of explaining a distinction between the good and bad of things; rather, I use ethnographies and empirical descriptions to augment a sociological or social anthropological understanding of how a query of life and its social embedding may be followed in the afterlife of mass violence.

I

The International Social

HUMANITY, CRIME, AND LAW IN SIERRA LEONE

The States Parties to this Statute,

Conscious that all peoples are united by common bonds, their cultures pieced together in a shared heritage, and concerned that this delicate mosaic may be shattered at any time,

Mindful that during this century millions of children, women and men have been victims of unimaginable atrocities that deeply shock the conscience of humanity,

Recognizing that such grave crimes threaten the peace, security and well-being of the world,

Affirming that the most serious crimes of concern to the international community as a whole must not go unpunished and that their effective prosecution must be ensured by taking measures at the national level and by enhancing international cooperation,

Determined to put an end to impunity for the perpetrators of these crimes and thus to contribute to the prevention of such crimes . . .

— From the Preamble to the Rome Statute of
the International Criminal Court

THE SIERRA LEONEAN WARS

Sierra Leone gained independence from British control in 1961. After several years of political instability, including several military coups, Sierra Leone became a one-party state in 1978 under the prime minister-ship of Siaka Stevens, leader of the APC, or the All People's Congress, which became the only legally recognized political party. Their main rivals over the years of political turbulence have been the SLPP, Sierra Leone's People's Party. The APC regime was, however, challenged in the late 1980s by the Revolutionary United Front (RUF), under the leader-ship of Foday Sankoh, an erstwhile corporal in the Sierra Leonean Army who was ousted in an earlier attempt at a coup. They came into being with the express purpose of overthrowing the one-party government. On the March 23, 1991, the RUF, with the help of Charles Taylor, then premier and leader of the National Patriotic Front of Liberia (whose alleged interest in creating and supporting the RUF was his intent to have them undermine the Nigerian Peace Keeping Forces, who were working against his rebel forces and were stationed in Sierra Leone), launched its first attacks in Sierra Leonean territory, which started a cycle of violence that went on for more than ten years. In 1996, in some form of democratic elections (boycotted by the RUF), President Ahmad Tejan Kabbah was elected. In May 1997, however, the president was ousted in a coup of Sierra Leonean Army soldiers who called themselves the Armed Forces Revolutionary Council (AFRC). A third protagonist appeared in the shape of a cease-fire monitoring group called the Economic Community of West African States (ECOMOG), which, together with a local band of militias called the Civil Defense Forces (CDF) and under the control of the erstwhile government, was successful in reinstating President Kabbah in 1998. As violence continued between the government forces and the rebel groups, there was international pressure on the president to negotiate a peace treaty with the rebels. In May 1999, a cease-fire was agreed upon, and subsequently, on July 7 of the same year, an accord was signed in Lomé, Togo, with the RUF. Violence, however, continued, and in October 1999, with the help of Security Council Resolution 1270, a United Nations Peacekeeping Mission in Sierra Leone (UNAMSIL) was established. Hostilities were said to have been permanently controlled by January 2002. During the same time, procedures for two internationally mandated justice institutions came into gradual being. The first was the Truth and Reconciliation Commission (TRC) for Sierra Leone, and the second was the Special Court for Sierra Leone (SCSL)—the latter was the first hybrid court of its kind. In addition, the simultaneous functioning of the TRC and the SCSL was also to occur for the first time in the history of international justice mechanisms.

Describing a civil war in any context risks error of measurement by numbers, where a higher number indicates greater, and thereby worse, destruction, when arguments about the futility of measurement can well be made. Given available figures, more than fifty thousand, by conservative estimates, were killed; approximately four thousand amputation survivors are reported; 2 million were internally displaced; approximately five hundred thousand refugees are estimated; and approximately five thousand children were believed to have been turned into child combatants. If a signature need be recorded, the amputation of limbs or cannibalism would stand out from the horrific list of atrocities that describe the Sierra Leonean Civil War, which lasted for eleven years, including abduction, forced child conscription, sexual slavery, gang rapes, kidnapping, and so forth. The *Final Report of the Truth and Reconciliation Commission for Sierra Leone,* which was made public in 2004, records in detail the findings of the commission and reports statistics of the exact nature and number of the atrocities reported to the commission.[1] The *Final Report,* in addition, seeks to find the causes for the conflict. My arguments here are not concerned in any direct way with these causes or with the conflict per se, except to say that while not intending to reduce the specificities of the violence in Sierra Leone to a deductive minimum, the overall causes cited seem to resonate with the usual suspects of distorted colonial governing mechanisms that divided the nation politically, culturally, and economically as well as years of uncontained greed and nepotism among the postcolonial elite. Regional alliances with Liberia and others undergirded the violence, and not least of all, the global capitalist networks associated with the famed diamond mines of Sierra Leone are considered as hidden triggers. Of course, varying opinions debate the relative importance of any of these factors, or others.

The afterlife that the Sierra Leonean Civil War presents for this discussion has a specific focus—the workings of the Special Court of Sierra Leone and its negotiations with international criminal law (ICL) against a larger backdrop of international justice mechanisms and crimes against humanity. As mentioned, the SCSL was a first of its kind, and its creation ushered in a new justice mechanism for situations of mass violence, moving beyond the usually applied TRCs. The workings of the court in negotiating ICL with the accepted standard of crimes against humanity allow the unique opportunity to explore how exactly notions of humanity come to be negotiated with punishable crime and, in effect, brought into applicable law. As the SCSL is a mechanism that is created under the auspices of an international community and negotiates its work through international law, particularly crimes against humanity, the justice effect here, so to speak, implies an international contour. In that sense, the afterlife that the Sierra Leonean context offers is one that informs the processes of how global intervention makes possible a construction of humanity and also how that intervention furthers a sense of protected life in contemporary discourse and practice. This intervention is global insomuch as it emerges from the participation of an international community (however partisan) that decides and makes prevalent a practice of protecting humanity and life. With such a reach, this afterlife, then, presents the possibility of understanding how a localized episode of suffering can generate a global sense of a social and, through it, an articulation of life.

THE INTERNATIONAL SOCIAL

A notion of life seems implicit in the transactions of humanity, not so much as an equivalence as an assumed coming together, where the business of protecting threatened and vulnerable life will imply a meeting of humanity that needs saving with a humanity that will save. The homage to life that does not survive also calls for humanity. The afterlife in the case of Sierra Leone provides an epistemological orientation with which the notion of humanity meets a legal understanding of human life. This orientation will be secured through an exploration of international humanitarian law and justice mechanisms, the work of criminal law in these mechanisms, and the implications of "crimes" against humanity. I will argue that humanity, in legal effect, remains subservient to the supreme value of life and that inhumanity facilitates that valuation by becoming a measure of injuries and threats against life and a listing of what betrays and destroys it—effectively recording transgressions of its supreme sanctity. I will suggest that such a valuation of life is supreme because it works as the final sovereign, above any state sovereignty and in the name of which aberrations to humanity can be tried as crime and due punishment can be accorded. In the end, it will be the symbolic logic of affective legal effects, distilled from a global humanitarian sentiment, that will define that crime and punishment but, in that process, communicate a powerful notion of life as legal value and, ultimately, an affirmation of life.

I presume the discourse that an international moral community channels an intent of protecting a sense of global humanity by sanctioning international justice mechanisms, which, through their institutional innovations and expansion of law, inscribe, through careful procedure and principle, the codification of humanity into law as a norm and a practice. ICL and the International Criminal Court (ICC), created under the Rome Statute, make this kind of criminal prosecution of offenders of humanity possible. What becomes crucial in this is the legal procedure and work in recognizing a crime as one against the notion of humanity and then determining a course of punishment. The challenge I identify here is understanding how humanity indeed has been violated—in that sense determining a meaning of humanity. My arguments here take the position that the complications of the term *humanity* for the work of law are indeed challenges for legal procedure and argument. However, these complications present the potential of looking for another line of reasoning, which shows that the concern for protecting humanity is not about humanity at all but rather is more about making life appear in law. To arrive at that reasoning, the argument begins with the extant discussions on crimes against humanity, where humanity is argued for as the final normative principle in terrains of international criminal jurisprudence. It may well be said, then, that humanity works as the contemporary figure of the sovereign—analogously, like the body of the king, whose sovereign sanctity is protected by the punishment of the offender against it—as in Foucault's opening arguments in *Discipline and Punish* about the spectacle of punishment.[2] The global community upholds humanity as a sovereign, one that will, in fact, stand above state sovereignty. Offenses against this humanity ultimately justify and validate the need, the power, and the implementation of international law that criminalizes acts against humanity.

I suggest that humanity retains an instability that arises from its qualitative inchoateness and that achieves meaning only in its transgressions (as in law). Conversely, unlike humanity, which is affirmed by its negation, what emerges from the workings of humanitarian law is the figure of life sustained as an affirmed value, whose expression depends less on acts of inhumanity and progresses more on the possibility of affirming forms of life. In situations of mass violence, as in Sierra Leone, in attempting to protect threatened life, international laws of crime and punishment pitch punishable life against protected life, thus making a distinction between life that is to be discarded and life that is to be sustained. To be sure, humanitarian reason and practice apply to particular geographies, histories, and kinds of human vulnerability. However, humanitarianism works with a value of life that works as the supreme universal standard which determines how threats against it, or how its diminishing, can be measured. Once again, like all humanitarian work, this universal is neither equitable nor all-inclusive; not all threats to human life are considered threats to valued life. Yet it is just this kind of articulation of what life is to be preserved that an exploration of mass crime and punishment reveals.

Given these transactions between law, life, and humanity, the questions guiding this essay are, how does this event of the SCSL and its operations in the afterlife of the civil war in Sierra Leone bring about a particular articulation of pathos and a bios, or a social sustaining an enunciation of life? Whose lives and what kind of sanctity accorded (or refuted) to such lives suggest the making of bios, in other words, the constitution of embodied life? In creating this particular notion of life, what kinds of affective relationalities—between agents, subjects, and objects—as well as the mechanisms through which these relationalities are made manifest or institutionalized, make possible the emergence of this afterlife's pathos? I pursue the answers in two threads: first, in the unfolding of a pathos that can be read as a trade between law and humanitarian "sentiment" or humanitarian affect, which leads to what I term an *international social,* and second, in the exploration of a bios that finds what lives are being denoted and connoted by that pathos, those subjects that are produced and made into carriers of bios such that they emerge as embodied and normative figures of that constructed life. In that intent, I will show, in empirical description, the injuries that are recognized and in what groups of people, how these injuries and vulnerabilities find responsible perpetrators, and, eventually, how both groups of people find redress or punishment. It is in the exchange between the endorsement of crimes (against humanity) and the according of punishment that the technique of law produces life, both as the final sovereign and as its affirmed forms. Clearly the singular event of the SCSL makes possible a social that establishes relationalities on a global level and, in their processing of how life need be protected, projects a value of life onto a universal level.

Marking this essay as the beginning point of a scalar discussion, I would trace here the contours of a pathos that is generated at the largest level of a planetary society. We understand that from the rather loaded phrase "civilized nations" (and its corollary, "civilized law," which makes possible international law), which describes the collection of those nation-states that amass as signatories to UN collectives such as the ICC.³ We also recognize it from the more dynamic, emergent, and ethically aspiring virtual communities arising from the worldwide connectivities of global human rights movements, or episodes in Wall Street, Tahrir Square, Delhi, or elsewhere. This scale is, in my reckoning, a steadily strengthening witness for the idea of pathos that I have anchored here. I suspect that this pathos is not something that remains as an inchoate expression of contagious affect that disappears when the episodes disappear. Rather, I see this as the gradual but certain crystallization of a global pathos into institutionalized normativities, into defined publics and public spheres of relationalities, of social life, and inevitably into law.

CHILDREN, WAR, AND AFFECT

International intervention toward resolving the conflict in Sierra Leone finds a significant moment in the signing of the Lomé Peace Accord and the subsequent establishment of the UNAMSIL on October 22, 1999.⁴ The Lomé Peace Accord also laid the grounds for a TRC in Sierra Leone, which was established to "address impunity, break the cycle of violence, provide the forum for both the victims and the perpetrators of human rights violations to tell their story, [and] get a clear picture of the past in order to facilitate genuine healing and reconciliation."⁵ Brokered by Reverend Jesse Jackson, the Lomé Peace Accord granted "absolute and free pardon and reprieve to all combatants and collaborators in respect of anything done by them, in pursuit of their objectives, up to the time of the signing of the present agreement"—an amnesty that included a complete pardon for Foday Sankoh, the leader of the RUF.⁶ Violence, however, especially under the command of the RUF, did not abate despite the signing of the accord. In fact, the UNAMSIL peacekeepers came under heavy attack until the time when British troops had to make a dramatic rescue in May 2000, when almost five hundred of them were taken hostage. Soon after this, as international pressure mounted owing to the continuing atrocities and human rights violations, the government of Sierra Leone wrote to the secretary general of the UN requesting the setting up of a special court. Proceedings for the SCSL were started after a Special Treaty was signed between the UN and the government of Sierra Leone following Security Council Resolution 1315 (2000) of August 14, 2000. The court came into operation in Freetown in January 2002. The Lomé Peace Accord and the accompanying amnesties granted at the time were also recalled. Foday Sankoh, at that time, was reapprehended.

It would be important to reiterate that the simultaneous working of two kinds of justice mechanisms—the TRC and the SCSL—was a first in any context of conflict and international intervention. The TRC was in operation from November 2002 to October 2004, whereas the SCSL was established on January 16, 2002. Although the institutions hold differing mandates and powers, there has been a good amount of debate on how these two models of transitional justice could, in effect, coexist or how they could be efficiently dovetailed.[7] Issues regarding the conflicts between testimonials produced at a TRC forum with the promise of amnesty and their potential in aiding criminal prosecutions during court proceedings indicate a strand of these debates. These issues do not, however, overshadow the simple fact that TRCs are meant to function as alternate accountability mechanisms where criminal justice prosecutions are difficult, that is to say, they are legally barred or impracticable.[8] The complexities being as they are, the point that emerges out of these developments in Sierra Leone at the time is that the justice mechanism of criminal proceedings that was to unfold combined a few firsts—the creation of the SCSL under the mandate of the ICC as a new hybrid institution, "a treaty based sui-generis court of mixed jurisdiction and composition" whose applicable law would include both international and Sierra Leonean law.[9] The court was to be composed of both international and local judges and other staff. In addition, the court was to make judgments that issued convictions against three "new" crimes against humanity or war crimes. A few further details regarding the mandate of the SCSL need be recorded. The jurisdictional limit of the SCSL was to try those most responsible for the eleven or more years of violence and civil war in the nation. In detail, the statute states the following:

> The special Court shall . . . have the power to prosecute persons who bear the greatest responsibility for serious violations of international humanitarian law and Sierra Leonean law committed in the territory of Sierra Leone since 30 November 1996, including those leaders, who in committing such crimes, have threatened the establishment of and implementation of the peace process in Sierra Leone.[10]

By September 2003, thirteen indictments were issued.[11] The three main groups indicted were members of the RUF, the CDF, and the AFRC, and accordingly, there were three trials. One indictment was brought against a sitting head of state, the president of Liberia, Charles Taylor. The SCSL wound down its activities with a formal closing ceremony on December 3, 2012.[12] In all, the court tried three cases widely known as the RUF, the AFRC, and the CDF cases.[13] The work of the court, over the eleven years of its existence, has been acknowledged (sometimes with criticism within international legal debate) as having made substantial contributions to what have been acknowledged as significant advances in international justice mechanisms. In addition to being the first court of its kind, the SCSL was also the first court to have made convictions in three "new crimes," as mentioned, under the charges of forced marriage and attacks against peacekeepers (RUF case) and the recruitment and use of child soldiers (the AFRC case).[14] Under the wider rubric of ICL and crimes against humanity, these new crimes suggest that the extant law has been expanded, through due procedure, to accommodate newer meanings to "crimes against humanity" and provide the foil for my propositions on how these accrue further metonyms for the sign of life.

A crime that otherwise may already be a part of the statute governing a particular jurisdiction (here the statute of the SCSL) or its related sources becomes a "new" crime when convictions are made under it for the first time. This sets a precedent, which currently, in the case of the SCSL, has produced a body of argument, both lawyerly and academic, that reacts to this as the violation of a legal principle in criminal law.[15] The "principle" under consideration is *nullum crimen, nulla poena sine lege* (hereinafter *nullum crimen*), or "No crime, no punishment without a previous penal law." The significance of this principle has been recognized since antiquity within the structures of general criminal law. In its foundations, it remains in clear protection of individual rights against unscrupulous penal proceedings. An enormous body of literature supports its inclusion in ICL, and it has been an integral part of the Rome Statute of 1998, which mandated the ICC. The principle is indeed retained to limit the power of the judges in proclaiming criminal responsibility, especially with regard to the inclusion of "new" crimes, without due deliberation of the authoritative lawmaker, however urgent the need may be.[16] Thus, in legal argument, its seeming violation occurs when new crimes are recognized and punishment is accorded to actions not recognized as violating existing law at the time of their occurrence. This obviously sets a critical transaction between the sanctity of law and its transgression through the violation of the *nullum crimen* legal principle.

The critique against these contexts of newness documents a legal and procedural logic finely tuned to legal procedure, technique, and argument, and it displays a nervousness in admitting to a transgression of legal sanctity, which expresses itself as admonitions against legal practice that seemingly go against accepted procedure. At the same time, there seems to be laxity in this specific aspect that paves the way for some interpretive freedom in the enumeration, definition, and subsequent inclusion of new crimes under the ambit of ICL. Those less wary of the violation and who support an interpretive laxity to this principle herald this as the only way in which ICL (or any international law, for that matter) can develop, expand, grow, and become a body of normative codifications that is adequate to the task at hand. In either, the question is of the recognition of something new and in setting a precedent such that the new becomes a part of normative legal reasoning. The work of law in making these new crimes, under the aegis of ICL (and buffered by humanitarian intent), is a work that seems to continually struggle to balance the rule and procedure of international law, on one side, and sentiment or emotion, on the other. The particular "new" crime that I will dwell on is that of "conscription of child soldiers."[17] This event (and others like it), through the recognition and treatment of certain crimes and their eventual inclusion into the general ambit of ICL with due procedure and argument, suggests that the very "reasoning" itself is an inscription of affect into law. The substance of negotiation, the procedure and argument show the acute conscious-ness that, indeed, law here has taken recourse to its subservient alter, emotion, to make rational that which remains obstinate to its rationality. What, then, facilitates and makes possible this recognition? To set the tone, Susan Lamb, in her analysis of the proceedings and practices of the ICC, suggests that the "dearth of state practice to guide the ad hoc Tribunals has ensured that the definition of international crimes by the ad hoc Tribunals has had a somewhat emotive, de lege ferenda qual-ity."[18] By calling the term emotive, she thus recognizes this crucial place of affect in law.[19] She supports her statement with a further remark by Theodor Meron:

> The "ought" merges with the "is," the lex ferenda with the lex lata. The teleo-logical desire to solidify the humanizing content of the humanitarian norms clearly affects the judicial attitudes underlying the "legislative" character of the judicial process. Given the scarcity of actual practice, it may well be that, in reality, tribunals have been guided, and are likely to continue to be guided, by the degree of offensiveness of certain acts to human dignity; the more heinous the act, the more the tribunal will assume that it violates not only a moral principle of humanity but also a positive norm of customary law.[20]

The qualifying of a humanitarian "norm" as emotive underlines this sub-terranean consciousness that something other than that which makes law positive or objective has been involved in the development and making of newness in international criminal jurisdiction and practice. This outside is the domain of affect, the disorderly social pathos that enters the jurisdic-tion of ICL by crystallizing into separate responsive motifs against human-ity. Each context (like the tribunal mentioned by Susan Lamb) seemingly reveals a scene of inhumanity, a crime against human dignity, which is recognized in that capacity and through that recognition—each names, defines, and categorizes a legal precedent which is then encompassed into the ambit of ICL. Each such event and its recognition, in my argument, is a moment of pathos in creating a social relationality of suffering and witnessing (sanctioned by humanitarian intent) in the afterlife.

The issue of child soldiers is included in the jurisdiction of the SCSL under Article 4, titled "Other Serious Violations of International Humanitarian Law." To reiterate, the exact formulation is as follows: "Article 4 (c): Conscripting or enlisting children under the age of 15 years into armed forces or groups or using them to participate actively in hostilities." The identification of child conscription as a proscribed action is not unique to this court's mandate; however, its criminalization and the first conviction, as mentioned, were made in the AFRC case, where the three defendants were Alex Tamba Brima, Brima Bazzy Kamar, and Santigie Borbor Kanu.[21] The RUF judgment also convicts its defendants, Sesay, Gallon, and Gbao, of child conscription, and this judgment also summarizes most of the court's findings as regards child conscription in both the AFRC and RUF cases. I describe in what follows some of these findings,[22] listed as "Factual Findings on the Conscription, Enlistment and Use of Child Soldiers" from that judgment.

The forcible abduction and use of child soldiers throughout the years of the Sierra Leonean conflict were common to both the RUF and the AFRC. Children who were ten years old or younger were taken away from their families to be trained and used in the hostilities. After they were abducted, they were screened for their suitability for combat or for other logistical requirements of the RUF and AFRC forces. Those found unfit for combat were used in other duties, such as cooking, food foraging, or carrying looted goods. Those found suitable for combat were sent into military training. Many children died during training or were killed if they tried to escape or did not follow orders. In training camps of varying durations, children were taught how to use weapons, how to conduct ambushes, and the tactics of advancing on and attacking enemy positions. Some children received basic immediate training, which taught them how to "cock and shoot."[23] Those trained in these camps were also expected to be involved in other duties, such as collecting information from civilians or opposition factions, and some were bodyguards for higher-ranking commanders.

Male children, upon completion of their training, were inducted into what was called the "Small Boys Unit," or SBU (by the RUF), a term which came into such common parlance in Sierra Leone that the court mentions this as evidence for the institutionalized and entrenched pattern of child recruitment. Female abducted children, sometimes younger than age fifteen, were forced into sexual relations with their captors and were often sexually abused or even executed if they did not comply. Male children have also testified that they wished to be married as they had been habituated to sexual intercourse because of their continual experience with raping. There were also "Small Girls Units," or SGUs, and most of these girls, after training, remained with their captors or their captors' wives, working as cooks or in other duties.

Very briefly, what follows is an example of the military training of these recruits and eventual fighting by these child combatants:

> Boys in SBUs underwent three-part practical training at Camp Lion training base. The first part of the training involved learning how to dismantle and reassemble a gun. The second part of the training was known as the "alaka" which involved recruits, mostly SBUs and SGUs but also some adults, entering a circular structure which had a single entrance and exit. While inside, the recruits were required to cross their hands behind their backs and crawl on the ground as instructors beat them with canes. The recruits also traversed the "monkey bridge," which consisted of a layer of sticks, by walking on their hands. Alternatively, recruits were forced to cross the "monkey bridge" while holding sticks to maintain balance. Those who fell landed on barbed wire and at times were shot.[24]

> TFI-093 started fighting for the RUF at 15 years of age and took part in approximately 20 battles from 1996 to 1997 in Kailahun. TFI-093 followed orders issued by Superman to fight and kill under the threat that she would lose her own life if she refused to obey. Other children between 8 and 17 years of age also fought for the RUF. Fighters were armed with sticks, knives, cutlasses, guns and RPG's, with which they would kill children, elderly men and women, and teenagers. They also engaged in beating people and raping children, and those children who are permitted to live were forced to join the movement.[25]

Drug use, forced upon these children, during, before, and after combat, was common. The findings state,

> The RUF habitually gave alcohol or drugs such as marijuana, amphetamines, and cocaine to child fighters before and during combat operations. The children testified that after ingesting the drugs, particularly cocaine, they felt no fear and they "became bloody." The children's legs would sometimes be "cut with blades (so) cocaine (could be) rubbed in the wounds," which

made them feel "like a big person" and see other people "like chickens and rats" that they could kill. Drugs were often ingested by smoke inhalation or by sniffing or mixed into a child's food. If a child-combatant refused to take drugs he would be "beaten and, in some cases, killed."[26]

The following excerpts are from a transcript recorded from a male child soldier called to witness by the prosecution.[27] The witness suggests that he was about twelve when he was abducted, and his age at the time of prosecution was seventeen. The testimony starts with a few biographical details of the witness's life before he was abducted. The questions that follow are about the rebels attacking his village, his abduction with several other young boys, his experiences in the training camp, and his subsequent time with the rebels:

Q. You described seeing amputations.

A. Yes.

Q. How were people amputated?

A. When they placed their hand and on top they stick and use a machete knife, they cut it, and they said, "Go to the government as they want to provide hospital for you."

Q. Who said that?

A. The rebels.

Q. Why were they saying that?

A. Well, they were saying that the people were in the support of the government, so let them go to the government, the government will provide medical service for them.

Q. What happened to the other people in your village?

A. Well, the others as young boys and also the adults we are—we are too placed in a single line, you know, and they started pointing their guns in front of our mouth and they said, "Presently you're going to move with us and you're going to stay with us." So they command you in that way and they called the other commanders to come and choose their—those they like, their choice, I mean. So that we call them the SBU. They said all the commanders should pick his or her own SBU, Small Boys Unit. After choosing really small boys and the adult they said they were going to train all of us so that we would be part of them.

Q. Were there any girls in your group?

A. Yeah, there were so many girls in the group.

Q. How old were these girls?

A. Some were 12 years old, 13, some were 14, 15 years.

Q. What happened to these girls?

A. Well, these girls were taken by them. They said the girls were their wife.

Q. How were the girls taken?

A. The girls were forcefully taken along with them. We said—because I heard one of the commander saying that "this was my girl—was my wife," I mean, "You're going to be my wife."

Q. —what did you see these girls doing?

A. These girls slept with them.

Q. What else did you see these girls doing?

A. Because after, after taking me from my village, the journey continued for some days. Day and night we were walking and any village they arrived with us, they burned houses and they will loot property from houses and food, people's food was removed from various houses and they would collect these properties, and people would be captured and we would continue the journey.

Q. Where were you taken?

A. Well, from my village through this journey, when we arrived to a town or a village called Bafodia where we met another group of rebels, you know, in the village there, as their camp.

Q. . . . What did you do at Bafodia?

A. At Bafodia, when we arrived my commander started training me how to shoot a gun, you know, and also how to—dismantle some part of the roll, really, and by then I was given a small machine gun, an AK-47, the name of the machine gun.

Q. When you were an SBU—

A. Yeah.

Q. —were you given anything?

A. Yeah. I was forced to a drug called marijuana, you, for the first time in my life. My Commander lit this—he first wrapped it in a paper and he lit and he said, "smoke it." He said, "xxxx, smoke this thing," and he command—he command me to smoke it. I said, "No, sir," I said, "I didn't want this thing." He said, "If you don't took it, I will kill you." He forced—if I didn't even took it, he just put it in my mouth. He said, "Draw it," and I drew it and the thing started growing in my head.

Q. Witness, did you ever take marijuana any other time?

A. Yeah. And this marijuana purposely went—when they went on attack, you know, they will make sure that all the—they themselves, the SBU, took this marijuana. They said, "this will help you to be comfortable during the attack."

Q. What else was done while on attack?

A. On attack, like some particular mission they succeed, you know, they make sure that they burnt down the houses there, they cut people limbs and they use—force the girl child, they will use them, you know, publicly. Like my own commander, you know, he used a girl in front of me.

Q. What do you mean when you say "use a girl"?

A. Well, use a girl. He sex her. I mean, in front of me he command the girl to lie down on the ground, he took off all her clothes she wore and after taking off her clothes he lie on the girl and he used—he had her.

Q. Did you ever use a woman?

A. Yeah. I was out on attack. When we succeed on the attack in a village. I mean, my commander captured a young girl who was—who was also a 15-years-old-girl and he said, "xxxx"—this girl was small—"you too should use this girl." Oh," I say, "Marrah," I say, "Please sir." I was so—I was a young man—I was a young boy, I mean. I was so small for this, I have never done this. I said, "Please sir." He said, "If you don't do this—if you don't do this I will shoot you." "Oh please." Then he cock his gun as soon as he want to shoot, then I say, "Okay, please sir." Then he put me in a room with the girl, he said I should use the girl and then opened the door. He said if I don't use the girl, then he will kill two of us there. The girl lose her—her clothes, I mean. After taking off her clothes, then I lie on the girl. And he said, "You should use her, if you don't use her, if you want to challenge me." I said, "No, sir." And I just lie on top of the girl and after awhile then I stood up and he said, "Okay, two of you fool me," and I finished with that.

Q. Did this ever happen again?

A. Yeah, this happened also on another attack. You know, when we went on the attack, we succeed and after that he said, "xxxx, you should did [sic] this, you should did this and since you have help me, I believe what I did, you must do it. Okay. Here is another young girl again, you should use it. You should not be given to me as impotent." "No sir." I was a very young boy. "I'm small to do this particular act. I didn't—I wasn't able to sir," and he forced me to do the same act and I did it.

Q. How did you feel about doing this act?

A. Ah, really my heart was so mixed up, you know. I was thinking all the time in the bush and I also prayed to God that I would—I might survive, you know, because of this evil act they introduced to me.

The testimonial continues with details about his time with the rebels (the RUF). He describes incidents of trying to escape and displays the machete scars on his back that were inflicted as punishment for attempting to escape. His narrative for the court ends with the time when he and many other child combatants were handed over by the rebels to the interim care centers that were established by UNICEF around the year 2000, in accordance with the peace accord of the time. Although accurate statistics are very difficult to come by, a UNICEF report of May 2000 indicates a count of seventeen hundred child soldiers, nine hundred of whom were in interim care centers opened across Sierra Leone.[28] A large number of these children were in fact handed over by the RUF forces to these care centers. The mean age of these children was fourteen.

During the prosecution of the AFRC case, where convictions for child conscription were to be made for the first time, the defense for the accused argued that the indictment of child enlisting was not viable as a crime in 1998, that is, the time when the indictments against the accused were made. Though that plea was dismissed, Justice Geoffrey Robertson of the SCSL noted his dissent with arguments where he distinguished between the notions of enlisting and conscription, eventually stating that there was no clear-cut evolution of enlisting as a criminalizable offense in international customary law. Whereas conscription implied some degree of force, enlisting could be both "voluntary" and "compulsory," and thus the prohibition of enlisting had emerged only as a humanitarian rule that obliges states or armed factions in states.[29] This would imply that the relevant article of the SCSL statute is in clear violation of the *nullum crimen* principle. Reacting to the prosecutor's idea that the principle of *nullum crimen* cannot be called on too strictly, especially when the act under consideration is universally held to be a condemnable one, and when it, in the words (quoted subsequently) of the prosecutor, "deeply shocks the conscience of humanity," Justice Robertson offered a firm and finely nuanced note of dissent about how the "when" of criminalizing an act should be kept distinct from the separate question of "should" an act be criminalized. Keeping his emphasis on the *nullum crimen* principle, he stated,

> It must be acknowledged that like most absolute principles, *nullum crimen* can be highly inconvenient—especially in relation to conduct which is abhorrent or grotesque, but which parliament has not thought to legislate against. Every law student can point to cases where judges have been tempted to circumvent the *nullum crimen* principle to criminalize conduct which they regard as seriously anti-social or immoral but which has not been outlawed by legislation or by established categories of common law crimes. This temptation must be firmly resisted by international law judges, with no legislature to correct or improve upon them and with a subject—international criminal law—which came into effective operation as recently as the judgment in Nuremberg in 1946. Here, the prosecutor asserts with some insouciance that,
>
> . . . *the principle of nullum crimen sine lege is not in any case applied rigidly, particularly where the acts in question are universally regarded as abhorrent and deeply shock the conscience of humanity.*
>
> On the contrary, it is precisely when the acts are abhorrent and deeply shocking that the principle of legality must be most stringently applied to ensure that a defendant is not convicted out of disgust rather than evidence, or of a non-existent crime. *Nullum Crimen* may not be a household phrase, but it serves as a protection against a lynch mob.

It is through dismissing such dissenting opinions that the SCSL still went forth to convict many of those accused on charges of child conscription. As Justice Robertson had said, these are crimes that are as "young" as the Nuremberg Trials of 1949. In fact, while the condemning and prohibition of the use of children in armed hostilities can be traced to relevant Geneva protocols, it comes to be criminalized only with the formulation of the Rome Statute in 1998. However, legal argument finds it hard to categorically state its place as a crime in customary international law, thus generating arguments of clarification as regards differences between abduction of children as a crime and enlisting and use of children in hostilities. Notwithstanding, the judgment at the SCSL remains the first such conviction.

The inscription of emotion in the arguments for and against the *nullum crimen* principle appears clearly in how the judgment makes its final decision. However, if the affective *epistēmē* is indeed the pathway here, if affect merges into a site and its emotion and becomes local—that is, humanitarian sentiment at large hones into framing the child soldier in Sierra Leone as childhood and a form of life or bios to be protected—how do we then approach this affect as occurring within a global pathos of alleviating human suffering, of restoring humanity, of giving political meaning, that is to say, how do we make a morally convincing principle or a social norm into a legitimate politics that can become a universal in the shape of a "crime" against humanity? What politics is thus generated from that pathos that will constitute a life that will demand an exchange between the universal of humanity, on one hand, and the localized transgressions of life, on the other? The crux, it seems, lies in this movement between the local and the universal political.

In view of the legal reasoning that I have parenthesized from the SCSL proceedings, I return, in the following, to the questions that initiated this essay, on how the social here comes to construe the notion of bios and pathos in this afterlife. First, what is the implication of humanity here in forging an idea of life? Second, how does affect allow that forging? And third, what do they reveal in the arena of crime, punishment, and international law?

INHUMANE CRIME, EMOTIONAL LAW, AND
THE MAKING OF LIFE IN LAW

Crimes against humanity as a phrase, it is largely agreed, entered the international legal order with the Nuremberg Charter of 1946, where it is listed alongside *war crimes* and *crimes against peace*. Almost five decades later, the 1998 Rome Statute of the ICC became the second most powerful notification of this list, which remains the same, except for the addition of the crime of genocide. What seems to continue to intrigue and challenge within this discourse is the idea of "humanity" and its implications within the legal ambit of "crimes" that could be committed against this "idea," so to speak.[30]

In terms of the construction of what humanity is, such that crimes against it may be committed, Norman Geras,[31] culling from a variety of deliberations on the matter, understands "humanity" under a dual classification—humanity as "the human race or mankind as a whole" and as referring to "a certain quality of behavior," or "human sentiment," "covering some or all of kindness, benevolence, compassion, philanthropy, and, indeed, humaneness." With regard to the first, he tabulates the following: "diminishing the human race," "threatening the peace and security of mankind," "breaching the sovereign authority of humankind," "shocking the conscience of humankind," "threatening the existence of humankind," and "all humankind are the victims." In terms of the second, he names "inhumane acts," "grave or 'inhuman' acts," "acts against the human status or condition," and "genocidal acts."[32] Running some risk of oversimplification, I read the preceding and similar as fundamentally understanding crime rather than the idea of humanity. In looking for that in humanity that can be injured and naming that as a quality of humanity, we attempt to understand humanity by its transgressions.

Without diminishing the skill of insight, or argument by fine casuistry, that would be required even to attempt such a circumscriptive definition of humanity, I find in this pursuit the futility, if it could be called so, of endless metonymic signification, invoking Lacan's chain of signifiers, where he suggests (and I interlocute very simply) that the search for meaning in and through language and words could be the endless pursuit of a desire fulfilled only by finding more associative words or signifiers where one set contiguously connects with another.[33] The endless metonymy of signifiers remains at the level of signifiers but does not cross the bar to the signified of meaning.[34] Contiguity by association is the kind of meaning that the preceding accretive meanings of humanity lead us to: they represent the signifiers used to pursue the meaning of what humanity could be—breach of peace, security, sovereign authority, conscience— and when they are found, they are inadequate and incomplete. "Associating" meaning with the idea of humanity represents a metonymic chain of its transgressions, where one kind displaces the other. Going through a detailed process of arguing and counterarguing the ideas carried in each phrase, Geras thus arrives at a summarized definition of sorts, which is worth quoting in some detail:

> Crimes against humanity are offences against the human status or condition, which lie beyond a certain threshold of seriousness. They are inhuman acts. . . . Humankind may also be said, loosely, to be the victim of crimes against humanity. Or perhaps not. It depends on the judgment about how

widespread and severe the terrorizing effects of these crimes are. But nothing decisive here hinges on this judgment.

That an act is inhumane is not sufficient, and that it diminishes (all members of) the human race is not sufficient for this either—though crimes against humanity are inhumane, and it is also plausible to think they diminish humankind. To be accounted a crime against humanity, an act need not threaten the peace and security of humankind or the world. *In itself, it may do or it may not.*[35]

However one argues for or against one or another notion of humanity, and especially the crimes that can be committed against it, the impulse toward contiguous association returns the pursuit of meaning to a generic inchoateness, to an unfulfillable desire, to a displaced meaning. Richard Vernon captures this inchoateness as well but hints at the crucial point that I use—this principle of humanity, however unavailable to law, remains the certain principle on which the international legal order, especially in its business of monitoring offense against it, is founded. As he says,

it is clear that the idea of crime against humanity expressed a sense of moral outrage before it became an international offense—it was wrong before a law could be contrived to condemn it. . . . The idea of crime against humanity does not operate only in a legal context. Both before and after the crime's incorporation into criminal law, invoking "humanity" has been one of the standard means of expressing horror and revulsion at acts of great evil. . . . And, since Nuremberg, it has remained a way of expressing outraged revulsion that owes nothing to international law at all.

. . . Indeed it has sometimes been suggested that it is not just legal thought, but discursive thinking generally that is unable to seize evils of great magnitude; that only poets and novelists, not lawyers and philosophers, can convey any real sense of what is at stake.[36]

Thus we again return to the seeming impossibility of defining what humanity could be (outside of poetics, perhaps) but yet remain certain about its normative work in legal thought. Notwithstanding, both Geras and Vernon move on to the question of the sovereign authority or normative principle under which these crimes can indeed be tried as crimes against humanity, with legitimate universal jurisdiction. Succinctly, it is clear that the very origin of an international order, especially international humanitarian law, bases itself on this collision between nation-state and sovereignty, and that collision will be trumped, vexatiously, by an intricate phrase, "humanity." When the evident atrocities of states, by logic and necessity, demand a higher sovereign that can offer, in the least, another forum of address or redress, then the burden of legitimating that authority has to be a principle, not an entity, as no political body above the sovereign nation-state exists. It would seem, thus, that the source of legitimation of the international order is a principle—abstract and inchoate, resistant to definition (endlessly desirable but unanchored in meaning), yet with surety and certainty of moral claim and ethical immunity and, above all, in the functioning of law, sovereign power.

What appears clearly is that any attempt at defining humanity runs the risk of overinclusion or underinclusion (more serious or less serious, how outrageous, how heinous) of the absurdity of scale (how many? how long?), of the inadequacy of pluralisms (cultural relativisms, subjectivities)—to list a few of these possible features. When these features still achieve enough coherence to validate universalism, then questions of institutional pragmatics haul in the extra heavy baggage of jurisdiction, the overriding of state sovereignty, finally, to return again to the supreme legitimation of a moral principle. When humanity does not find meaning in an endless metonymy of signifiers or in endless displacement, can it be suggested that this meaning be sought, invoking Lacan again, in a metaphoric gesture? This is a meaning where the signifier crosses over to the signified, secures meaning because its choice of language or words offers a substitution, a condensation of meaning rather than a displacement by association. Metaphoric meaning, it would seem, captures an inherent signified of meaning that association cannot: it crosses over the bar from the signifier to the signified, uniting both in a way that a sign—a meaning—can be achieved.

When Lacan suggests that poetry is more potent in conveying meaning, he refers to poetry as metaphor, as the substitutability of words that resonate the sense, the interiority, of meaning. Echoing that, the endless chain of signifiers, the metonymic displacements that the pursuit of the meaning of humanity seems to trigger, has a common, substitutable core of meaning—one that can be grasped as and by the metaphor of life, its forms and its living. It is the possible metaphor that implies the presence of a core sense in each of its metonymic enunciations. Life as a metaphor is open to the potential of as many substitutions of meaning that can be attributed to notions of humanity and inhumanity. Whether meaning is found through negative orientation, namely, inhuman crimes, or through positive orientation, namely, humane intent—both drive toward the amplification of what life stands for as a supreme value. To propose life in this way is not just in response to the lack of surety and certainty in conceptual categories or units of measure for humanity with which to codify law against it; rather, the response is toward proposing an intuitive and instinctive common denominator that does not necessarily serve as the source of morality and, eventually, law but rather serves as a belief that lies embedded in a social universality.[37] Its immanence (and not transcendent concept) is justifiably universal, but it does not seek the qualifying attributes provided by the metonymic meanings of humanity nor its historical, civilizational underbelly that courses through a chronology that reveals itself in those endless metonyms.[38] In this sense, it is the ideal metaphor where one life can reach out toward the "meaning" of life, so to speak, on one hand and, on the other, each life is substitutable by another by the very meaning of being a form of life.

It is not the highest moral principle but rather forms the basic founding ground on which the questions of morality and normativity can be debated as aspects of sociality.[39] Moralities and ethics associated with humanity become a secondary process, another level of affectivity or affect generated in this case, within the discourses of humanitarian sentiment (I will develop this a little later when I reach the workings of humanitarian sentiment in law). Geras's classification of humanity mentioned as metonyms is an illustration—for instance, "diminishing the human race," "shocking the conscience of humankind," would imply a socialized affective sense of what constitutes a conscience or what could diminish the human race. But metonymy cannot be released from contingency or from context (or the historical, civilizational underbelly noted earlier), and context will carry its own politics, so to speak, of inscription into what will indeed be the "belief" of life in a given situation. When forms of life are recognized, it will only be too true that they will carry the politics of the time. As I have said, social affect is a way through which life is recognized in its form, and this affect is bound to the pathos of the contemporary—if humanitarian sentiment is the zeitgeist, its markings, political or not, will be sure and certain on the forms of life that are found.

How, then, does this social affect of humanitarianism and its recognition of life rather than humanity find place in law? I reckon its basis in the reading of humanitarian discourse and practice as a history of emotive progress, or what I would call discursive regimes of sentiment. This is an unfolding of the terrain of affect through both time and space in ways that it influences and guides, motivates and limits and sometimes jeopardizes, the humanitarian effort. I encompass this strand under the rubric of affect, one that can produce the relationalities constitutive of a pathos. Simply stated, the way in which I propose international law to be "affected" is by the presence of emotion in its proceedings and its final codification, as I have shown earlier. An emotive legal governmentality emerges that makes possible my claim that the affective response, emerging from an extant humanitarian pathos, makes possible the recognition of certain forms of life—claiming some for sustenance and removing others from the social.

I suggest a complicity between the notions of morals, ethics, and affect that inform the understanding of sentiment, on one hand, and, on the other, the progress of humanitarian thought and institutional practice—sometimes called the "sentimentalist thesis."[40] Illustratively, the history of humanitarian discourse and practice is often thought of as a corollary to the progress of human rights—in both, the dilemma has been about what consensus there is about their constitutive fundamentals. One of the abiding debates seems to be about what implications of morality, or ethics, or faith, or sentiment account for the rising global concern and, in effect, success of the humanitarian movement as well as the apparent rapid universalization of human rights regimes. Thomas Laqueur makes his historian's answer to the same query by stating,

> Once we get past the uncomfortable irony of speaking about the "astonishingly rapid progress of sentiments" and the ideological and institutional elaboration of a "human rights culture," in a post-Holocaust age —— in the shadow of Darfur, the Terrorism Act, and so much more, we can recognize that there is a great deal to be said for Rorty's[41] claim, both philosophically and historically. We are, in fact, more likely today to have sympathy for, and even to do something to alleviate, the suffering of people and animals distant

from ourselves—geographically and culturally, in their species being—than were men and women three centuries ago. . . . Laws and norms that mandate human rights as well as the mechanisms that make their violation exigent were and are rooted in "sad and sentimental stories" even if they are at the same time justified, and come to have efficacy by other means. In the end, one needs to care in order to legislate.[42]

Following even a bare historian's chronology, which I can hardly summarize, the following listing, starting with the abolition of slavery, which most historians of humanitarianism would consent to as a beginning, through Henri Dunant's creation of the International Red Cross based on his intense reaction to the sufferings in the battle of Solferino, the various conventions and declarations monitoring the conduct of war, the treatment of civilians and the injured in war, and the regulation of weapons used, all of which add to the mandate of international humanitarian law, which, in turn, contributes to the Universal Declaration of Human Rights by the United Nations, seems, at the least, to be an adequate point of departure to argue for the progress of sympathy.

The progress of humanitarian sentiment into criminal law marks the inscription of affect into law, through the techniques of contemporary institutional mechanisms and legal devices where emotions are offered to bureaucratic management and control—as in the SCSL and ICL discussed earlier. At the same time, it articulates the pathos that makes that inscription necessary and possible. Suffering and—much more potent here—its witnessing construct an assembly of participants, a significant collection of powerful agents embedded in a pathos that unites those who appear in the discourse and practice of humanitarianisms. Horrific violence and the heinousness of atrocity are too banal (to borrow from an "infamous" phrasing), too much of an everyday occurrence. However, when such atrocity commands the attention deemed necessary by the international agents of justice—the international community (in the shape of the UN and its constituent bodies, in this case)[43]—by those who can stand guard over the transgressions of life, the pathos makes way for the bios: the bio- and geopolitics of sanctified life, so to speak. In due course of procedure, when deployed by the international justice mechanisms, bios gradually embodies itself by finding the location of those transgressions and violations in groups of people, in criminals and their victims—literally in the bodily carriers or transgressors of that intuited notion understood as life. This life is apprehended through a pathos of sentiment that sanctions the knowledge of what kind of life need be valued. It is not the biological self, the corporeal body as much, that extrapolates to classify a population (or its vectored reversal, from population to biological) but more an emotional judgment that determines what indeed is life and, in that process, both the population and its individuation. The population is known not biologically but rather affectively—the subject so produced is measured not by the markers of the biological species (or a typical racist interpretation) but rather by an emotional quality—that runs common to both the subject that knows and the subject that is known. This emerges as the function and meaning of a form of life made supreme—thus the place of bios emerging along with pathos.

I have suggested that the collision of the principle of *nullum crimen* and the event of child conscription takes place in the horizon of affect, within the crystallized parameters of the humanitarian sentiments of sympathy, compassion, or empathy—also often phrased as a politics of pity. I see the paradox in the face-off between the *nullum crimen* principle (which is meant to safeguard a fundamental human right) and the recognition of a "crime against humanity" or an "inhumane act" (which would protect rights in another context). In this judicial triage, an argument about how the struggle over which meaning of humanity, or, in my language, which form of life, need be privileged finds shape, and this argument relies on the affective *epistēmē*. While neither sentiments nor events (nor the accompanying politics of pity)[44] have been unknown in the critical history of humanitarianisms, it is their codification in the institution of law that has international mandate, which drives toward the understanding of affective governmentality and, ultimately, governance in the name of life. Insofar as these mechanisms are counted under the label of provisions that are designed to come into play after the devastation caused by an episode of war and violence, they inhabit an afterlife. In their ultimate goal, they suggest the promotion of a life, formulated through and against the condemnation of another. This is a "making live" that is at first constructed in legal procedure and judgment and then regulated through the future practice of law—thus contributing to a formulation of life as such.

The final argument that remains is to apprehend how the metaphoric idea of life finds a double functionality—it claims the place of a sovereign and, with that claiming, uses legal procedure to achieve multiple meanings of life, or what I have called the forms of life—the bios in this afterlife. First, the question of a sovereign seems to appear with the motivation for crime and punishment, or in another way, it is not that the sovereign is required to legitimate the dispensation of punishment but rather, in this case, it is punishment that calls the sovereign into presence. Punishment, to have potency, must be sanctioned by and made in the name of a sovereign or else it disintegrates into private vendetta. When state authority is no longer legitimate or the state has abdicated its legitimacy to represent the body politic, this betrayal of trust, or, in another way, the inefficacy of the political concept of social contract, dissolves the idea of sovereignty at its very core. The debates around crimes against humanity establish humanity as the principle that appears above and over: a hierarchically higher norm that can take the place of the betrayed trust of state sovereignty and legitimate punishment against the perpetrators.

What we have read so far as crimes against humanity is reiterated further as this—when a distinct sense of harm and violation is suffered, whether by one or many, combined with the necessary condition that no forum of redress is available or no authority can or will respond, the international community, the *international social* cohered by a pathos, invokes the highest principle of sovereign authority. This cannot be humanity as we understand it, as it is measured and understood only by possible transgression, leaving uncertain its stability of meaning. Life as a value commands an affective response that remains immanent, and at the end, this belief is raised to a principle of law, rather than the attributes of humanity leading to codifications in law. I am persuaded that an understanding of life as a belief is useful for a consideration of how the institutionalized workings of humanity in effect lead to constitutions of life as a supreme value in the contemporary. I am persuaded not because I can detract all the critique that is leveled at the inchoateness of the idea of humanity but rather because I rely on this belief as knowledge of life as the intuitive force that explains the human capacity to witness and respond, time and again, despite repetitions or surpassings of horror and without falling back into the skepticism or irony of already knowing what that violation is and thereby resign to nonresponse. It is also the same belief that drives its violation, the awareness that the violation of life is, indeed, the supreme violation.

Once this affective sensibility is codified in law, it proceeds to embody that life into bios, into forms of life. Unlike Foucault's description, where he shows the transition from the public sacrifice of the punished body as a ritualized spectacle of sustaining sovereign sacrality and power (where crime is offense against the sovereign) into the techniques of biopower that subjugate and control behavior,[45] I argue for a line of reasoning somewhat in reverse. I argue that legal tenet, when it deals with mass crimes, mandates that there be punishable bodies (for crimes against humanity, they would be "those most responsible" or those with the charge of "command responsibility"). The punishable bodies, in these situations of mass crime, become the figures that embody within themselves that life which is to be desacralized—made profane—by pitting them against those forms of life that are to be protected. In the technique that is generated by crimes against humanity, law, using life in the position of supreme principle, cannot define it but recognizes it as life saved and thereby privileged, or its other, as life condemned. It achieves a definition by increment—sustaining the assumption that law can only work, almost aesthetically, to provide signs for the potential meaning of life but can never construct an exhaustive classification in legal knowledge. With the recognition of a particular offense against humanity, those who commit those offenses become those discarded from the moral sphere of global society. At the same time, the victims of those crimes embody the lives that are to be protected, in the course of which an enunciation of life valued emerges.

ICL, which operates under the sign of life, does not endorse the death penalty but rather condemns a form of life and produces a particular condemned subject. In some sense of an ironic twist, the withholding of the death penalty in ICL appears to suggest that in the modality of international punishment, life is not desecrated; rather, its sanctity is retained by dividing its forms into the sacred and the condemned. Here I maintain the sacred–profane relationship in the symbolic logic of a ritual—the ritual of criminalizing and punishing. This can, perhaps, also explain how life can indeed be sacred, sacred enough to separate it from life that is profane, immoral, and unethical.[46] The affective discarding of profane life, the outrage felt against perpetrators of inhumane crime, the impulse to disavow a criminal against humanity in the universal arena, is to hold that form of life as that which is profane against sacred life or universal life, which has to be protected. The idea of *hostis humani generis,* an enemy of all mankind, was applied to the slave trader or the pirate, perhaps as precursor to the criminals now tried against humanity. This is the profane form of life that has to be discarded such that the sovereign sacrality of life is maintained. The distinction between a sacred form of life and the profane calls into presence the sovereign—the sovereign in whose presence punishment to the *hostis humani generis* can indeed be conducted.

The forms of life so identified become the replaceable, substitutable, paradigmatic metaphors for others, in other episodes, that may occur in the future and may have occurred in the past in locations already heard of or yet to appear. Its "detachment," the unleashing of its representative capacity from the local, happens as an effect when, first, forms of life are created in its localized sphere—the child here and her violators. Second, they move back, by an endorsement of exchange and collaboration with the humanitarian *dispositif* into the global arenas of international institutions, mandates, and law—completing their forms as bios. Pathos surrounds the episode in capturing life in both its hypersingularized real on the ground and its generic virtual, making possible the actualized version of what must be let live and what must be discarded. Thus the ability of ICL to render a form of life universally protected calls for the parenthesizing of specifics in the SCSL—African Child Soldier v. African Warlord (so to speak).[47] The question of the "African savage warlord" does trigger the critique against international "civilized" communities' hypocritical outrage and their questionable reification of a racial other. The fact that similarly vicious, brutal acts of heinous harm occur particularly within the realms of the powers that be renders their legitimacy to bestow universality on the racial other heavily suspect. In that tone of argument, condemning profane life against sanctified life is not an empty statement, emptied of history, or of the dynamics of historical power—it will carry the trace of who decides.

As best as the record of ICL can document (starting with Nuremberg, extending to the former Yugoslavia, Rwanda, Sierra Leone, and, lately, Cambodia and Uganda), state sovereignty has been suspended or found inadmissible when mass crimes are perpetrated. These are crimes where culpable perpetrators are so vast that no local or international court can meaningfully prosecute and try all those responsible. This is why alternate justice mechanisms like TRCs are created, where no criminality is judged but the minimum of confession and acknowledgment of offenses can be hoped for. Criminalization, or criminal law, alternatively, is effective only when specific persons can be brought to trial when arguably, in situations like Sierra Leone, there are many more than those held most responsible and who carry enough culpability for prosecution. In these circumstances of criminalization, the question of the most culpable gestures toward more than the pragmatic proceedings of law—it implies the symbolic logic of a scared-profane relationship in the ritual of international law, which produces the forms of life, the bios.

Drawing these sets of issues to a close with a recapitulation—the specific agents in the institutions generated or mobilized (the ICC and the ICL), the groupings of people and their agencies that are assembled, the lives that are recognized as human and whose protection is warranted, and the lives that are recognized as inhuman and therefore to be disavowed—these have illustrated the scope of the bios here. The pathos, conversely, has emerged from the relationalities that have been cohered by an affective *epistēmē*, by regimes of sentiment that have been generated within the global humanitarian community and its legitimating norms and practices, which buffer the sanctification of life in law and find their way into local contingency. Both notions of bios and pathos have drawn from the workings of law; they find their contours in the effectuations of reason extracted from affect, conveying and securing that which could secure an analytic of life in the contemporary. In the global reach of the illustration here, it is the impact that I will call the international social. In a simple arrangement of scale, I am persuaded that the importance of understanding afterlife in all its constituents of bios and pathos must start from the largest rubric that lends itself to analysis in the contemporary world. This rubric I have accessed here through the Special Court of

Sierra Leone, established by the international justice community under the jurisdiction of ICL as the constitutive part of a life-social that assembles a network within the afterlife of this episode. The analytic, however, steps outside the temporal or spatial boundaries of the actual episode of Sierra Leone to circumscribe universalizing intuitions of virtual life. And as I would like to emphasize, it becomes immanent insomuch as it is in the intricacies of the flesh and blood of damaged life that the actual of life is once again sought and, to the extent possible, found.

2

Compassionate Citizenship

NYAYAGRAH, GANDHI, AND JUSTICE IN GUJARAT

The fact that there are so many men still alive in the world shows that it is based not on the force of arms but on the force of truth or love. Therefore the greatest and most unimpeachable evidence of the success of this force is to be found in the fact that, in spite of the wars of the world, it still lives on.

Thousands, indeed tens of thousands, depend on a very active working of this force. Little quarrels of millions of families in their daily lives disappear before the exercise of this force. Hundreds of nations live in peace. History does not and cannot take note of this fact. . . . History then is the record of an interruption of the course of nature. Soul-force, being natural is not noted in history.

—M. K. Gandhi, *Hind Swaraj*

THE GUJARAT VIOLENCE

The Gujarat 2002 episodes of violence are widely understood to be a calculated attack on the Muslim population in the western state of Gujarat in India that began on February 28, 2002. The immediate trigger was the burning of two compartments of the Sabarmati Express a little away from the Godhra station on the early morning of February 27, 2002. On that day, the train arrived at the station carrying a number of Hindu pilgrims, or *karsevaks* (those who worship through service), who were returning from the north Indian town of Ayodhya, where they had been to participate in the initiation of the building of a temple on the site of a sixteenth-century mosque, the Babri Masjid. This mosque has been a site of immense political turmoil and communal violence in India since its demolition in 1992. The frenzied destruction of the Masjid in December 1992 was based on the belief that the mosque had been built on the grounds of a temple that was demolished earlier by the Mughal emperor

Babar during the sixteenth century. The 1992 destruction of the Babri Masjid is seen as the culmination of intentions carefully nurtured by Hindu extremist organizations over several years. The legitimacy for the destruction was made on the claim that the temple that had occupied that site was built to commemorate the birthplace of Ram, a deity of great significance and popularity in the Hindu pantheon. This site has since become the cause of immense contestation, fanned duly during periodic election phases and symbolically serving as a place for which and in which to flex political muscle by Hindu extremists. The Vishwa Hindu Parishad, or World Hindu Council, along with its youth wing, the Bajrang Dal, organized such traveling groups of *karsevaks,* who would go to Ayodhya to participate in rituals of consecrated rebuilding.

The recounting of the facts of what actually transcribed that day has been produced by a number of sources, which include civil society and citizen's initiatives, journalists, filmmakers and writers, and government-initiated inquiry commissions. The common threads begin with the karsevaks indulging in provocative behavior with the Muslim vendors on the platform and ends with two compartments of the train being engulfed in flames, resulting in the horrific death of fifty-eight people in coach 6, who were trapped by the raging fire. One burn victim died later, bringing the death count to fifty-nine. The instated inquiry commissions—the Nanavati Inquiry Commission and the Banerjee Inquiry Commission (BIC)—offered competing official versions of the fire, where the latter, in 2004, submitted that the fire was an accident, whereas the former, in 2008, held that it was premeditated. The Gujarat government discredited the BIC report. From February 28, 2002, for a period of three continuous days in Ahmedabad and continuing over months in that city and in other areas of the state, a pogrom of killing and mayhem ensued, targeting the Muslim population.

Calculating damage in these pogroms once again runs into the absurdity of numbers. An estimated twenty-five hundred men, women, and children were killed (official figures are around two hundred); approximately two hundred thousand were rendered destitute and homeless; homes, private property, and farmlands numbering around three hundred thousand were destroyed; business establishments were plundered and destroyed; and religious structures were razed. Images of burning alive were widely circulated; gang rapes and gruesome attacks were the mode of attacking women and girls; and they were so prolific and brutal as to accord their place as among the worst in any episode of communal violence in India. Those rendered homeless were forced into makeshift relief camps organized by citizen and community efforts with the persistent absence of the state in providing any relief measures, let alone the setting up of emergency relief camps. The involvement of the whole continuum of state agents, particularly police officers, on the ground during the days of violence, standing as uninvolved bystanders, and, in later months, their cooperation in allowing the genocidal pogroms to engulf the state are well witnessed and archived. The bureaucracy responsible for providing immediate relief and protection to the thousands driven out in plain threat of imminent slaughter refused any form of organized relief management. In whatever form or function, all efforts at providing any support or succor to the survivors were carried out by various concerned citizen's groups and nongovernmental Muslim community organizations, despite extreme conditions of hostility and threat, including consequent government pressure to close down the existing camps. As days turned into months, no real accounting of the carnage, as is typical in these situations, was done, and the destitution of the survivor-victims became alarmingly precarious as they were unable to return to their lives or homes in areas of relentless hostility.

The afterlife that I trace and follow in the damaged worlds created by the episodes of violence in Gujarat is about the monumental failure of the basic social contract of citizenship in the use of power to dismember the sanctity of law and justice and the triumph of translating citizen life into embodiments of desecrated sectarian identity. State complicity in all of this, while acknowledged and widely discussed, is a presumed given in my arguments; however, I do not privilege that in my analytic. Though I endorse the argument of still extant negligent governmentality, I extend it further afield to explore a sociality (literally, the "social" of the social contract) that privileges majoritarian politics that can trample on any and all aspects of civic, public trust. I draw attention to the ability and action of people who have been responding to the episode from within their damaged worlds, in ways that pave another way toward justice, while being surrounded by perpetrators who are cloaked in protected impunity.

These are ways that, on one plane, attempt to recapture justice from the machinations of unethical power and, on the other, make possible the making of a social that realigns the torment of violence and injustice with a politics of compassion. On yet another plane, it devalues the divisive capacity of ascriptive identities to claim a citizenship that seeks an affirmation of justice through an obedience of law. Through a movement called Nyayagrah, I locate an afterlife of the Gujarat carnage, where the pathos of communal tension finds survivors who, despite all odds, seek to inhabit the bios of citizenship through a pursuit of law for justice. This is, though, a pursuit that does not value the ends of success and failure but more so values the process of achieving the individuation, the bios, of citizenship.

SURROGATE POWER AND MAJORITARIAN PUBLICS

The responsibility of protection against threat, of support during vulnerability and benign sustenance in quotidian life—these necessary conditions are written into the edifices of the nation-state through the concepts and arguments of social contract and sovereign power. However, this has been one of the most profound betrayals of contemporary political society. The fact remains that when state apparatus in power choose to abandon their mandated responsibility and aspired ideals, they can be the most vicious, brutal, and complete threat against life—in its collective living or in its individual experience. When such intents become implicit, an excess of vulnerability cloaks the citizen, especially when even her ontological status, at its moment of definition as a citizen, risks her own annihilation through the double edge of sovereign state power—a formulation that Agamben has skillfully made available in wider discourse through the combined force of the "state of exception" and its product, "bare life."[1] This argument of bare life, or a politically stripped life circumscribed into a state-crafted zone of exclusion, is inclusive of the place of ascriptive identity in state-supported pogroms, where populations who are recognized as threatening are faced with annihilation. Apart from the atrocious political misfortunes of sovereignty and statecraft here (especially in the ideals of parliamentary democracy), the aporetic relationship between citizenship and community identity poses a critical turning point in understanding the biopolitical. Although my reading in this chapter will retain that theoretical framing, it will also show a different inflection by way of which I imagine the possibility of return into citizenship after abandonment—a fragile but crucial possibility I find in the Gujarat afterlife.

Incidents of mass violence in India, especially those often termed as *communal riots,*[2] are known to be allowed to run their course and beyond, with state "cooperation." While *state complicity* is a widely used phrase in these descriptions and techniques of cooperation, which range from blatant administrative negligence to the suspension of formal justice mechanisms, I draw the focus away from state power per se and ally my arguments with an extended understanding of state power. This is not an examination of the state's propensity to misuse its legitimate control over violence against its own citizens; rather, it focuses on the ability of the state to work from within its structures and move beyond to extend relationships of *surrogate* power with chosen, majoritarian publics. This is an argument that seeks an explanation about state-supported violence that appears to transform supposedly secular state institutions into sectarian ranks of bureaucrats, judges, and armed militia fueled by hostility and hatred, legitimated by majoritarian sentiment.[3] This is where the Weberian idea of the state having legitimate monopoly over violence is often unfortunately interpreted in situations of state "complicity,"[4] when in effect, what could be argued for is that the legitimacy of violence is an extendable relationship where the state apparatus transfers a surrogate monopoly to its agents and its chosen public to play a more insidious role of reacting against unwanted populations in political–public space. In the Indian body politic, where democracy is less about individual citizenship and more about community membership, majoritarian rule legitimates this surrogacy of power and complicates state complicity in violence. This legitimacy channels a blasphemous exchange between publics, law, and statecraft, which does not just nullify the enactment of illegitimate violence against excluded others but also makes invisible the nature of the violence, and this ultimately works toward keeping the violence immune from any prosecution by administrative or legal measures.

This "illegitimate governance"[5] takes us to Richard Vernon, who makes a point that "belonging to a state is a colossal risk, the greatest risk that the vast majority of people are exposed to in their lives—and thus requires a correspondingly enormous degree of trust."[6] When discussing crimes against humanity, he suggests that the morally compelling principle that legitimates international justice mechanisms to make an intervention is when this trust is betrayed—when the state, which is ultimately responsible in prosecuting crimes against humanity, is itself a perpetrator of such crimes. Vernon's discussion is about crimes against humanity where international intervention is legally and morally justifiable—as it has been in the cases recorded so far in the historiography of international justice mechanisms. Sierra Leone, as discussed in chapter 1, is one such arena. However, this chapter signals the difference when the international community cannot intervene.

The moral frustration and the political dilemma that find shape in the context of the Gujarat violence is that, going at least by the precedents of what crimes against humanity are, this episode can be proposed as one such episode; however, any attempt at definition here was muffled once again to serve illegitimate governance. The then union home minister and leader of the ruling Bharatiya Janata Party (BJP), L. K. Advani, stated that nothing happened in Gujarat 2002 that was more untoward than any other similar episodes around the country—his obvious reference would have been to the other event of carnage, the first of significant proportion in postindependence India, the one aimed against the Sikhs in 1984, when similar complicity of state power under the aegis of the then ruling party, the Congress, was equally acknowledged in public sentiment.[7] The political dilemma of appeal toward international intervention is clearly ruled out, given India's nonsignatory status in the ICC, in addition to the invocation of India's sovereign assertion. Upendra Baxi, in his foreword to a rare volume on mass crimes and international standards in India, notes that India's stance of nonratification of the ICC Rome Statute, on grounds of sovereignty, may yet have to be reconsidered, given the nation's seeking of expansion of the permanent membership of the UN Security Council. Until then, though, the dismay, in his view, that I resonate with here remains in the easy collapse of immunity into impunity. As he says,

> all too often "impunity" cloaks itself in the languages of "immunity." For about four decades plus, the constitutional Indian State claimed immunity for performance of sovereign function. Students of public law in India know well

how the constitutional State argued before the Supreme Court of India—and for several decades—why public officials may not be sued for torts (harms caused to citizens by official conduct). It pushed the doctrine of sovereign immunity to some obscene limits.[8]

By any argument, this also means that nothing must prevent any obligation on the part of the Indian courts to prosecute crimes against humanity under customary international law, with or without any international pressure to do so.[9] When one of the few controversial cases concerning the Gujara violence found its way to the final court of the nation, the Supreme Court, that court did not find enough concern to detect sufficient "miscarriage of justice" in the Gujarat courts. However, issues of federalism appeared to "limit" central state power to negotiate beyond political instrumentalities in the Indian legal environment.[10] The Human Rights Commission of the country issued statements and reports that condemned the violence and demanded an ethical and procedural response from the Gujarat state courts. The state of affairs, at the time of writing, continues to comprise a small handful of cases, some of which have achieved a mediatized high profile: cases in which, after controversial procedure, convictions have been made. Justice mechanisms in the aftermath of the Gujarat Violence—as elaborated through the arguments in the following pages, will have to be recorded as "Gujarat's second catastrophe," in the apt words of Upendra Baxi.[11]

In this context of betrayal of the social contract, in the immunity of Indian sovereignty and the perversions of justice mechanisms, I pursue what does appear in the afterlife in Gujarat—an arduously paved path toward extracting formal justice, one that reclaims the contract of trust, but without the usual structures and institutional dynamics of formal justice mechanisms. It is a socially initiated, personally inspired, and collectively pursued movement called Nyayagrah (roughly translated as "Justice Force," constituted by its carriers, the Nyayapathiks, or those who follow the path of justice). I will argue for an interpretation of this movement that will trace the lines of life and the social in this afterlife—in the specificity of communities embedded in the harsh envelope of hostility and in which visceral expressions of violence and atmospheres of legitimated hatred live on as traumatic remembrances, as tormented presents, and even as fraught futures of repressed trauma. I explore Nyayagrah and its Nyayapathiks as an assemblage of social relationalities that emerge out of an innovative participation in the pathos of suffering and compassion. I explore how that participation finds embodiment through the individual experiences of being survivors, victims, saviors, perpetrators, legal workers, peace activists—to bring forth a bios that transforms them into the individuated category of citizens. And in that, they signal the potential of a figure of life that can extend to populations that have existed in the past (in the shape of those excluded or violated, such as the Sikhs and, further on, the Dalits, the poor and the "minor" others in India)[12] or those who will appear in the future. In the course of this interaction between bios and pathos in the Gujarat afterlife, the constitution of life will emerge as a challenge to the forced occultation of the citizen, when its political presence as life affirmed is kept opaque in the perverted transactions of justice that the surrogate violence of the state sustains.

COMMUNAL PUBLICS, EMPATHY, AND JUSTICE

Approaching justice in the aftermath of mass violence has outlined a history not too distant from the genealogy of crimes against humanity mentioned in chapter 1. One direction has been that of crimes against humanity, which literally frames the idea of crime and which can then be pursued with due punishment through legal procedure. The other direction has been toward invoking justice where punishment is not the goal but rather the intention is to develop structures of accountability, which will allow crimes to be acknowledged in a duly designated forum where both survivors and perpetrators share a space in which to confess, record, and publicly seek acknowledgment, namely, TRCs. In most or all of these situations, the state or state actors as perpetrators of the violence are well recognized, and the establishment of these public fora is the marking of a regime as ended, especially by a newly motivated regime willing and able to make a gesture of addressing the wrongs committed. The temporal feature becomes central insomuch as the episode of violence has been allotted a definite location in the past and some form of surpassing of that violence—a political victory, some form of state transition, or otherwise—has been achieved. These mechanisms are thus applied in the appropriately named transitory regimes and the form of justice well documented in the cases of South Africa, Argentina, and Sierra Leone, among many others.[13]

This sketch outlines a model of justice whose core features measure its distance from the Gujarat context, which brings into focus what is entailed for the cause of justice in Nyayagrah. Two issues are crucial in this measure. First, justice in transitory regimes is indeed about marking a transition where the past is given a place. Without doubt, the past lives on in the multitude of experiences and remembrances or in continuing inequities and trauma, yet the fact of transition marks a movement away and forward from a designated time of turmoil, which ostensibly will not be repeated. Second, the new regime, whether under international pressure or local demand, makes a gesture of response toward acknowledging the nature of the violence and the need for its accounting. The aftermath in Godhra is diametrically opposed to these features—there is no transition of the existing regime, and neither has there been abatement of similar episodes of "communal" violence in locations other than Gujarat.[14] In particular, it is possible to say that Muslims versus Hindus as sides to a particularly marked form of communal hostility in India[15] (others exist as well) is a condition of its independence—India's independence from British rule in 1947 is also the year of its partition from Pakistan. There is no dearth of reflection on these putative conditions of India's making. While the 1947 Partition battles its way through revisitations, repressions, or oblivion in the narrations of anamnesia or amnesia, communal hostility is the underbelly of the nation—repeated instances of violence are enough testimony to that. Justice as a mechanism that will deal with a particular past and achieve some form of mandated closure is an anachronistic aberration in Gujarat and in the nation.

Second, there is no existing gesture of response that makes a formal acknowledgment of the fact that the violence in Gujarat was a serious crime against citizens or society at large. Added to this is the unavailability of any other avenue, such as the ICC or any of its mandated institutions, that could have acknowledged that and initiated any intervention—how well advised that would be is, of course, a matter of debate. The episode of violence related to Godhra has been another incident where "law and order" has spiraled, allegedly, out of control. The repeated techniques of administrative subterfuge (described in the following) retain the usual myth of "law and disorder," with its attendant issues of difficult administration, where there is neither need nor motivation in most structures of state authority to evaluate the situation any differently.

Nyayagrah, under these circumstances and in this environment, is a properly organized effort born out of the vision and commitment of a dedicated individual, Harsh Mander, and his trust in social justice, a commitment that he has carried forth in a long-sustained set of beliefs translated into practice in diverse contexts, of which the Gujarat carnage is one. His efforts are undoubtedly buffered and supported by a host of actors and agents that have found it necessary to either join his cause or provide professional contributions—all of whose experiences combine to make possible the exact social assemblage that makes the profile of Nyayagrah. Mander is not the necessary focus of the narrative that is presented here, nor is an appraisal of his social activism.[16] However, his presence remains center stage in the play of pathos, where the bearing of witness and the expression of testimony for a realm of suffering make possible the approach toward what indeed is at stake in the constitution of life here, in sentiment and in practice.

Nyayagrah, at the time of writing, has extended its sphere of activity from Gujarat to situations that have since arisen in various parts of India, namely, in the northeastern state of Assam and in the northern state of Uttar Pradesh. Gujarat, in that sense, is a first case, and an analytic of the movement needs a tracing of its formative steps in Mander's initiative. The following, quoted at length from some of Harsh Mander's work, forms the semantic and semiotic ground in which the movement is embedded.[17] Most of all, for my arguments, this ground reveals the web of pathos that brings into being a network of people and emotions that experience the immediacy of suffering and, through that experience, create a social. That social gives shape to a form of life, a bios—that of a legal person aspiring toward citizenship in the frame of this afterlife. Mander stated,[18]

> I will argue that especially in a democracy, in situations of persisting injustice, hate and fear, efforts for legal justice help powerfully to create conditions

in which egalitarian spaces are created for estranged and divided people to renegotiate and rebuild bonds of mutual trust and amity. It can do this by shattering aching and suffocating silences that are born out of dread and intimidation, by establishing their equality before the Constitution and law of the land, regardless of the god they worship, their caste, gender and ethnicity. For the victims, it can challenge their resigned or sullen despair. For the perpetrator, it can deter further violence by convincing him of the legal consequences of his offences. For the organizations that manufacture disaffection and divide, and State authorities that enable or even organize hate crimes, it can break the norm of impunity, which, if unchallenged, destroys the foundations of secular democracy.

It *can* do all this. But efforts for, or even the eventual achievement of the ends of legal justice, need not necessarily facilitate egalitarian reconciliation. I will argue that there is a much greater chance for strivings for legal justice to achieve authentic reconciliation if the battle is actually fought by large numbers of the victims of mass hate violence themselves, and not remotely by lawyers and human rights agencies acting on their behalf and in their name. The chances of healing are even greater if local members of the community that meted out the violence are also encouraged to partner efforts for legal justice. Not just should the contest for legal action justice be a mass, community based, peaceful enterprise of democracy in action, people themselves should use the instruments and institutions of a democratic State to affirm their equality before the law, which the sectarian violence had threatened and challenged. It should also be bound by ethical rules in which the means deployed in the struggle are consistent with the ends of the battle. There must be vigilance and self-critical reflection to ensure that the victim is never instrumentalized or taken for granted. Instead, every decision regarding the process of the case should be taken based on the informed consent of the victim. And, most importantly, at every stage, the legal struggle should be based on truth, with no bribes and inducements, and no manipulation of the truth during evidence.

The clear message in this vision is the appeal, first, to a notion of law and justice, grounds on which to claim citizenship. Second, this claim to citizenship has to appear from within the damaged community itself, as the demand for an entitlement that makes use of a sense of parity rather than of status of minority. And third, the demand itself has to follow a path that makes the means to the end an ethical one—an ethic that exposes the malevolence of state power by its very formula. It is in the last that the Gandhian legacy finds expression, but in an adaptation that molds itself, I would suggest, to a political condition different from its origins. Mander speaks of this legacy when he states,[19]

> We propose ... the idea of "Nyayagrah," or a people's campaign for legal justice and protection, for peaceful action to use the law, and democratic instruments to secure justice. Satyagraha was a form of mass resistance to unjust laws. Nyayagrah (literally "justice-force" or people's resistance for justice) is proposed as mass campaigns not to disobey its unjust laws, but to hold the state accountable to enforce and not to disobey its own just laws, and to uphold the rights guaranteed by the country's constitution and laws and by international covenants.

Mander's words do not need amplification; however, understanding Nyayagrah as a legatee of satyagraha requires some reflection on what Gandhi's satyagraha is, and I will return to that later. Mander then constructs his principles as four founding elements of what he understands as an essential part of an authentic process of reconciliation. They are acknowledgment, remorse, reparation, and justice—each of which is quite self-explanatory in context. This cluster of justice effects that Mander outlines literally lists a discursive set through which denied justice writes the history of the state apparatus and communal violence in India (not least of which have been the Gujarat 2002 and Sikh 1984 contexts elaborated in the explorations here). Nyayagrah, then, takes off in the following environment.

In the few months after the Godhra-fueled mayhem in the state of Gujarat, 4,252 cases, directly about the murders and other crimes of the time, were registered in various courts around the state. More than 2,107 of these were closed without the minimal issue of a charge sheet. Marking the extent of bias through the judiciary, about two hundred lower courts in seventeen districts closed these cases, in clear violation of any legal practice. In about three hundred cases, all accused were acquitted after trial, within months of the carnage. The accomplishment of these numbers in a span of less than eighteen months, in a system that is known for absurd delays of procedure, is enough evidence of the concerted intentions of state officials. The specific procedure through which this is achieved starts with the fairly well rehearsed technique of police work in these situations, where large numbers of complaints as well as long lists of accused are summarized into single omnibus "First Information Reports," some of which were filed in advance by the police.[20] The large numbers make these reports impossible to investigate and, predictably, preempt their closure without due process. Even when complainants have listed names of witnesses and accused, the names of the main accused were often obfuscated with the euphemistic yet insidiously potent turn of phrase "violent mob." In effect, the erasure of both accused and survivor, as embodied individuals in directed attacks, is effaced by a singularly powerful label—thereby pitting one group against another rather than recognizing perpetration as acts of individual volition and responsibility. Nor are the survivors, by this same maneuver, given a face or particularity other than that of an ascriptive identity. In those cases where investigations were ordered, those responsible were police officers who were known to have aided and abetted in the massacres or to be openly biased. Some public prosecutors were active members of the Sangh Parivar and had no qualms about being openly discriminatory, threatening, and dismissive with regard to the plaintiffs. Witnesses were openly threatened and coerced into agreements where their silence was bought in exchange for their alleged ability to return to their homes in some pretense of safety. Loud and clear signals about what it would mean for this community to seek the mandatory protections of the state apparatus became the audible mode of "justice" in post-Godhra Gujarat.[21]

However, even within this paralysis of any kind of justice mechanism (which should have been normative to a democratic polity), there was enough response from civil and public spheres, at the least, to document and, to the extent possible, reveal, acknowledge, and pursue the massive betrayal of state function in Gujarat. In a response by the National Human Rights Commission, as per a report of April 12, 2002, a clear statement was made about the "comprehensive failure of the state to protect the Constitutional rights of the people of Gujarat."[22] A few cases, pursued relentlessly and controversially by human rights groups and lawyers, were referred out of Gujarat under extreme conditions of witness coercion, which then went forward to win convictions. A brief sketch of one of these cases, which has a direct bearing on the beginnings of Nyayagrah, is as follows—the Best Bakery case, where (in an absurdly quick judgment made as early as June 27, 2003, allegedly in a "fast-track" court) all accused were acquitted, allegedly because no evidence could be found to the contrary.[23] The incredible effacing of all possible evidence by the unscrupulous manipulation of not just court proceedings but police work only strengthened the growing concern about the Gujarat government and its intentions. Eventually, the National Human Rights Council made a petition to the Supreme Court asking for a mistrial, which the apex court of the nation took cognizance of, and the Court transferred the case, in 2004, to a special court in Maharashtra, which eventually led to the final convictions.[24] Soon after this, Harsh Mander, on behalf of Aman Biradari [25] and together with the Lawyer's Collective, filed an interim application and a writ petition that sought a proper implementation of the Supreme Court's directions, made at the time of transferring the Best Bakery case to the Maharashtrian court, which ordered the Gujarat government to reopen the two thousand or more cases that were closed, mostly because of the impossibility of investigating the summary reports filed by the state police.[26] The Supreme Court directed that the state government actively pursue litigation through filing appeals in higher courts against the mass acquittals. After a long period of contestation, the Gujarat government, in January 2006, ordered the reopening of all but twenty-two of the closed cases.

This reopening was responsible, in many ways, for the beginnings of Nyayagrah. The campaign started with the express purpose of and attempt at reclaiming the law of the land, not as much to ensure the punitive burden on perpetrators as to congeal through the tenets of citizenship an equal contract of social status, dignity, and civic presence, insomuch as the applicability of law itself can ensure that experience of contract. The Nyayagrah intervention, in the shape and form of a double goal, intervenes in both the formal contract of citizenship the relationships that sustain a community, in all its fragile balance of give and take. I refrain here from using any eulogistic or aspirational brush on the possible outcome of what Nyayagrah will achieve or overcome (the experiences and discursive practices that will emerge from it will be evidence for the future to record or forget), because in Mander's own reckoning, Nyayagrah does not necessarily endorse good policy potential. Reconciliation may or may not be achieved, in whatever way that can be measured; nor can justice necessarily be ensured—yet a kind of healing sociality can be aspired to with certainty, which will be located in individual experiences and individualized narratives. These are a testimony to the making of a social, and that is what I privilege here. As I will propose, the Nyayagrah movement is a counterforce to prevailing sanctions of violence, which are endorsed by techniques of surrogate power that empower a majoritarian visceral politics of hatred. This counterforce—in all its fragility and inchoateness of subversive emotion, on one hand, and, on the other, concreteness and conviction of reasoned empathy based on the practical use of law and justice—lays the groundwork for a politics of compassion. It envisions a pragmatic alternate path in contexts of mass damage where state impunity together with malevolent affect create one of the most formidable forces that repeat a history of violent damage. Exploring Nyayagrah, therefore, is to understand what it means to counter sabotages of formal justice in a democratic polity as well as what is entailed in countering affect with affect—socializing, as it were, emotions of hatred into empathy and solidarity.

The following account covers aspects of the first two years of the work that Nyayagrah has put on record.[27] The campaign has focused on five districts in Gujarat, which account for around 60 percent of all criminal matters relating to the 2002 event—Ahmedabad, Gandhinagar, Anand, Kheda, and Sabarkantha. Survivors involved in more than 1,263 registered criminal cases in four of these districts have been individually approached, and approximately 226 of these cases, which involve approximately four thousand survivors, have been revived. Those representatives who have chosen to pursue the Nyayagrah "option" are doing so in an atmosphere of pervasive insecurity and turmoil. Needless to say, the nuances of what this movement could imply in the generic discourse of justice in mass violence are larger and more complex than the focused argument I develop here. Nonetheless, reiterating the overall analytic, I explore this afterlife by tracing the affective concatenations through which networks of individuals are affectively assembled through the practical aspects of the Nyayagrah movement, the first of which is the question of "voluntary choice."

The choice is a result of Nyayagrah's founding equation of seeking and offering complete solidarity and resolve between those who will choose to pursue their cases and those who will support them through that effort. An initial acknowledgment is made of the fact that the cases that have so far been successful in procuring convictions, like the ones I have mentioned, have been much in the mold of showcase trials, highly publicized, deeply fraught with controversy, and involving high-profile legal and human rights activists and lawyers. A distance emerges between the lawyers and activists and those they represent, given the toxic environment of witness coercion—for instance, the Best Bakery case found the witness Zahira Sheikh formally stating that she was being coerced into involvement by Teesta Setalavad, the human rights activist lawyer who was spearheading her cause.[28] This claim was set aside, but with other unsettling information about Zahira having been paid substantial amounts of silence money by political functionaries of the ruling party, that is, the BJP. These situations may well be the destructive result of nationwide attention—however, it stands to opinion that the survivors and their representations in justice, or their involvement, can be a situation less of solidarity than of other, however benign, instrumentalities.

Not least of all, the Nyayagrah belief further substantiates the fact that legal proceedings can themselves be too opaque for the survivors, who, more often than not, are challenged in any kind of literacy—thus hampering the route to justice. In consequence, thus, setting aside these less than 10 percent of "high-profile" cases, a prime motivation in this movement is the fostering of legal education.[29] The aspiration is about the mass of survivors whose initiation into that consciousness could only come from their reengagement with a society and a polity that recognize them as much as they recognize their own agency. This mutuality, Nyayagrah insists, has to take place in the realms of common, quotidian worlds of everyday sociality compromised by undue immunity and triumphalism of majority rights and actively pursued on the ground—among and between those in the compromised sociality. Thus the voluntary choice to pursue formal and elusive justice, and the bases of its support in the movements' solidarity, effectively, are the main guiding principles through which Nyayagrah proceeds.

In terms of the voluntary choice of those who expect to pursue their cases, as mentioned earlier, the Nyayapathiks have individually approached those involved in more than twelve hundred cases, where they have explained their motivation and sought consent to pursue the legal option, which would mean complete and total involvement of the claimant. Consent here means a host of factors that an uncomfortable environment of fear, suspicion, and obstinate antagonism could imply. Moreover, many of these survivors are utterly poor; they live in conditions of social expulsion, and most have had to give up their original homes to live in far from desirable "rehabilitation" camps or ghettoes, often trading in their homes for alleged protection within these makeshift spaces. Some live on in their own homes, in complete, terrified silence, under threats from their neighbors and the larger community. Economically, the Muslim community has almost no chance of employment in any form within the locale, as this "boycott" has been a consciously produced outcome of relentless hostility—their meager trade efforts are limited to select places and produce barely enough for basic sustenance. Choosing to fight the case would mean naming older or existing neighbors as perpetrators, making their intentions public in a formidable environment of threat and intimidation, physical, sexual, or verbal. For those who choose to pursue their cases, the Nyayapathiks' foremost norm is to assure complete, unwavering solidarity and support, both in legal and social–personal terms, to sustain these efforts as a combined struggle. Since the volunteers are, by design, members of the community themselves, survivors and those from the perpetrator community as well, a meaningful sense of empathy—a foundation for the notion of egalitarian compassion, a phrase that Mander uses and that I argue with—is generated. Significant legal aid is augmented here through the help offered and volunteered by some of those Nyayapathiks who are recent law graduates. In addition, no monetary inducement is offered to any of those whose cases could be reopened, as this is believed to mar the decision to pursue this path to justice. In that sense, a complete sense of self-reliance and voluntary involvement in this regard is reinforced.

Another set of ethical principles mark the Nyayagrah code.[30] First, they are committed to not paying or offering any bribe to any official on any occasion. In a system whose functioning is marred by many other obstacles, bribe taking is one of the most widespread, not just in Gujarat but across the nation. For the smallest piece of everyday bureaucratic function, money makes an exchange out of daily official duty. Extracting difficult information out of various offices, police stations, or courts would include bribery as a given; however, the Nyayagrah commitment to this has been steadfast, to the best of all available information. The ethical obstacle that this poses has been understandably huge and has frustrated and puzzled many of those pursuing the difficult task of preparing long-buried cases. However, the stringently honored commitment continues to strengthen and keep alive this pursuit of justice, in ethical integrity.

Second, the movement maintains a resistant position with regard to the many ways in which survivors can indeed be instrumentalized, and it is cognizant that their actions are not just about securing a conviction (which may or may not materialize) but also aid the cause at its core. As has been evidenced by the Best Bakery case mentioned earlier, the enveloping atmosphere of fear and intimidation puts the survivors as witnesses under enormous strain as to where the burden of truth lies in the goal of justice. Making the survivor responsible in the procedures of law also entails the complicated tangle of how witnesses are coerced and threatened by the prevailing powers, often with monetary inducements, into either taking back their statements, changing them considerably to settle the case, or closing it. Effectively, they become those on trial, get demonized when their statements waver or withdraw, and, conse-quently, become figures of betrayal for the community, those who have spoken and worked for them, and the ideal of justice. Underlined by a simple but enduringly incisive dictum *sach bolo, saaf bolo* (speak the truth, speak it clearly), the Nyayagrah principles combine a set of goals. The first involves the complex procedures of law, which often build a gap of knowledge between lawyers and their survivor clients that the movement suggests can be overcome if legal support is provided in such a way that lawyers and their clients work together every step. As the volunteers are largely from the community itself (with help from the young volunteer law graduates), there is an educative and empowering strategy that engages the survivor and her support in a bond that speaks of solidarity; however, in my argument, it does more. Effectively, the active encouragement of educating the victim about the procedures of law—engaging with her own sentiments as well as their reasonings and questions in the everyday following of legal procedure by volunteers who themselves are part of the fraught community—makes possible the fusion of two discursive agents who remain separate in most pursuits of formal justice, especially in contexts of mass crime. On one hand is the affect of suffering, and on the other is its translation into a reasoned legal plea. The legal learning and egalitarian compassion that the Nyayagrah movement parenthesizes together bring forth an instance of affect and reason as *reasoned empathy*. Adding to this is the contrapuntal effect—that of making an individual an embodiment of citizenship as much as of community identity. The question of whether that is a possible outcome is not the judgment I suggest but rather the process that makes its imagination possible.

The account moves now to the Nyayapathiks, a large number of whom are drawn from working-class environments and other humble milieux, and crucially, they come from both sides of the conflicted locale, comprising Hindus and Muslims, the former obviously lesser in number.[31] The insistence is on the site, however fragile and ephemeral, as the focus of an emergence of any reconciliatory process. Although community action in reconciliation processes is widely acknowledged in discourse and practice, the significant nuance here is the idea of enablement where legal knowledge and practice are seen as something that need not remain removed from the people. When legal action is indeed sanctioned or any formal reconciliatory process is initiated, the survivor community is the recipient, rather than being the agents themselves, in the formal decision process, whether that involves local state sanction or international intervention. Circumscribing social actors, as such, within the spheres of sociality and keeping that action separate from formal legal action is usually the case in spontaneous efforts of reconciliation. Within the Nyayagrah milieu, both formal legal action and rehabilitated sociality are the strategized goals.

The formal tasks of the Nyayapathiks and the ethical rules they must follow (aspects of which were discussed earlier) are listed along with a concise set of guidelines regarding the exact nature of the cases to be considered; the steps to be taken in imparting legal advice; the actual stages in pursuing, documenting, and following the cases; understanding and following charge-sheeted cases; ensuring impartial legal help if it has to come from outside the Nyayapathiks; the possibility of challenging acquittals; and other similar details, which also include considerations of compensation.[32] Nyayapathiks are expected to help and support the most vulnerable, widows and young children or older people, with any assistance required in building up their homes and shelters or their livelihoods—all in all helping the survivors in coming back to some semblance of normalcy. The legal part of their duties is equally supplemented with the insistence that there be a conscious involvement in the experience of the process, in all its travails and challenges, in the personal and social lives of those who choose to fight this battle.

The Nyayapathiks, so volunteered, are a group, therefore, who have emerged from these circumstances of hate and fear; they understand the failure of legal justice and see their role as something that can challenge and overcome both. The following brief descriptions are of a few of these Nyayapathiks as well the witness-survivors they support:[33]

> Imranbhai came to the largest relief camp in Ahmedabad based in the Sha-halam Dargah, from Naroda district, where he and his family lost everything they owned to the fires that engulfed their homes. In the relief camp, he worked with children, teaching them and trying to keep his own self and the children in the camp from remembering. Eventually, over five years of penury, he has acquired a degree in journalism and has committed himself to being a Nyayapathik and has been working with the movement for the past 8–9 years. His words: "As a Nyayapathik, I have learnt so much. Earlier I would feel hesitant going to a police station, but now…I know…I can demand information from them—it is my right…. I cannot describe the feeling that you get when people (carnage survivors) thank you…then one feels as if everything has been worth it; the pain, the tears, everything."[34]

> Manibhai is an advocate and works for Nyayagrah in the village of Kavitha in Anand. He is a Dalit and in his village, the only individual working for the cause. The pressure on him from the Hindu community is expected, but he believes the carnage was not about religious sentiments and hostilities, but more about political instrumentalities and believes that many Hindus did not support the killings. He states: "The people who have done wrong will always try to protect themselves. I know what is right and will stand by that…. This is not just about a case. It is really what my profession really teaches me—to fight for justice."[35]

Afroz Apa and Altaf Bhai are siblings who have grown up witnessing communal violence across generations. Their grandfather, a well known left-intellectual was killed in the 1969 riots in Ahmedabad and they both carry that memory as well as his ideals. Their father was killed in the 1984 riots. Afroz Apa fights her own battles of widowhood and raising four girls of her own and clinical depression to join in the Nyayagrah struggle. Before 2002, she was not accustomed to stepping out much in public, but she was one amongst those who worked, against fatigue and innumerable obstacles, in the rehabilitation camps after the 2002 events. As a Nyayapathik, she finds herself in police stations and courtrooms, finds herself emboldened by the process and confident in her own self and capacity. Both siblings have also been the first to extend support to Hindu children orphaned by the Sabarmati Express fire. They have also challenged a local rich Muslim who was known to be exploiting widows of the carnage.

Usman Bhai, while having "participated" as a younger man in the mayhem of riots in the past, throwing stones, staying away from work etc.; his participation seemed indeed to follow the mindlessness of mob contagion, which did not quite engage with the ugly underbelly of hatred and organized killing. His involvement, starts with him accompanying his uncle to a camp, which he was running, for about 3000 people, after the 2002 carnage. His anger against the perpetrator community changes to the potency of empathy when he realized what the sense of solidarity in that situation could mean for the survivors. While his admiration and commitment to Mander's cause is the man's humility and depth of involvement, his personal statement in his own words, says this, "When you help someone else, somewhere from their inner soul, they must have prayed for my wellbeing. Sometimes they say it. Sometimes they don't, but it can be read in their eyes. What better platform could I wish for? My biggest personal development is that people are with me. . . . After seeing such suffering, I wanted to fight back for my community. However, for the first time I saw that an explanation with love was more powerful than by force, that helping people would be more effective than throwing stones in revenge."[36]

Kishorebhai, in Ahmedabad, is a non-Dalit Hindu and who has been active in working for Dalit rights, with his father and grandfather in Rajasthan. They had moved from there to Gujarat for better livelihood opportunities. After witnessing the 2002 killings, he was involved as one of Action Aid's workers in the relief camps set up immediately after the Carnage. Forty five members of his family, driven out of their homes, had to find their way to shelter in his home and eventually to the camps. His work as a tailor and that of all other family members had come to a halt after the Carnage. In 2005, when Action Aid was sizing down their activities and Nyayagrah was taking shape, Kishorebhai joined in. Nazirbhai, another Nyayapathik in Ahmedabad, wanted to be a police officer, but family responsibilities and lack of resources or opportunity prevented his ambitions; Nyayagrah, in the course of time offered him an opportunity for the same when he worked with the Action Aid team.

From profiles of these men and women as well as others in Nyayagrah, two clear nuances of their experience need emphasis. First, the involvement with legal learning has made it possible to understand the notion of citizenship as a way of negotiating a sense of personhood in a democratic, constitutional space. The fact that a constitution exists that delivers rights and securities to all citizens and that, in effect, could remove people from their entrapments in social regimes of identity discrimination, oppression, or hate and occasions of extreme violence is often a knowledge that has been revelatory for these people. For some, it was an unknown fact that made them accustomed to and also accept the treatment they would receive from state authorities like the police, courts, and their social environment as an inevitability of ascribed identity. The potential of approaching these authorities under these trying circumstances instills in them a sense of assertive visibility in ways that are foreign to their own experiences of hatred and disdain, on one hand, and, on the other, the impunity of authority. The understanding of themselves as entities that can demand and retain the law of the land is, to say the least, empowering, in addition to garnering respect from their own communities in life worlds of defeat and hopelessness. Observing that empowerment in action, so to speak, when the cases are reopened and their pleas have found a second chance, supported by institutions and edifices larger than their immediate spheres of fear and terror, is, to say the least, a place found in a public leveled by citizenship and not by identity. The sense, then, of what society is and what social relationalities entail takes on a consciousness that, while perhaps not potent enough, yet instills some potential against rampant despair and insecurity.

There is enough realization among the Nyayapathiks that intimidation and threats can certainly get the better of people and circumstances and that their efforts are not always going to succeed. Many have had to succumb, by choice or force, to abandoning any pursuit of justice, opting for other, less than desirable options. In addition, not only is the movement weakened by these moments of "failure" as such but it has its critics from other assemblies of nongovernmental organizations, activists, or official fora that do not see this mode of approaching the violent particularly efficacious. Despite all these hindrances, Nyayagrah has sustained itself to move beyond the context of Gujarat to other similar situations in India. What remains indelible is the community that is finding greater strength through its emergence as an assemblage based on social relationalities that do not reinforce the claim only of an identity population of dispensable people but rather as a terrain of contesting publics of equal standing.

This prevailing sense of shared equity leads to the second nuance of the Nyayagrah experience. As part of their efforts, the emphasis for the Nyayapathiks has been to build a bond of support and solidarity with those who have chosen to fight for a renewed goal of justice. This is not support that is part of the institutionalized, and thereby possibly faceless structure of, say, large aid organizations; rather, it is more intimate involvement in quotidian life. Nyayapathiks are keenly aware of the relationships and bonds they have built with their compatriots, and they see that part of their work as a mutually enriching development. Their investment has, in their own admission, instilled a sense of fulfillment and, simultaneously, a sense of responsibility about what they mean and offer to those with whom they have related in this cause.

I parenthesize the nuances sketched here as instances that contour the social in the Gujarat afterlife—they remain as the form of this pathos here as well as its embodied vehicles. In adding to those who constitute this assembly of the social—the Nyayapathiks—this section ends with a few, much too brief sketches of those who have chosen to fight the second battle for justice:[37]

> Hanifbhai lives in the slums by the river Sabarmati in Ahmedabad. A 700 strong mob attacked their shack, carried away his nine-year old daughter and burnt her. Living in penury, he continues to hope for justice.

> Hameedaben was married to Sulemanbhai, the village postman. On the last day of February, she accompanied him as he went for his routine monthly

visit to a nearby town to clear the village phone bills. On their way home, he stepped off the bus in another town to look for a newspaper. A mob spotted him and recognizing his beard as that of a Muslim's and killed him, as his wife watched. As she screamed and shouted for help, she herself was hit on the head and left for dead. After two operations, she now has settled into her life in Himmatnagar re-settlement colony and has had her case re-opened and continues to fight for justice for her butchered husband.

Ayeshaben was a widow of ten years, when in 2002, the shop that she had opened on the outskirts of her village to support her family, Kishangarh, was looted and burnt. Her family was one among a group of eleven Muslim families in the village. She was closing down for the day when she heard a huge mob approaching and she ran to hide. From where she was she could see all those who razed her shop. Later when she tried to have the incident recorded in a FIR, naming those she saw, the police wrote them down as an "Unknown Mob." She was able to get the case re-opened again and the accused, all rich and influential, spent a week in jail. Ayeshaben is now in Himmatnagar, a re-settlement colony, still seeking justice for her case. She reports that she gets regular visits from members of the RSS (the *Rashtriya Swayamsevak Sangh*), a militant part of the Hindu Parivar, who threaten her politely, to take her case back. Walikaka, similarly, continues to live in his damaged house, next door to the neighbors who burnt his home, refusing to repair or to move. His statement got his accused a week in jail, but he now continues to fight to have some justice delivered. Niaaz bibi, Jan Mohammed bhai, Qadirbhai, Shamsuddin bhai, Roshneeben are others like her, who have lost every bit of their lives' earnings, their work and homes and now live in resettlement colonies, pursuing their hopes for justice. Mohammedbhai, ironically, was a staunch supporter of the BJP, but his house was not spared by the mob that razed it. He named and filed cases against all the familiar faces in the mob, tried calling his BJP contacts/friends, only to be rebuffed. He had "settled" the case and then he was threatened, and now he fights two cases . . . his first one and a second when he was arrested by the Anti-Terrorist squad and jailed.

The preceding sketches underline two aspects: first, the affective relationality that makes up the constituent space of Nyayagrah, one that directly confirms the pathos of witnessing and participation in suffering, and second, those who participate, in other words, the embodied vehicles of that pathos, the bios. Together they form the social in this context, one that makes available another value of life. The following section suggests the interpretive tropes through which this becomes possible.

COMPASSION AND CITIZENSHIP

Nyayagrah owes its legacy to Gandhi's satyagraha, but it engages with a contemporary environment. Notwithstanding, that legacy is worth exploring in its implications for a justice movement initiated in today's India, and I choose a few strands from Gandhi's movement for reflection, especially regarding the question of justice after mass violence.[38] Gandhi's satyagraha, as initiated in South Africa and then brought to India as a final strategy to oust British rule, was a political tactic against colonial subjugation. His couching of it as a struggle through notions of truth, nonviolence, and self-sacrifice was in a profoundly religious idiom that I would read much more as a formulated ethic of being, as *dharma,* rather than as fundamentalist Hinduism, as is often done in the usual co-optations by divisive readings of political instrumentality. In my reading here, it was a philosophical and spiritual questioning of the crisis in a particular juncture of European legitimation of politics, especially colonial control. The question of unjust laws, whether in South Africa or in India, perpetrated by a regime legitimated by, as he saw it, nothing but coercion, was the leitmotif of the struggle he launched and was ultimately successful with. In essence, this was a struggle against externally imposed power structures—the British colonial regime whose illegitimacies hardly need any new argument. In the motivation that Nyayagrah espouses, however, it is not a struggle against an external power but rather the question of state failure in delivering its already existing powers of justice, powers that Mander clearly reads as just laws made unavailable to forsaken citizens. This is a context where the challenge is not the illegitimacy of an imposed colonial regime; rather, it is the daunting dilemma of a sovereign state perverting its work of statecraft and, in that process, empowering a malevolent public. The negotiation with truth, nonviolence, or self-sacrifice here imagines a political struggle that seeks to imbue an already established democratic space with principles that continue to be, in substance, European. That is a strand of Gandhi's deliberations that applies in post-Godhra Gujarat and to India as a democratic state at large.

Gandhi had a powerful counterrhetoric on democracy as a viable model of colonial government by European powers, especially when, in his reckoning, it was inevitably the imposition of the majority (*ghana*—density of numbers, in a sense) over the minority (*thoda*—or the less in number and status). For him, republican democracy could mean government of the powerful, not necessarily a just government for the free. Ajay Skaria describes this succinctly when he mentions,

> Gandhi takes issue with the consensus, with republican democracy's claim to institutionalize a space for the minor through human rights. Indeed he is not willing to accept the sovereignty that the British exercise over themselves as "true *Swaraj*." ... For him in such a politics, what always prevails is the major—not simply numerically as in the term majority, but also conceptually and ethically, where the major names what is dominant.[39]

What emerges strongly from this, in Gandhian conception, is also the rebuttal of the rule of law under this kind of a sovereign, where justice itself (or the judges themselves) become, consequentially, an extension of dominant, oppressive power. His rejection of republican democracy rests on the incommensurable space between the will of the majority and its protection of the minority. Satyagraha as a means to achieving *swaraj* (self-rule) is a rejection of colonial dominance over the colonized minority (not in numbers, certainly, but in status), a rejection that was, in principle, a refutation of the republican democracy that the European ideals upheld.[40] Nyayagrah, in a contrapuntal movement, challenges this seemingly inevitable tension in the nation space of India between the *ghana* and the *thoda*—the majoritarian subjugation of minority presence. It appeals to citizenship to effect a resolution of this tension, thereby understanding citizenship as a medium to justice.

In this resolution, Nyayagrah rejects neither the law of the land nor the statutes of democracy through which it is delivered. Rather, it seeks the exposure of corrupt, unjust governance that reproduces itself in empowered publics, and it seeks the reification of law through its correct implementation. This is a commitment that is envisioned through a claim of citizenship, one that constitutively constructs, at least in concept, equitable existence within Indian sovereignty. Reclaiming that space of citizenship through an appeal to law and the justice that it could deliver is the goal. In pursuing that goal, the reliance on truth, on the devout and stringent following of ethical means, makes Nyayagrah a Gandhian struggle. This is a form that does not just adapt itself to a contemporary condition in India but rather uses the Gandhian ethic of nonviolence to express cooperation, *not non*-cooperation with the ideals of democracy—a strategy that could hold universal appeal in the diabolical perversions of democracy rampant around the globe. Using democratic citizenship to combat injustice through the commitment of an ethic of nonviolence against the atrocity of violence is the transformative potential that satyagraha holds for Nyayagrah.

However, there is another thematic that reifies my parameters of argument here—one that channels an aspect of a Gandhian legacy that reverberates within Nyayagrah. Gandhi understood just government of the free through the notions of Ramarajya (the governmentality of Ram, the ruler and central figure in the Hindu epic *Ramayana*). Notwithstanding the co-optation of that ideal by Hindu fundamentalism that reads it as the prerogative of dominance in Hindu nationalism, Gandhi's Ramarajya was the benevolent ruling of a ruler whose ability to rule justly did not emanate from the power bestowed by a majority; rather, it was the ability to encompass all through a pious commitment to what he called *dayadharma* (the religion of compassion).[41] Ajay Skaria, in a strong argument that suggests the symbiosis of a religious virtue with an ideal of political rule, approaches the question of *dayadharma* as one that brings into sharp texture the movement of an abstract notion of compassion into the political sphere and, in that, reconciles equality with totality. In totality, if a government of the majoritarian will treat the minor as subjugate, that is not just rule, it is coercive rule. A political virtue of compassion, in Skaria's words, reconciles the totality of the major and the minor with the "equality of deference, or absolute equality. This equality which is constitutive of *satyagraha, ahimsa* and *Ramarajaya,* not only contests domination whether in the form of abstract equality or virtue, but does so without seeking to become dominant or the new major or center."[42]

Dayadharma and its infusion into compassion as a political virtue is what I keep as an argument here to lead to the social relationality that informs the conditions of life in the Gujarat afterlife, particularly its incarnation in Nyayagrah. It is an argument that finds Gandhi's *dayadharma* in Nyayagrah as that which seeks a potential of finding absolute equality through the trope of citizenship, but a citizenship that does not emphasize individual rights alone; rather, it constructs a formation of the social of compassion, empathy, and sympathy. Reading this notion through the construct of compassionate solidarity, I suggest that the pathos that is embodied and the life that is constituted in this arrangement of mass violence and its aftermath are the formation of a social that takes empathy and compassion as forces of social relationality. It is a relationality that is initiated in the realms of face-to-face intimacy but that moves to create a public sphere of political action. The political action is the reclaiming of citizenship on the grounds of equality that does not acquiesce the minor to the major but seeks parity between them in the universe of just law and equal citizenship, brought together through sympathy and compassion—emotions that are allegedly anomalous as conduits of relationship in public spheres and politics where, instead, critical reason is meant to reign.

The Nyayagrah effort works within the consciousness of a political environment that has, in many ways, institutionalized communal tension. When the work of law is invoked here through the agencies of citizenship, legal justice is indeed the possible consequence, whether in denial or in commitment. However, justice for crimes committed during the violence is not the only aim that Nyayagrah purports to. As a collective effort, it seeks the making of a particular sociality that thrives on a partial endorsement of reconciliation, which may or may not appear in consequence. However, the sociality emerging out of connectivities made through the sharing of a compassionate and sympathetic relationship has the effect of a community of solidarity composed of both the saviors and the saved (sometimes both appearing combined in the same person). The making of this affective sphere, intended and realized through the reasoning of ideals of citizenship, marks a peculiar shift in conventional understandings of what citizenship entails and what place compassion has in that entitlement. As I propose, this is the crafting of a *reasoned empathy* that makes a new political space, a new political action, possible, one that sharpens the power of positive affect in formal public life and participation. Gandhi's satyagraha and his ideals of Ramarajya, *ahimsa,* and *dayadharma* resonate with the force of religious virtue, of a pious commitment to spiritual values. Nyayagrah borrows its form in commitment to justice and equity but substantiates its content with a quotidian consciousness of shared affect made forceful politically in the pursuit of civic public life, that is, through notions of legal learning and citizenship. It does not, as I have mentioned, reject democracy but demands its correct implementation. This play of affect in public life or the place of reasoned empathy requires a connecting thread that understands affect as politics or, in this case, specifically, sympathy and compassion as redemptive political action. In that focus, the proposition that emerges is the notion of a compassionate politics as a meaningful conduit of political action, especially when this politics coheres a strategy in the aftermath of mass violence and suffering where basic justice is elusive.

If Nyayagrah is a form of politics that seeks the reascription of identity from the minor—the subjugate—into equal citizenship, then a notion begins about what this could imply in the wider context of life in the body politic of a sovereign state. In a preliminary comment at the beginning of this essay, Agamben's notion of bare life, or *homo sacer,* as it emerges through the ontologies of sovereignty was mentioned. His methodical excavation of a political theological genealogy of sovereign power leading back to Greek philosophy and a crosscutting of that narrative with a parallel reading of Foucault's biopolitics lead to the final formulation of bare life, or life that can be killed but not sacrificed. Sovereign power, whose condition of being is the responsibility of supreme jurisdictional power over life and death, becomes that very power that holds the maximum ability to suspend that protection of life through the paradoxical yet logical use of legal privilege—when a state of exception legitimating that privilege is declared. Posing this figure of life as a resolute shape of modern politics, Agamben completes that genealogical trajectory of the figure of bare life excluded from the domains of law, but produced by sovereign law itself, by finding its place in the Nazi camp.

In a state of exception, where a clear and present threat to sovereign power is seen as the condition under which the suspension of law is mandated, the threat is recognized in a particular population—a biopolitical recognition. This ties in with Foucault's parallel formulations about governmentality—an interpretation of statecraft that recognizes populations rather than individuals, populations that are identified by their biological or species attributes, which readily translates into ascriptive identities of communities, ethnicities, race, and so forth. In this governance of populations, in a state of exception, the criteria of recognition of populations determine the principle of who can be let live and who let die. Agamben's use of the concentration camp as the logos of such modern sovereign power reigns in his formulation of bare life—the production of people without rights, relegated to a zone of exclusion from the political realm of citizenship. These are people who, then, can be killed without penalty but not sacrificed within the rituals of state like those killed in "legitimate" war. The state of exception in sovereign power thus produces a zone of abandonment, making the legal transformation of citizens into those without appeal to law. Understanding this in the terrains of sovereign violence is not difficult in the contemporary global scape of abandoned citizens/*qua* bare life, where state power demands the annihilation of populations for the sake of its own existence. Agamben is thus able to conclude that this modern form of power to produce bare life is the norm, rather than a state of exception, of current political power.

However, this argument requires a twist of understanding when the abandoned population of the subjugate, minor population of India, made recognizable by state-complicit violence, is examined in Gujarat, that is, the population of Muslims in the post-Godhra context. Contrary to popular readings that give enormous legitimacy to the idea of the state of exception in Indian politics, I would propose that sovereign power in India has stopped short of a state of exception, because power by other means is able to create similar zones of abandonment,[43] fulfilling the diabolical need to exclude populations from legal domain and citizenship. While India has known the declaration of a state of emergency in the past (1975–77), during Indira Gandhi's prime ministership (as leader of the Congress Party), it does not suspend the procedure of law. Despite the misuse of the practice of law or the execution of emergency on the ground, even states of emergency are not, in legal code, states of exception. What, then, are the stratagems by which power by other means can be deployed to effect zones of abandonment?

In a preliminary outlining of Indian politics, particularly where state complicity in episodes of mass violence is acknowledged, I have mentioned the notion of how majoritarian politics creates the possibility of outsourcing, so to speak, the power of violence to a surrogate—the majoritarian public, which takes over, in a semblance of sovereign legitimacy, the right to violence. This semblance of legitimacy emerges out of a domain of affect that is created and sustained within a majoritarian public sphere, such that emotions and sentiments of hatred, suspicion, belligerent hostility, and aggression become the mode of recognizing populations and effecting mass behavior. Whether triggered by an event of political manipulation, like the destruction of the Babri Masjid and its consequent violence in 1992, or in conditions of spontaneous eruption in atmospheres already charged with hostility, which the Godhra episode could be explained as, the sentiment of aggressive majoritarian hatred is played out to its diabolical extremes by a cooperating public. A majoritarian public so created and sustained by affect becomes the vessel of incubation where surrogate power is nurtured and given form. The majoritarian government need not take on the burden of calling a state of exception against the threatening minor or subjugate population—its affective politics produce a *quasi*-state of exception. Its public, empowered by surrogate power and sustained by malignant affect, works with sovereign authority to create and sustain zones of exclusion and, certainly, inclusion. Thus, without having to negotiate questions of sovereign decree in calling for states of exception, a quasi-exception is successfully effected and, in that sense, a *quasi*-bare life. Techniques of separation are aided and abetted by the technologies of everyday administrative power, by state functionaries who are part of the majoritarian public but who work through the space of an emboldened public, without whom a complete zone of exclusion—socially, economically, culturally—is not possible. The state does not take responsibility for its illegitimate government but rather feeds off majoritarian sentiment and a public that populates the rank and file of its apparatus. In turn, the public, with majoritarian government at its disposal, does not fear the sovereign dictum to protect life, because sovereign power has indeed transformed into majoritarian power.

A fissured and fraught society emerges, with clearly marked lines of exclusion that denote a zone of abandonment—one that is created and sustained by public affect translated into legal denial. The passing over of citizens who have been attacked and who can claim the law for justice to people without recourse to justice shapes the biopolitics of this community of the excluded. This is society demarcated along lines of affective disposition, a disposition that can carry the effect of political action in a majoritarian nation-state. This is thus the political affect (of hatred and suspicion) that creates the abandoned community of those now circumscribed by their own affect of fear and acquiescence to the major—this is how the affective division of publics into those excluded and those included carves the political space of the post-Godhra landscape, the Hindu major versus the Muslim minor. Ascriptive identity, not citizenship, recognized by affective politics, either in acceptance or in disavowal, is the criterion through which this kind of biopolitics operates.

While Agamben creates the figure of bare life in the zone of abandonment and exclusion and inscribes the movement into disavowal of political being by sovereign power, he does not suggest the possibility of a reentry, because he is indeed working with the complete state of exception, the completed project for creating bare life. However, in a created zone of abandonment that is sustained by a majoritarian sentiment, can there be a figure of life that can negotiate a reentry in the space of politics and legal right, if not spaces of socialities? Can there be a temporal progression into a potentiality of reinclusion, once having been excluded? An answer can be posed in the desire for justice in the Nyayagrah movement read as a movement of reentry, where ascriptive identity of the minor is negotiated for the identity of the citizen. The expectation of justice from the state apparatus of law and courts attempts a reassembling of the cognitive cartography that separates those who can access and claim the protection of law and those who cannot. The right of invoking law is the right of a citizen, not the prescribed action of a subjugate minor. This is where ascriptive identity can be trumped by egalitarian citizenship, which the sovereign nation has not yet suspended by a call to the state of exception. However, this task of reclaiming citizenship is not just an act against an unresponsive or diabolically biased state apparatus; it is the domain of public affect.

The Nyayagrah movement, with its pursuit of justice through building a community of empathy that congeals around a solidarity of sympathy, produces another domain of affect. This is a sphere that produces another public, bound by the pathos of sympathy and compassion that conjoins this affect with the reason of law to fashion a strategy of reasoned empathy. Resculpting the rights-bearing citizen, from a zone of exclusion through an awareness and knowledge of the reason and procedure of law, combined with the affective adhesive of compassion, paves the path of reentry into a zone of inclusion. Where hatred and suspicion made possible the making of a vitriolic public that could effect a division in the body of citizens into those who can be inside and those who are to be discarded, the use of compassion and sympathetic solidarity provides another affective domain to suture the separation. This is the creation of another public that stands in defiance of the malevolent public—whether they succeed could be another story of Goliath versus David, but in terms of a strategy in political action, its force must not be denied. If Gandhi's ahimsa could stall the might of colonial violence, then this may yet be a neo-Gandhian force; however, the measurement of success is not the analytical agenda here. Rather, it is the making of a politics out of compassion, especially when the common or even discursive understanding of compassion as a sentiment is best left outside the realm of hard political negotiation.

Martha Nussbaum, in her long-standing work on political emotions, elaborates on the possible emotions that could have a place in a public:

> Respect on its own is cold and inert, insufficient to overcome the bad tendencies that lead human beings to tyrannize over one another. Disgust denies fundamental human dignity to groups of people portraying them instead as animals. Consequently, respect grounded in the idea of human dignity will prove impotent to include all citizens on the terms of equality unless it is nourished by imaginative engagement with the lives of others and by an

inner grasp of their full and equal humanity. Imaginative empathy, however, can be deployed by sadists. The type of imaginative engagement society needs, . . . is nourished by love. Love, then, matters for justice—especially when justice is incomplete and an aspiration (as in all real nations), but even in an achieved society of human beings.

But if we agree that love matters for justice, we still do not have an account of *how* it matters, how a decent society might arrange, compatibly with liberal freedom, to invite citizens to have the sort of emotional experiences that the theory imagines.[44]

It can well be argued that Nyayagrah is the answer to the query posed here—how, indeed, it could be possible to reconcile a society composed of individuals with rights, as it were, through the formation of a public of sentiment.[45] The use of love, or in the language of Nyayagrah, a compassionate solidarity aiming at legal rights, brings both spheres together, constituting a public that understands the potential of justice in securing a future of democratic citizens and not one made of hostile communities of ascriptive identity alone. In India, that potential is crucial, and that was a recognition that Gandhi was vehement about. Compassion, or Gandhi's *dayadharma,* recognizes not just a public sentiment and, specifically in the latter, a spiritual ethic and virtue but pays attention to the locatedness of compassion, a point that Nussbaum emphasizes in underlining the engagement with the "lives of others." A careful understanding of what will make compassion work for justice is when that emotion is not dissipated in a mere abstraction but located in the actuality of context. Involvement in the narratives of injustice, in the specificities of the collective as well as the personal, the private, and the public, makes possible an engagement with the here and now of legal procedure (as the Nyayagrah work does). This engagement underlines the entry of reason into empathy and compassion, making the pursuit of justice the consequence of reasoned empathy. This is where the kinetic energy of compassion as a politics is harnessed and made available as a public action that imagines a reentry into democratic space.

What, then, is the figure of life that finds form in this pathos of the social, and what embodiment does it recognize in its making of this life? With my arguments here, I propose that the movement of denied citizenship (on the grounds of minor identity) to its reinstilling in citizenship marks the movement from a biopolitics to a politics—from bare life to life. Surpassing the creation of affective populations that is constructed through sentiments and technologies of hatred directed at assigned identity, the endorsement of secular life speaks of a pursuit of empowerment that positions itself against the governmentality of majoritarian power. In Nyayagrah, finding this movement in those named individuals and bodies, through the actual reopening of closed cases and appealing to the procedures of law for secular justice, underlines the embodiment in grounded political action. Making these embodiments into a collective based on reasoned empathy reveals the tracings of the pathos—the making of a social through shared witnessing of suffering. To be sure, there is the underbelly of fear (one that Nussbaum in her arguments also identifies as one of the greatest threats to love and compassion) that makes for a politics of *ressentiment* in the making of that collective among the Muslims in Gujarat, or among the same in the nation at large. In any which way, this making of a life in secular politics—the citizen articulated in compassion, so to speak, who also understands the meaning of justice in claiming citizenship—makes for a singular relationship in this afterlife here. Giving and taking compassion, en route to justice, is the underlining of a political form of life that takes citizenship from its relegation to a dangerous opacity of subjugated populations created by hate politics, to their legible transparency, created by a politics of compassion in secular public and political life.

The afterlife of Godhra in Gujarat presents an articulation of life that retains the value of life where compassion is as yet a generative force and indeed a small part of the motor of politics—one that is made possible through the public pathos of commiserated suffering. At the same time, it upholds the embodiment of justice in the real lives, contexts, and narratives of those individuals who are threatened. Politics of and in life, not just assigned identity in public space, lifts the human out of identity and, more so, life out of identity. What is crucial in this recognition is the pathos of compassion that works with the making of political life. The value of life as one that can speak to a politics of fissured identity and, in that process, understand life itself as a political goal suggests how indeed the creation of a social can find its specificity in this afterlife. It is a social that seeks stability through justice but does not relegate justice to the impersonal workings of law; rather, it inscribes compassion into legal work and procedure. If such a pursuit of life as citizenship politics can find legitimacy and force, then it is a potential that needs some reckoning in the landscape of perverted democracy that is much too common in contemporary times.

3

Wounding Attachment

SUFFERING, SURVIVING, AND COMMUNITY IN DELHI

That which everyone fears in the *munus*, which is both "hospitable" and "hostile," according to the troubling lexical proximity of *hospes-hostis*, is the violent loss of borders, which awarding identity to him, ensures his subsistence. We always need to keep these two faces of communitas uppermost in mind: communitas is simultaneously both the most suitable, indeed the sole dimension, of the animal "man," but communitas is also its most potentially disintegrating impetus for a drift in meaning of that dimension of the animal "man."

—Roberto Esposito, *Communitas*

THE DELHI SIKH CARNAGE

On the morning of October 31, 1984, the prime minister of India, Indira Gandhi, was walking toward her morning appointments in her official residence when her accompanying bodyguards turned their guns on her and shot her down. Her bodyguards belonged to the Sikh community, and this assassination of the country's reigning political leader was connected to the prevailing Sikh militancy of the time. The north Indian state of Punjab, the territorial home of the Sikh community, had been in violent political turmoil for several years leading up to this event. Led by a charismatic religious leader, Jarnail Singh Bhindranwale, the overall political demand of the ideologues and leaders of the political movement was Sikh separatism, with their own independent state, Khalistan, a demand made in apparent rebellion against the hegemonic Indian state. Indira Gandhi and her regime (the Congress Party) officially recognized Bhindranwale and the Punjab militancy issues as a problem of Sikh terrorism. Following many failed attempts at supposed reconciliatory meetings with Bhindranwale, Indira Gandhi is said to have endorsed the Indian Army's decision to access and capture him from the premises of the Golden Temple in

Amritsar, the place of supreme religious significance for the community and where Bhindranwale had ensconced himself since 1981 with his skilled, loyal, and heavily armed militants. This maneuver was called Operation Blue Star and was conducted over the first eight days of June 1984. Apart from the numbers killed, the pall of infamy was more about the invasion and near-complete destruction of a sacred place cherished by an already offended community, which, at the time of the attack, was housing many hundreds of civilian pilgrims. Last, but not least, the attack was commandeered during one of the holiest weeks of Sikh belief.

Over the seventy-two hours following Indira Gandhi's death, a genocidal zeal gripped Delhi, the capital city, where mobs went on a rampage of ruthless killing of Sikh men, ranging from mere infants to elderly men. Burning alive with torched tires around their necks, throwing kerosene and setting people on fire, or hacking them to death are just some of the ways in which recorded testimonies witness the horror of those days. While numbers dead in Delhi are unofficially reported as between three thousand and four thousand (numbers that surpass even the killings associated with the Godhra episodes), incidents around the nation claimed close to eight thousand lives. The explanation was that this was a public driven to unreasonable violence because of the intense grief felt at the loss of a great leader. However, all possible reportage of the time and, eventually, well-documented proof show the involvement of the ruling Congress Party. Starting from members of parliament to the rank-and-file of party functionaries, many party members were actively part of instigating the attacks or organizing them. Truckloads of galvanized men were driven to city neighborhoods known to be Sikh localities—there they unleashed mayhem, took any and all male lives they could find, and destroyed all forms of property. A few women were killed in their attempts to save the men, and sexual violence was also reported but still meagerly documented. Subsequent to the events in Delhi, unlike in Gujarat, a few official relief camps were set up. Several civil society groups and individuals also volunteered help and assistance while the nation tried to take cognizance of the magnitude of the event, the first of its proportions in independent India.

In the aftermath, when the time for accountability came, once again, in an environment preempting the Godhra situation, justice or the basic work of law was abandoned in the murky domains of political subterfuge. This time, as far as state complicity was concerned, the accused was the Congress Party, most of whose loyal soldiers involved in the 1984 events still stay free from any accountability or prosecution. The techniques of violence and subsequent obfuscation were the same: party hench-men provided information from voter's lists, ration card lists, and so on, about where Sikh households could be found, especially the poorer ones. Voluntary groups, invigorated by the call for revenge, went on a rampage, and the police remained ineffective through the three or so days of bloodbath in the city of Delhi. When survivors and victims tried to register the crimes committed in police stations, police chose to file omnibus FIRs, which successfully obliterated names of the accused with the use of the ubiquitous euphemism "violent mob." An enormous body of evidence implicated party officials, including high-ranking politicians in government, as well as numbers of the lay public. However, the number of cases successfully pursued and convictions attained remains a paltry few as compared to the number of murders.

The Sikh episode suffers its location in a past where neither media coverage nor wider civil society involvement had the same influence or presence as it does now, as in instances like the Godhra episodes. However, current interventions into these subsequent episodes of "com-munal" violence have had their influence on revisiting the Sikh episode or strengthening the work of those who have tried to pursue justice for the crimes and other casualties of that episode. This chapter revisits the episode after a period of nearly twenty-five years. The afterlife sug-gested here circumscribes the lives of some survivors associated with the event and who continue to live in Delhi. The ethnography and narratives presented are largely from two sections of the survivor community, one located in a widow's relocation colony established by the state in Delhi (probably the only widow's colony in the world established in the wake of such an event), and the other another locality in Delhi, well known as a largely Sikh neighborhood, that was attacked in 1984. In the former, as the name suggests, live widow survivors and their remaining families, and in the latter, the survivors are those whose properties and businesses were destroyed.

My arguments develop a sense of an afterlife here in which I follow how life is and has been lived in the interstices of community life and surviving. The conditions in both afterlives, Gujarat and Delhi, resonate strongly, and my interventions in the Gujarat afterlife may well echo here. However, here I suggest a movement into an interiority that takes the focus away from negotiations within the circumscriptions of a national space; rather, it takes a path into community life. How does the idea of living from within the identifications of a beleaguered community, and its internal negotiations, affect life and the social in this afterlife? This separating out of analytical trajectories does not imply that the question of national space or the issues of citizenship and justice do not influence the Sikh experience—they are certainly a part of it. The pathos that catches the light here and becomes visible is one that suffuses an emotive environment of and within the community (which has absorbed the inflections of the wider national environment) and thus embodies another form of life, or bios, in the social that this environment creates.

I, WE, AND WOUNDING ATTACHMENTS

Ressentiment, or "wounded attachments,"[1] could well be a defining trope with which to recognize a community that forms in the aftermath of political violence. Experiences of shared suffering, marginalization, and victimization or, in the same trope, experiences of solidarity, however contingent their terms of gender, religion, race, or more, outline the borders through which groups of politicized identities congeal. When that identity is religious, the community of suffering often draws on affiliations that trace belonging in a span of pasts (sometimes a history of persecution) that hovers above present-day hostility. Violence against embodied identities and its time of occurrence is at a historical juncture, and that temporal moment marks a particular constitution of "who, why, and where" of those moments of trauma, which, while being a possible repetition of past patterns, still effect a singularity in that moment. The question of locating an afterlife paradigm, for my arguments here, in the particularity of the Sikh Carnage negotiates a discursive temporality that is both a real time duration of a recognizable event and a duration of surviving. Here I invoke a time that is also captured by anthropological knowledge forming insomuch as this essay traverses the distance between the present of my writing and past anthropological deliberations on the same "event"—the Sikh Carnage of 1984. And in those discursive vectors, I find the making of an afterlife through the experiences and representations of a specific survivor community emerging out of Sikh identity as such, which shapes its presence in the twenty-five years after the 1984 episode. It is through that duration that the notion of a community of "wounded attachments" is explored, revisiting the question of how, once again, the possibilities of excavating a sense of the social and life in that afterlife play out.[2]

The Sikh community does emerge as one of wounded attachments, struggling for their politics of recognition in the contestations of their suffering. These contestations, not unlike those in the Gujarat context discussed earlier, also invoke the question of citizenship. However, citizenship and wounded identity begin to interact in ways that disrupt attachments among the wounded in experiences that persuade another understanding of a community brought about by ressentiment. The identity that violence targets here is certainly one that arises out of religious ascription, and when a part of that religious collective becomes survivors, their identity deepens almost in the likeness of a vivid scar. At another level, the apparatus of recognition also involves a tangle of bureaucratic labeling and categorization, which subjectivizes further and makes that collective eligible for compensation, rehabilitation, or any other classification that contingent governmentality can produce. In a domesticating bureaucratic technique, these "victims" are offered material compensation, but the state's obfuscation of possible procedures of justice for the murders committed makes this collective an accusatory one and their presence disorderly. A double subject emerges—one that combines, on one hand, incomplete bureaucratic victimhood that sides with citizenship and, on the other, an identity scar that disfigures the body politic. I had explored this earlier in the template of a double subject, first as a bureaucratic category (acknowledged citizenship) that seeks to normalize surviving and suffering with compensation but also works to silence the question of justice. This, in effect, draws out the second, that is, the subject of political identity seeking recognition (the wounded community) in the social and political spaces of continued life.[3] It is in the amplification of the social that the current discussion explores the place of community as something that reveals itself in experiences that break open the homogenizing and domesticating tendencies of politicized ascriptive identity.

As I have mentioned, a well-defined community of ressentiment formed in the aftermath of violent invasive destruction is well founded. But, when the focus moves from that exteriority to another plane—that of an interiority of experience—the community cracks and makes its emblematic aspects fragile. Through a framing of that interiority of participation, suffering, and survival in this afterlife, I show how that pathos exposes fissures within the community itself. To be sure, this pathos is indeed one of a community experience of shared suffering, but a clear distinction of experience arises when the catalog of losses involves murder or loss of material property. This may be a facile division when the question of community identity as a whole is under threat and attack. But, experience and its representation combine to unfold in separate trajectories and, in that separation, work out differing levels of subjective experience.[4] Taking that distinction as a starting point, I extrapolate the following fragmentations of community experience.

There is a subterranean tension that builds up in the dynamic of a triad—first, the historically congealed, shared community of those who share the Sikh belief. The community here is made up of abstract, constitutive members that carry the emblem of that community, and that identity is, so to speak, transcendent over history and geography. Second, from within the first collective emerges a group that occupies the contingent space and time of the event of suffering, and this forms a grouping of victims or survivors. The already political community of Sikh identity subdivides further and now subscribes to the meaning of ressentiment by forming a here-and-now collective of victims and survivors. Third, these victims and survivors are in their personal experience individual embodiments of that suffering, making possible an experience that is about subjective and subjectivized selves—the "I" and the "we" within the same community.[5] In this multiple layering and fragmenting of the space of a community, incommensurable experiences among different lives/vectors of this afterlife appear. This is where the sense of a community of ressentiment seeks another understanding that could clarify what indeed could be the nature of bios and pathos in this afterlife—where the former recognizes the embodiments of community and the form of life that expresses and the latter, the affect involved in being with others in wounded attachments.

Life here is thus a figure that captures these subjects, subjectivities, subjectifications, within the terrain of a violated community and its afterlife, where life forms differently under different experiences of surviving. Through striations of experience, the question of pathos now moves, in the continuum that I have suggested,[6] to that of affect or the emotion of participatory suffering within the boundaries of a community. The accounting of that affect and its embodiment in those who experience that affect find expression in the following account through representations. These representations show the varying intensities of suffering, the compromises and concessions of subjugated life, as well as the perceptions and acknowledgments of life triumphed over atrocious threat. These domains of affect are, I argue, the relationships that show the density of pathos in an afterlife. The breaking up of a collective of suffering engendered by violence shows how this kind of pathos finds its way of calling into presence emotional experiences that intersperse between or separate the "I" and the "we."

MASCULINE RESILIENCE, FEMININE GRIEVING

In the three days following the assassination of Indira Gandhi, the city of Delhi was paralyzed by a gruesome orchestration of targeted killing. As mentioned, Sikh men of all ages—infants, young, or old—across the city were attacked, with a seeming intent to efface the future of that community in the city. The preferred mode of killing was by pulling men out of their homes, taunting and humiliating them, before burning them alive or beating or stabbing them to death. Hordes separated men and boys from their families and killed with impunity, leaving burning corpses while the women, and others who could manage to, fled or hid, only to return to find their sons, husbands, and fathers as remains of inhumane death. The worst affected areas in the city were Sultanpuri and Mongolpuri in southwest Delhi and Trilokpuri in east Delhi, all of which are working-class neighborhoods. Although most other parts of the city were affected in terms of sporadic attacks, arson, and looting, the devastation in these colonies was terrible—entire stretches of homes were razed to the ground; sons, brothers, husbands, and fathers were wiped out, leaving almost only womenfolk and very young children. The city, for those three days, was engulfed in fear, with mobs roaming the streets with impunity, leaving hardly any part of the community, however privileged, untouched by the terror on the streets.[7]

Stunned by the occurrences in Delhi, numerous concerned people from a variety of backgrounds joined hands to provide relief and support to the terrified survivors. Some even marched the streets in open retaliation to the marauding mobs. Relief camps were set up by government order, and other efforts to bring some shelter and help to the victims took shape in the form of citizen's organizations. Foremost among these was the Nagrik Ekta Manch, a number of whose volunteers carried out the important tasks not only of helping out and organizing the daily work in the camps but also recording the first handwritten narratives and reports of the survivors, obviously mostly women, in these camps. A number of these members have dedicated years of their lives to pursuing the cause of justice and healing for one of India's worst bloodbaths.[8] Some of this documentation was also eventually compiled into one of the most searing and bold statements against state complicity, a report titled *Who Are the Guilty?,* with detailed testimonies of the victims and names of senior political functionaries who were witnessed as being directly involved in the directing and organizing of the attacks.[9]

A few years after the 1984 event, Veena Das, at the time teaching at the Department of Sociology at Delhi University, wrote her first essays on the Sikh episodes with the intention of addressing the conceptual lacunae on violence and social suffering in the disciplinary discourses within sociology and anthropology. It is largely her work that I juxtapose to our own[10] ethnographic etchings among the survivor community of widows—with a time span, however, of about twenty years in between.[11] The ethnography on Bhogal is, however, separate in both analysis and description from the gendered experiences of the widows—the following narrative starts with Bhogal.

Bhogal is a dense residential/commercial, largely middle-class neighborhood located in south central Delhi. One distinction of the area was its earlier history, when people displaced by the Partition of 1947 were allotted residential plots as part of the relocation plans of the time. A large section of the neighborhood is made up of families from that group, alongside others. The goods transportation business, largely associated with the Sikh trader community, has its main hubs here, which meant that there were a large number of trucks parked within the area with their owners living in the Bhogal area. During November 1 and 2, Bhogal was attacked by mobs, and although no lives were reported to have been lost in that attack, property, in the shape of trucks or shops and other business establishments, was destroyed in targeted arson. Sikh-owned shops and houses were identified and gutted and a substantial amount of looting took place; however, the most significant and symbolic damage done was the burning of about one hundred to three hundred trucks, another example of the very calculated "frenzy" of the mobs.

During summer 2004, we visited Bhogal and spoke with a number of residents in the area, and the following fragments of conversation were with those who were willing to talk to us about their memories and experiences of 1984 as well as their continuing lives after the event. Our conversations followed a pattern of understanding their experiences after the damage—what kinds of effects they perceived in their personal biographies, how much of the neighborhood, and in what way, still carried traces of the event. In all our conversations, it was striking that there was a clear expression of 1984 having been an event in the past, one that has been now firmly relegated to an unfortunate incident best left behind. From their narrations, this sense of surpassing of the event in their personal and collective biographies was initiated by a recollection of how, as a community and as a neighborhood, they were able to fend off the attacking mobs during those days. There was an emphasized sense of how this was a resilience not only born out of the fact that the neighborhood as a whole had a sense of unity but also arising from the Sikh community's ability to combine forces spontaneously to fend off even a heavily armed, maddened mob. An illustration of masculine pride, but more a recall of an emblematic community ability to stand up strong against any threat and attack, seemed to be the underlying sentiment.[12] They spoke about how their young men came out with their *kirpans* (knives that Sikhs carry as part of religious doctrine) and charged back at the attacking mobs. They mentioned how the attacks in other localities were much more devastating, but in their own locality, they were firm in their resolve to face their fate at any cost, some even suggesting that, during the Partition, their community had killed their own children rather than have them taken by their Muslim attackers. A sense of continued community resilience, in fact, a reinforced community identity of resilience, marks these narrative fragments, especially when they consciously tie together the events of 1984 with those of 1947—often saying that if they could withstand 1947, 1984 paled in comparison. A temporal equity marks the way in which the community emerges as a coherent whole through the past into a present, the coherence marked by the continuity in the sense of collective solidarity and strength. The possibility of replacing material losses seems to be the thematic that underlines this particular neighborhood's ability to relegate the event to a disruptive past that has been successfully overcome. The representative motif, or the iconic image, that mediates this articulation of resilience is indeed the recourse to the enveloping sense of a community—a named identity, that is, the Sikhs as a historic collective that delivers their resilient reputation in times of critical fracture, but also as a continuing framework of pride in community existence—it is a sense of "we" that pervades.

One of the younger residents, whose two trucks were saved from the fires because they were parked in front of his home rather than in the lot where all the loaded trucks were normally stationed, said,

> You already must know that they burnt all our trucks. They burnt our businesses, all of our work. We started out again from the very beginning. There is, of course, the mercy of God. We people do not beg. In our community we have no beggars, we earn what we eat. We worked hard and God has rewarded us for our efforts.

Other younger men, who were able to replace the losses their fathers suffered in the 1984 episode, spoke with visible pride that they were able to make up their losses, for instance, replacing by four trucks the one that was burned. In another conversation, a resident said,

> I cannot tell you about the others, but I know about my community. They are very enterprising; they do not shirk from any work. Of course they suffered

losses but they have restored their losses. Some help from insurance, some of their own courage, some help from friends—from one they made two, then three and like that they managed to stand their businesses back again.

However, a chink in the armor seemed to emerge when some gave us their opinions on how monetary compensation and insurance claims were dealt with. This appeared to be a contentious issue among residents of Bhogal. A comment on community consciousness could be hazarded from these conversations. Some alleged that a few in the community had filed false claims and received loans and insurance payments, an action seen as defaming the values of work and enterprise associated with their recovery.[13] Notwithstanding, the rigorous emphasis was on the fact that, indeed, it was a matter of community pride and character that something so heinous could be thought of as an obstacle passed.

Moving toward the widow's colony,[14] our work there was also conducted during 2004. A few months after the October–November event in Delhi, the state authorities, faced with a large number of widows left homeless, identified a newly built set of residential blocks meant for lower-level government employees and allocated them to the group of widows, calling it the Tilak Vihar Widow's Relocation Colony. Sitting adjacent to an already vibrant, also largely Sikh neighborhood, the colony was made up of tiny one-room apartments in small blocks of nondescript government housing. From around March 1985, about 950 families of widows and their surviving children were relocated there. Around 250 of these consisted of sons and daughters of men killed in the Carnage.[15] Once again, in Tilak Vihar, our attempt was to grasp a sense of what entailed the work of surviving through the twenty years after the 1984 event. Briefly, accounting of the event in terms of either compensation or legal justice, the proceedings were abysmally inadequate. Although material compensation was made in the form of the houses allotted or sums of money,[16] justice continued to be a fraught issue.[17]

The colony, in all its existential implications, marks a spatial containment, one that creates boundaries between the marked residents of the colony and the rest of the city.[18] Within this space itself, a sense of ressentiment is sharply articulated—a widow who was very young in 1984 had spent the last twenty years in the colony, and she had a sense of a comparatively successful life—her children are educated and employed. When I asked whether she ever thought of leaving the colony for a better place, she said, "Here I can talk every day about 1984. I can share my burden every day. But anywhere else, people will just be tired of me—the madwoman who only talks about one thing." A community of suffering or of shared victimhood emerges from an implosive moment from within the larger collective, a moment that is anchored to the 1984 event. Just as in Bhogal, it was compelling to note that a sense of community consciousness, one that takes recourse to the solidarity of historical identity, but at the same time actualizes it in a moment, emerges distinctly at that moment of violation. From the narratives that gathered shape from our conversations in the colony, the transformative moment indeed comprised the days and nights of the violence, moments that were etched deeply in their minds and that they described to us in detail. Even when we reiterated our intent not to reopen old wounds but instead to talk more about life afterward, about coping and surviving, the residents of the colony felt a need to retell their stories from the moment of the Carnage. Ressentiment seemed to have a moment of origin in both Bhogal and the colony, an anchor that marks the striation of a community of victims of identity into communities of survival. However, unlike in Bhogal, where there was a quiet sense of triumph of surviving in pride and resilience, the vignettes of conversation that follow represent a community acutely aware of its fractured destiny—a sense of futile mourning, as Judith Butler may call it.[19] This sense of futility is an experience that, in turn, as the following suggests, also draws the boundaries of separation more clearly between this group of survivors and others.

The invocation of the larger community of Sikhs appeared in a few striking ways during the time of our visit, one of which was the sweeping victory of the congress and their assuming government with a Sikh prime minister, Professor Manmohan Singh. At the time of our conversations, the Delhi Sikh Gurudwara Management Committee, an apex body that looks after the running of the Sikh religious places and also provides various kinds of community support, had discontinued the monthly pension that it had been providing to these widows since 1998. Another presence was the Sikh faith-based organization called Nishkam, which had set up permanent operations in the colony since its inception. They supported the colony residents with a repertoire of provisions, such as a Sewing Center for the widows to eke out a living stitching garments for sale, schooling for children, medical services for colony residents with subsidized care, special vocational courses for young people, and a meeting center for the same. All of these find their presence in a poignant conversation we had with one of the elderly widows[20] of the colony. She spoke of how their holiest site had been vandalized, how their men had been martyred, and how they now wait interminably for justice. She referred to how her community feels that the current government, being led by a Sikh prime minister, would support their cause but how she feels that they have no hope, except perhaps for divine intervention. She said that her community (her reference is to larger groups of Sikhs who are seen or heard in public politics) has no qualms in welcoming back into power those same people who were responsible for the killings. She lamented how even the Gurudwara Committee had stopped their pensions, claiming that the widows now have children old enough to work and earn. But for her, the greater tragedy was that because many of these children (the boys) had to be left behind at home while their mothers went out for work, their "neglect" turned them into drug addicts. She reiterated, time and again, that "all we want is justice":

> Go to Nishkam, they tell you—forget 1984. How can we forget, even if a dog in the house dies, we are sad. We have lost our young children, our world has burnt with them. Twelve men, we are just waiting for them to come home, we are waiting and on the way, petrol is poured on them and they are burnt. ... Our living is not living.

Their negotiations with the community become a multifaceted engagement—the return of a ruling government that was considered responsible for the event and their destinies, ironically with a Sikh as leader, and the daily negotiations with organizations like Nishkam, which runs solely on community support and donations, that are clearly crucial for their everyday lives, if not for long-term sustenance. The multiple layering of community consciousness forces a subtle yet compelling experience of a fractured community—which, in its way, transforms the sense of ressentiment based in identity to one that also displays cracks in its coherence. The residents of the colony cannot but be recognized by their ascriptions of Sikh identity, an identity that has come under severe attack. At the same time, they are not the same as other survivors, like those in Bhogal, where the support required for sustenance came largely from within the group itself—those in Bhogal did not require support from the community at large. In the colony, the acknowledgment and, subsequently, also the experience of betrayal from the larger community seemed acute. The lack of justice for murders contributes to the abiding sense of rancor and is the cause of the intense sense of betrayal and forgetting. Once again, the striations became clear and, in effect, have been made more visible as this collective of ressentiment affects a future group, the next generation. Beyond the lifetime of a single generation, a nuanced community consciousness seeps into a younger generation that experiences this, as if in proxy. The temporal grip of ressentiment demands a future as well. The young people whom we talked to were mostly men between the ages of nineteen and twenty-four. Most of them were infants or very young in 1984 or were born soon after.

> A: We have not received any support from the government. They had said that they will give you these things, they will give your children jobs, they will make your children stand. They have done nothing....
>
> Some time ago there was a fire in a cinema hall in the city. The government has given them a lot, they are still giving them a lot. That was an accident. But with us, it was done to us, still they give us no help. With us it was no accident, it was done to us. The government should have once thought, there were riots, let us look at them—do they have all facilities or not. There is nothing here. They send two to three people—they talk to the leader here and that's all.
>
> ...It's twenty years since 1984. But the government has not thought of keeping fifteen seats for the children of the 1984 people. They have not done anything until now.

Flowing underneath, in the same breath, was also the double bind of community loyalty bordering on vengeance and betrayal:

> B: But, the day we get our turn, this is just a matter of opportunity, those people took advantage of the situation, the mistakes of the police...

A: ... You know what kind of mistakes these police made. All of our people had come together, do you know what the police said? No fights are taking place, go home and leave your weapons with us.

B: Never mind a day, if we could get just an hour. They had three days. They should give us an hour and see. The day we get a chance we will show them. The community can say what they like, but anger inside never dies. Those who can kill their own and win cannot be considered manly [*namard*]. I cannot live like that. What are the *sardars* [men of the Sikh community] doing these days? There is no *sardar* now who has any humanity—in spite of them showing their piety. Tytler has come again to contest—the man who killed our fathers, burnt them alive, he is again being put up. Why do the *sardars* have no courage, couldn't they have shot this Tytler, this Sajjan? Why are they standing again? They only keep fighting behind the gurudwara.[21]

The sense of a trapped future becomes clear when the community of shared victimhood draws its containment tighter, when it implicates stigma, as the following vignette suggests:

A: A friend of ours had learnt the work of air conditioners. He went to an interview and everything was fine. At the end they asked him, where do you stay? And he said, Tilak Vihar. They said you have to go, we cannot take you. Because you are from Tilak Vihar. Just because of this word. They say, everybody is aberrant here, we are disreputable. Someone is a pickpocket, someone is a thief, you catch them and they say they are from Tilak Vihar. ... They say you are from 1984. There is such dirt there [in the colony], you must also be doing the same. We can only say that five fingers are not the same. If along with four bad ones here there is another, he will also be considered bad.

C: Shahpura [another slumlike locality] is even worse than Tilak Vihar. All bad things happen there—chain snatching, kidnapping—but only Tilak Vihar is considered disreputable.

The alleged "dirt" in the colony, as this young man narrates, is associated with the very high incidence of drug addiction among the young men in the colony. Although such problems are equally serious in various similar economically disadvantaged colonies, here the problem takes a different hue. As touched on earlier, we were told by many mothers as well as others that this was a generation that had grown up without proper male parenting, which is required to keep young people firmly in hand. A colony of widows, a large number of whom[22] had to leave their homes to work, to eke out a livelihood, meant that their young were left to fend for themselves. This, in their opinion, led to a generation of young men who could do no better than to lose their way. Here not mere poverty, or the other usual disadvantages of opportunity, was the culpable factor but rather the expected destiny of a "victim" community.

In the preceding narratives, the theme that I underline is the polytonality in how community consciousness affects experience in the work of surviving. Through that thematic, I gesture toward the expressions of succor, solidarity, and betrayal that striate the politicized community, one that in the first place was made coherent by an act of violence—striations that appear to form literally smaller and smaller circles of containment. To add a further facet to this striation, I invoke Veena Das's portrayal of a young widow, Shanti, who was moved to take her own life soon after the events of 1984.[23] Over the course of their conversations, Das weaves together a narrative that, gradually, draws a path toward Shanti's expressions of the "destruction of her soul," beginning with Shanti's description of the night that her husband and male children were killed:

> Some people, the neighbors, one of my relatives, said it would be better if we hid in an abandoned house nearby. So my husband took my three sons and hid there. We locked the house from outside, but there was treachery in people's hearts. Someone must have told the crowd. They baited him to come out. Then they poured kerosene on that house. They burnt them alive. When I went there that night, the bodies of my sons were on the loft, huddled together.
>
> It was my own *mama* [mother's brother] who had advised my husband to hide. He revealed the hiding places of the Siglikar Sikhs to the leaders of the mob. He bartered their lives for their own protection. Go and see his house. Not even a broken spoon has been looted.
>
> They hurled challenges upon my husband to come out. If he was brave he would have come out and then my little children would have been spared. But he remained mute. The mob burnt the house.[24]

In the flow of a few sentences, an intense fragmentation of the bonds and trust that are expected of one's own community takes place. Das comments on the betrayal meted out by a kinsman and the "cowardice" of Shanti's own husband. As Das continues the narrative, she locates Shanti's implacable torment that finds no solace in her daughters who had remained alive. Nor did she find any solace in the sharing of mourning with the other women with similar losses around her. Her constant iteration was her inability to save her children when other women could. She blamed her husband, her eldest son, her eldest daughter, and the community itself responsible for the unbearable torment of the loss of her younger sons. Shanti recalled that during the hours when she was hiding with her daughters, she had sent one of them to their father, her husband, who was also trying to keep his sons from harm at the time, to send back their infant son to her. Her husband had refused, saying she was too feebleminded to protect the infant boy. Later Shanti could not stop herself from beating and blaming her daughter for not trying hard enough—she felt she knew that the crowd was not out to kill children. Other women were able to save their younger children, but she had failed. Her agony was her own, one that could not find any comfort in the fact that many around her had suffered the same fate. The force of shared feeling that must be felt appears starkly, when Das finds Shanti inconsolable in the company of others, one of whom says,

> She carries on as if she was the only one to suffer a loss. Look at the world around us. Everyone was affected. A storm came upon us and destroyed everything in its way. Can we save anyone from such a storm?[25]

The gestures of all those who surrounded Shanti during the time leading up to her suicide—her own mother, her father-in-law, and the ever-present neighbors—combined to put up, it would seem, a stage performance of understanding Shanti's agony, at the same time reinforcing her inability to cope. Undoubtedly, these were compulsions of affect that emerged in the torturous double bind of empathy and disdain, especially when one struggles with one's own pain. It was the constant reiteration of the futility of a woman's life, of a woman's female community, even of her own daughters, and the guilt of having to participate in that community while not affirmed by a male presence. In Das's words,

> She was the only survivor who committed suicide in the colony. Her willingness, even compulsion, to take her own life was the only proof she could offer herself that her guilt could be assuaged by joining her husband and dead sons in their destiny. She was not able to take the risks of re-engagement in the world, including the possibility that she might in time be able to "forget" what

happened to her dead. The forgetting would have included a forgetting of the dominant definition of a woman, as integrated individually into the lines of men and a reformulation of life in terms of female connections. Death and masculinity finally broke the hold of life and femininity.[26]

Das's reading of Shanti's experiences, her death, and the surrounding world of a community made up of her daughters, mother, neighbors, patriarchal kinsfolk, and widow companions leads to a deep inflection of how the community reveals its presence and at what intensity. This is the interior world of a community that now moves into a negotiation of the "I" with the "we." The "I" here of Shanti is that of a woman "deranged" by grief, a woman who is unable to mourn successfully in a collective, a woman who refuses ressentiment. She, perhaps, finds herself acutely aware of a self that forces her to a subjectivity that the community otherwise had taken from her—in a way, she grasps her self back from the collective, even if that grasping back is one that annihilates her living in the community.

The duration of the Sikh Carnage over three days in Delhi and across the twenty-five years since makes this afterlife available in multiple registers of experience. Some of these experiences register the act of "successful" survival, others of compromised and partial coping, and finally, of someone who negates life in the pursuit of the dead rather than of the living.[27] The event itself produces these striations, as I have said, of community and of a subjectivity and a subjectification that negotiate the community. How, then, does this pathos allow an understanding of what the social is and what forms of life it embodies as bios in this afterlife?

COMMUNITAS AND THE UNBEARABLE GIFT OF IDENTITY

Without attempting a sweep of what the notion of community has connoted within political philosophy and theory or in anthropological and sociological concerns, it does seem that in contemporary distillation, there is an inevitable, almost formulaic understanding of community as spheres of human associations that are formed through shared bonds, contingent or otherwise. In addition, they imply a "social" dynamic of relationalities that are different from, and often exclude, the allegedly homogenous liberal space of citizen life. Illustratively, in classical sociology, a basic distinction has been made between *Gemeinschaft* (community) and *Gesellschaft* (civil society)[28] as analytical categories that identify these separate realms—identifying the former with shared values or beliefs and other personal connections and the latter with formal connections of duties, rights, and impersonal connections. In that distinction, community-life is led in realms separate from citizen-life; however, that distinction inevitably blurs in lived reality. In any which way, a community is a sociality that gives a certain form to the arrangement of a society, and it indicates assemblies of relations that underlie the essence of social life as one that implies, literally, being with others. This is not a standard contractual rendition, as in citizenship, of shared existence, where individuals exchange rights and duties, honoring the social contract as a condition underlying feasible civic society. The inevitability of shared life in communities outside of formal citizenship urges an understanding of what creates and sustains the conditions of possibility that make necessary a being with others (when life lived on one's own is clearly not a social possibility). As mentioned, the idea of politicized identity through Wendy Brown's ressentiment, which I will retain for the moment as a community brought about in shared suffering, offers the meaning of such sustenance in people whose social lives, rather, identities, are grounded in violence, threat, or marginalization.[29]

Whether we follow the legacy of paradigms that have been recognized, both in despair and in hope—like communism or communitarianism—or understand a collective, a group with a consciousness that effects an association of identity, or an association of affect, sacrality, or instrumentality, the desire and need for associative living are immanent. As much as that is, the acute consciousness of its lack as well—for instance, the alleged impossibility of the goal in communitarianism of adjusting individualism to common good—leads to a deeper etching, in these discourses, of the desire and the impossibility inherent in the aporetic experience of being with others.[30] The complicated relationships between identity and community, especially those emerging in ressentiment, have been posed by Wendy Brown as an interrogation of the tensions between liberalism's abstract "we," on one hand, and, on the other, the different "others" of particularistic identity. She suggests this tension as one of subversion, where the containment of individual differences through techniques of subjectification in a larger discursive arena of "disciplinary-bureaucratic" normalization negates the emancipatory project underwriting the intentions of politicizing identity. As she states in her argument,

> how can reiteration of these conditions be averted in identity's purportedly emancipatory project? What kind of political recognition can identity-based claims seek—and what kind can they be counted on to want—that will not resubordinate the subject itself historically subjugated through identity categories such as "race" or "sex," especially when these categories operate within discourses of liberal essentialism and disciplinary normalization? Second, given the averred interest of politicized identity in achieving emancipatory political recognition in a post-humanist discourse, what are the logics of pain in subject formation within late modernity that might contain or subvert this aim?[31]

Understanding Brown's project with her stated intent takes us closer to the point that I utilize in the following discussion. Her contention is that the subversion, or rather the containment, of the emancipatory project, within liberal democratic politics, is a form of discursive co-optation, one that skillfully transforms marginal identity categories into domesticated categories that deny them the political intent that they purport to, by the very act of recognition. As she says,

> this subordination is achieved either by the "I" abstracting from itself in its political representation, thus trivializing its "difference" so as to remain part of the "we" (as in homosexuals who are "just like everyone else except for whom we sleep with") or by the "I" accepting its construction as a supplement, complement, or partial outsider to the "we" (as in homosexuals who are just "a little different," a bit "queer").[32]

The inevitable tension arises from the perennial problem of abstracting the individual from the group, the "I" from the "we." The leveling out of differences, or in other words, the blurring of one's life circumstances, one's contingent constitutions of social position, to abstract out "an" identity is perhaps the making of the liberal citizen. The individuation of the citizen as an "I" remains in some tension with other forms of "we" identity necessary for a politics of recognition to be, and this brings into question the subjugations and negotiations inherent between citizens, on one hand, and other identities constituting wounded attachments in suffering, on the other. Following from this, can we assume that the "we" of a community of similar identity (of suffering) is always a homogenous one?

In political violence within democratic nation-states, community-identity negotiates citizen-identity in ways that apparently destabilize both, that blend both or create fissures between the two—a situation discussed as the afterlife of the Godhra event. However, when the focus moves to that of the community itself and explores what tensions emerge within, I have indicated the emergence of another level of subject and subjectification experiences, which are mediated through formations within the community.[33] I draw again from Roberto Esposito's work in *Communitas* to approach this clarification.[34] In a radical exploration of a genealogy of community, he reads Hobbes, Kant, Rousseau, Heidegger, and Bataille to expose in each the arguments for the putative conditions of community as well as its principles of sustenance or disavowal. Although I cannot claim to interpret his exposition in its deserved fullness and nuance, I refer here to his initial etymological excavations, which delve into a social or sociological/anthropological core in the semantic unraveling of *communitas*. The usual understanding of the social bond implies a give-and-take, a basic principle of reciprocity that understands social life lived within a group as one that sustains itself with the idea of a gift that is received and, in turn, returned. Instead, Esposito suggests, that *communitas* draws from its roots in *munus*, which, he says,

> is the gift that one gives because one *must* give and because one *cannot not* give. Although produced by a benefit that was previously received, the *munus* indicates only the gift that one gives, not what one receives. All of the *munus* is projected into the transitive act of giving. It doesn't by any means imply the stability of a possession and even less the acquisitive dynamic of something earned, but loss, subtraction, transfer. It is a "pledge" or a "tribute" that one pays in an obligatory form. . . . The gratitude that *demands* new donations.[35]

This sense of giving without any expectation of return turns the sense of reciprocal living with others on its head. First, it suggests that the social bond that sustains a community is one that demands an obligation without reciprocity. Second, it brings into sharp focus what is really given in this a-reciprocal giving. Esposito makes the claim that this giving is that of subjectivity—that property which is properly one's own. As he says,

> the *munus* that the *communitas* shares isn't a property or a possession. It isn't having, but on the contrary, is a debt, a pledge, a gift that is to be given, and that therefore will establish a lack. The subjects of community are united by an "obligation," in the sense that we say "I owe *you* something," but not "you owe *me* something." This is what makes them not less than the masters of themselves, and that more precisely expropriates them of their initial property (in part or completely), of the most proper property, namely, their very subjectivity.[36]

The startling reordering of reciprocity as something that does not build the foundation of a social bond puts into relief the loss that indeed becomes foundational in the making of a community. A community, so to say, founds itself on the giving of subjectivity rather than on the ensuring of a subjective position.[37] The perpetual giving of subjectivity, as the only property of one's own, makes itself precarious when living itself is so tied to the inevitability of community living. When subjectivized as members of a community—gay, lesbian, Muslim, Hindu, Sikh, Dalit, black—what we achieve as politics is lost in the coherence of a self, loss in the boundaries that make my self different from the other. This analytical turn around then takes us further afield in the loss of something that Wendy Brown hints at, in her way of approaching the coopted politicization of identities, the merging of the "I" in the "we" and the further merging of that "I" in the larger arena of multiple identity publics that make up citizen space.

Community living, or, in another way, politicized identity, is the invasion of the exterior into the interior, making belonging not an intersubjective collective bond but an acute confirmation of the pain of lacking subjectivity. A disavowal of community living could mean a withdrawal into some possibility of a coherent self, perhaps, but that would be a giving in to a void of nonbelonging and, in that sense, a lack of political, or even feasible, existence.

At the same time, it is also equally feasible to suggest that, to start with, the consciousness of my subjectivity and subjectification is impossible without society/community. I could not understand my gay marginality if it were not for the heterosexual society around me, nor would I understand the politicization of identity if it were not for the community of other gay people that I can belong to. If both are true, through my politicization and my subjectification (both presuming a subjectivity), I am indeed not losing but affirming myself as a member of either group.[38] However, in those who make the community of ressentiment that I explore here, I am emphasizing the work of subjectivity and subjectification in the making of a survivor community—perhaps a group that can be extended to politicized community per se. In that, when the putative damage itself is a liability induced by the contagion of belonging, the community becomes a burden rather than a source of succor. I give to belong (following Esposito) and I suffer to remain (following Wendy Brown), thus I give my suffering as well. Who can I be, when this belonging and this giving do not define me? My awareness of myself as something extant appears, it would seem, only when I acknowledge a burden of that belonging and of that giving. And in that, I know that I am giving something of myself to be a part of a community. My self, in these circumstances, is recognized only in its loss.

Esposito's extensive work delves into an exposition, a critique of the ingrained origins of community in political philosophy and the way it has channeled our discursive practice. A fragment of this can be a way of understanding how a community disintegrated by violence lives an afterlife where the unmaking of a community, its dispersed sustenance and experience, charts out the tracing of a life in the social. The politicized community, or a community of ressentiment, is one that sustains a bond of solidarity that arises out of common suffering, of shared victimization. Finding place in a threatening or hostile world could imply and provoke a need of belonging to a protective collective—in that sense, the community holds the final recourse for viable social and political living. When violence is aimed at identity, within a larger political space that is clearly hostile to that identity, the community appears as the place of succor, especially when the work of surviving has to be sustained far beyond the event of violence itself. However, it is this work of surviving that puts into question the solidarity of a community and, at the same time, makes tenuous the possibility of succor. In the experiences that are described here, the privilege of succor seems to be, in some measure, turned around to the perpetual giving of its community members to sustain the sense of solidarity and, in effect, to assert the community's presence. There is a giving of subjectivity for life to be continued as live-able, and when this living is mediated by the community that needs perpetuation, there appears to be a giving of one's private suffering, not so much to mark it as the claim of membership as to offer it in exchange for the community's perpetuation.

To make an extended case in point, the Sikh widow survivor of the 1984 event is not a figure that emerges just as a result of that particular moment of violence. The history of Sikh militancy that prefigured the 1984 event is one that underlines the masculine nature of a violent movement that preempts the making of a community of widows. Their coming loss was preempted in the Sikh struggle or militancy, insomuch as the years of turbulence[39] before the event had already circumscribed a collective of women who were left to bear the burden of mourning for their lost men. They were the prefigured collective that bore the scars of a masculine militant movement leading to the moment of Indira Gandhi's assassination, where again, it was the menfolk who faced the wrath of a vengeful public supported by a complicit reigning government and its foot soldiers who unleashed the mayhem. The loss of masculine lives left the collective of women who bore the identity of those who will mourn or cry for their men.[40] Even within the mechanisms of compensation, when the government allocated money for lives lost, the community decreed that it was the menfolk who should lay claim on the money and be the responsible awardees.[41] This is where the entire historic struggle of the Sikhs, their experiences and perceptions of persecution and victimization, their eventual irruption into violent struggle, forms the transcendent Sikh identity as a larger politicized identity that creates and actualizes the here-and-now community of widows, a community of ressentiment grafted off of its originary one.

In this preempted future, a present is lost where the past leaps into the future, marking the present only as a transformative threshold between a past and a future. This appears stark and acute when the younger generation of Sikh boys and girls living in the colony represent their experiences, live with that burden of a past, constantly reminded of their destiny in the name of which they are made to sacrifice their present. These are not circumstances that are born out of a "common" misfortune of death or poverty, but they are social afflictions that are caused-conditions that have an externality in blame. These are not changeable conditions that could, or are meant to be, dealt with by personal or social means. In fact, they are impediments to the movement of biography because they remove even a consciousness of agency from private life.

If the community of widows is a collective within the larger group, which is formed through their ongoing work of surviving and coping, framed through relationalities to the menfolk of their community,[42] the mark of masculinity appears again in the shape of a further striation that I have mentioned before. The loss of male life is the emblematic definition of the widow's colony, which finds a spatial form in a sequestered bureaucratically organized place in the city of Delhi. In another location, Bhogal, where not loss of life but rather the loss of business enterprise was the effect of the violence, the recovery of the community takes place through the masculine work of restoring that professional enterprise. Although the government made some gestures of compensation for losses through some recommendations of financial loans and insurance, it was the hard work of the community of victimized men that recovered their life-worlds. The work of recovery then builds up another division, another collective within the community that negotiates their identity in another way. While an experience of ressentiment ties this collective to the wider political body of Sikh identity, this would seem to be a passing ressentiment that does not retain its victimhood but rather surpasses it through masculine labor.

In the sum and substance of these two localities and their constituent members, the fragmentation of a homogenous political identity breaks down. However, the survivors' identity now remains within the experienced realm of the "we" versus "them," where the "them" could be those others bearing and practicing the Sikh identity but not suffering the same degree of loss and devastation. Or the "them" could be the larger nation of those outside the community. However, when the shared subjectivity of a "we" is measured with the "I," further fragmentations appear that can be found in within the group of survivors. Group experience is an amalgamation of individual experiences; however, private, individual experience within the community is a question, I would argue, not just of the transference or mediation of community into the individual alone, the permeation of a collective consciousness into the individual carrier. While individual subjectivity can be an experience of the social, there is an imperative in recognizing how life lived in an afterlife can make recognizable the way in which subjective suffering can trace different paths. On one hand, it becomes the equal, often substitutable suffering of each constituting individual of the community; or on the other, it becomes the ultimate privacy of suffering, of individualized experience. Both of these kinds of subjective suffering and their negotiations remain as sublations in the name of the community, in the name of ressentiment. With regard to the widow's colony, I had written earlier,

> These generations in the colony, both past and future are now a "community" of victims bound together by their common loss and grief to follow a common destiny, remembered on occasion as anecdotes in discourses of other "similar" events in the country.[43] But their lives have continued for twenty years of ordinary living in one way or another. What is the nature of this life? Have these lives been assigned any proper political subjectivity? Did their loss make for a "grievable life," i.e. a public political existence that moved into the realms of justice, closure or any form of retribution?[44] Have they been blended back into some form of cohered social fabric? If from Judith Butler's idea of a grievable life, I am to understand the legitimacy of their widowhood, their entitlement to legal or to any other kind of right, then the widows of the Colony do not have grievable lives. Their grief and mourning is the continued private trauma and memory (constituted "publicly" as well) that constitutes the other part of the widows' entity.[45]

The political existence of these widows without justice can well be called lives that have fallen outside the frame of grievability, their trauma remaining public and private at the same time, retaining a representation of community of common suffering.

However, with an instance from the ethnographic archives of the Sikh Carnage and the anthropological interventions made at the time by Veena Das (1990), I attempt to understand the suicide of Shanti, a widow who takes her own life a few months after the 1984 violence. I read that instance in an afterlife as a statement of private suffering that finds little place in public political suffering and in some sense breaks apart the cohesion of the community. In all of the preceding striations of community, or of ressentiment, I see the necessity of intervening with Esposito's explorative analytics of *communitas* as a legacy of the *munus,* which makes unstable the sense that a wider shared subjectivity, especially one of suffering, holds the community together, especially when political recognition is the desired leitmotif.

Politicized identity is a staple of a democratic polity, where the negotiations with power or even governmentality are seemingly best achieved not so much with individual claim to citizenship as with the combinatorial force of group membership. Not all politicized identity is about religion, but when it is, the question of secular society does give way to a difficult transaction with political society. In India, this transaction has been frequently violent, before or after British rule. An archival colonial genealogy marks the formation of a concept, as it were, of "communal" violence, one where real and alleged hostilities between communities, religious, sectarian, or ethnic, shape the perception of a particular kind of collective violence. In any which way, communal violence in India certainly forms a significant analytical category that prefigures the reading I attempt here.

In the ethnographic vignettes, I have described the experiences of groups within the collective that cover the range from gender differences to age and social class. The Bhogal men that we talked to are a group of middle-class businessmen; the widow's colony, on the other hand, is made up of women who are middle to lower class, with caste variation as well. The generation that suffered directly was of course made up of those starting from those who were very young children and had witnessed the time of the Carnage. Yet another age group that inhabits the collective of survivors are those who were born after the riots and are now living in the widow's colony. All of their expressions here endorse the point that, on one hand, social and kin positioning effect a variation in the experience of violence, to which I have added the dimension of material loss versus loss of life.[46] On the other hand, Das's forceful point about how the violent event was not the only form of devastation that the women survivors faced, but their continuing oppression in the processes of justice, compensation, meted out both by kinsmen and state authority, endorses the gendered dimension of suffering and survival.[47] The continuing generation, however, carries the burden of a perpetuated collective—in all of these striations, Esposito's notion about community as that which is formed by the giving of its members of a sense of self, or of a subjectivity, is incisive. I emphasize that here, to understand the pathos of suffering and its participations (within a community) as one that configures different embodiments of obligatory giving to the community. These differences in embodiment then express the forms of life that emerge in this afterlife.

The Sikh emblematic identity of resilience and work ethic is a resource that the men in Bhogal draw their sustenance from—it is their proud reconstruction of a group, which they are able to endorse after they have "succeeded" in recovering their losses, so to speak. While not equally true for all, the reemergence of a community identity performs the operation of suturing a portion of the larger group, over time, back into the overall community fabric. How was this suturing possible? I read in these men's experience an unremitting giving of their selfhood, their labor, and their resilience to the making of that emblematic identity such that it gains a perpetuation especially when it is under the threat of being dismantled. Community honor is the product of work and labor that is continually performed for that honor to subsist, to continue being the resource it does become in times of severe distress. The ability of these men to express themselves through an anchoring in their group identity rather than speaking of personal hardship and achievement speaks of the blending of the individual into the collective. In the first instance, their giving was marked by them being targeted as those who represent the community for the attackers—they carry the burden of victimhood. In the second instance, they sustain that marking by reversing their fate of targeted identity to that of resilient identity, thus recovering their belonging in a transcendent community that surpasses their individual experience. Here there is a distinct sense of the "I" aiding the sustenance of the protective cloak of identity of the "we" so as to maintain a social position in the afterlife. Once again, it is possible to suggest that the loss and regaining of material wealth alone guides the trajectory of the afterlife in this group as one that resumes its position within the larger identity—

those unable to make the same material recovery appear as chinks in the armor of resilience, making the community vulnerable to their nongiving, so to speak. Their subjective incapacities become an expression of the individual rather than of the community.

In the widow's experience, on the other hand, the subservience of any individual, singular subjectivity to the subjecthood of the whole of these Sikh women aids the work of creating a distinct political identity as much as it carves out the space for a group that stands separate and unique from the larger community that has been attacked. The voices that we hear in the preceding vignettes speak of a collective "we." These are the women who are collectivized in their suffering, in their mourning and their womanhood. Their trauma, which is undoubtedly private, finds itself blurring into the common contours of a group created not just by bureaucratic management (e.g., their relegation to a "widow's colony," their profile as victims who can get compensation) but also by the continuing denial of adequate justice for the loss of life they have endured. It is as if their private suffering has received a public affirmation that seals their identity as a group. It is the ascendance of the "we" in creating the foundations of ressentiment for a political identity.[48]

Earlier, I wrote about their coherence as a socially distinct group that also finds spatial containment in their continued life.[49] Their living together unites them in a further destiny of biographical commonality—one that focuses on their emplacement in the public gaze that perceives literal city spaces. The refusal of the state system to accord justice for the murders and the Sikh community's persistent appeals for it find their iconography in the widow's colony. Films, regular journalistic portrayals, and the recent rise in public appeals to justice (which may be linked to the similarity with the Godhra episode and the wider public consciousness on that) fix the widows as the unchanging face of Sikh victimhood. In that portrayal, the private individual suffering remains in concealment—this is a collective that suffers, however, individual narratives of suffering do not claim the same political presence. The pursuit of justice, it would seem, can only be conducted with an appeal from the group—whereas the actual procedures of justice, if they were to take place, will name the individual complainants or those who have been killed—individualized citizenship is the end result of a collective endeavor. In that sense, collective relief on a few of the convictions will have to substitute for those whose murders remain unaccounted for, or they are condemned to a waiting and a futility of mourning.

The children of these widows find their fates tied to this destiny of futility. It would be incorrect to say that all among the youths are unsuccessful in leading lives with potential—some are able to pursue paths as best as the opportunities in their socioeconomic circumstances can allow. However, the question of a common identity does not leave them, nor does the occasional outburst of the burden of avenging meaningless deaths caused by that community identity. The coherence of this collective of victims rests on the giving, following Esposito, of their personal biographies, their individual biographies of grief and loss to the collective, so that the political presence is not diminished. The continuing project for justice and other accounting of the crimes committed can continue only when private life is subjugated to public life—this is the gift they give for the community to exist.

But Shanti's biography troubles this giving without obligation to receive. While private subjective experience is subservient to the political collective of widows, there is an underlying reciprocal demand that emphasizes a return of compensation in justice or in material goods. This return may not be made to individual members, but the community as such will be vindicated, as and when these compensations have happened, however inadequate, or will happen. However, in Das's account of the circumstances leading to her suicide, we see her gradual withdrawal from all the collectives that form around her—from the most proximal of her kinsfolk, her mother, her remaining female children, or her father-in-law, to the women who gather in mourning around her.[50] Her constant litany is the need for an inner peace, a consciousness of an overwhelming interiority that makes her unable to participate in the outside community.[51] She is compelled by a subjective experience to withdraw from giving; she cannot be a member of the community of victimhood that demands her presence as the constituent of a collective, and not as a subjective biography of anguish. This is the inability to give, and in this inability, the seeming seed of community destruction and disentanglement is apparently sown.[52]

Shanti's suicide is a claiming of a subjectivity that can be read as defeated life, as failure to survive. But it does call into question how the "I" can indeed assert itself in a community of suffering. When it does, ressentiment is a failed force and leads to the unmaking of a political project of gaining acknowledgment in the document of atrocious suffering that society registers. This acknowledgment is one that uses the subjective to manufacture the community and thus is dependent on the continual giving of the subjective. However, when the subjective is claimed for one's own self, when the singularity of experience is prioritized as against the need of the collective, the sense of the community is dismantled. How does this movement away from the collective of suffering negotiate social suffering?

The inability of an individual to socialize suffering is also, it would seem, the movement away from society. However extreme these particular examples, like that of Shanti may be, it will not be very difficult to find disturbingly long lists of those who have taken their own lives in the process of "surviving," and not just in the temporality of an afterlife. To extend the movement away from society in this act of self-killing seems to startle a notion of society where it is possible to note, quite starkly, that suffering without society could mean the annihilation of self. In an extraordinary double bind that swings between individual freedom to claim a singular subjectivity and surviving with the exteriorizing, or the "giving," of one's biography to the collective,[53] in the latter, as I have argued, it could be both a condition of succor and sustenance, or it could be the relentless subservience of the personal to the collective.

How does this afterlife discern the notions of the bios and the pathos; what questions of life and the social emerge from this? In the here and now of the Sikh event, subjects and subjectivizations emerge that offer for speculation a striation of community. Through these striations, subjective experiences come to be foregrounded, ones that bring into question the nature of community itself. Through the making and unmaking of community, selfhood or its negation appears as the bios of this afterlife, the lives lived in the work of survival. They are no longer as much about community as about the fissures and sutures between the personal and the collective, each of which now becomes a figure that embodies an experience, the emotive experience of belonging in a community—the pathos in this afterlife.

4

Emotional Geographies

WAR, NOSTALGIA, AND IDENTITY IN BEIRUT

"Container" in Greek is *periechon,* literally a having or holding around. To be in place is to be sheltered and sustained by its containing; it is to be held within this boundary rather than to be dispersed by an expanding horizon of time or to be exposed indifferently in space.

... It is the stabilizing persistence of place as a container of experiences that contributes so powerfully to its intrinsic memorability. An alert and alive memory connects, spontaneously with place, finding in it features that favor and parallel its own activities. We might even say that memory is naturally place-oriented or at least place supported.... Unlike site and time, memory does not thrive on the indifferently dispersed. It thrives, rather, on the persistent particularities of what is properly in place; held fast there and made one's own.

—Richard Casey, *Remembering*

THE WARS IN LEBANON

The cycles of violence in Lebanon, particularly in the capital city of Beirut, are about the nation's multiple genealogies of ethnic hostilities and arguably also about its location in regional hostilities that involve Israel, Palestine, Syria, and the larger Middle East as well as the Mediterranean. Be that as it may, the sketch here does not take on the formidable task of summarizing the historical political conditions leading to violence in the region or the nation; rather, it focuses on the city of Beirut, outlining a set of events and rendering a reading of them.

The first set of events flagged here relates to the 1975–89 civil wars, the beginning of which is traced to a clash between a group of Christians and Palestinians on April 13, 1975, a date commonly considered as the triggering moment that led to the snowballing of civil hostilities in the nation. A prolonged cycle of armed violence, immense devastation, and social turbulence ensued, which was then called to an end with the Taif Accord signed during September 1989. The second set refers to a later cycle of violence, the July–August 2006 war, which was an episode of the ceaseless armed hostility between Israel and the Hezbollah that resulted not only in massive destruction to life and property but also in an uncertain cease-fire. This later event is considered in the past continuous, more in its ability to qualify as evidence of a future already prefigured in the city's horizon. During the thirty-four days of that warfare, Israeli bombardments, provoked by yet another incident of Hezbollah cross-border firing, succeeded in pulverizing the Dahiye,[1] the area where the headquarters of the Hezbollah is located. Approximately twelve hundred are said to have lost their lives, and approximately three hundred thousand were displaced—all of whom belonged to the uncertain category of Hezbollah "supporters," labeled so because they lived in Hezbollah territory or were simply Shia civilians.

Both of these sets of events are bookmarks or temporal points in which to locate an afterlife, especially to emphasize one where transformations provoked by violent episodes are about a peculiar interplay of temporal and spatial experiences and in places where hostilities are suspended rather than closed. Once again, the issues discussed have very little focus on the violence itself, but they provide the grounds of engagement for understanding the question of faith-based identity in space. The episodes of violence in the city take on a spatialized or place-related character of hostility, and conflict bears a particular relationship not only to the localization of disruption but also, in reference to my own problematic, to the localization of an afterlife.

Traditionally, the sociopolitical networks in Lebanon were contoured predominantly along confessional lines somewhat in the manner of a patron–client relationship, where religious identity, kinship and community ties, and village or area loyalties organized social and political life.[2] The family or leader who traditionally held the highest authority in any community sought and dispensed favors and was promised loyalty and, when the time came, armed protection. Militias and gunmen were a common appendage to every leader and community. Even in independent Lebanon, after the French mandate, the democratic institutionalization reflected the confessional patterning of the nation. Political figures rose out of their traditional roles as patrons of religious groups or areas and held positions in the government, but their operations remained largely aimed at maintaining their positions as leaders of "a community" rather than of a civic society. After independence, for about three decades, the pattern of shared governance held up remarkably well and came to be considered a model for institutionalized democratic coexistence in a multicommunal state and one of the few viable examples to follow.

However, once the many episodes of armed hostilities among confessional groups commenced, it was obvious that a political apparatus, which, in its formality, guaranteed participation and representation to all confessions, could not, in its execution, overcome the divisive factors of changing demography and confessionally defined power rivalries and economic disparities. A striking feature of this particular form of sociopolitical organization was its literal mapping onto geographical territory. The expanse of Lebanon, even when it was not included within the present boundaries, was in actuality a conglomeration of patches, each patch representing the historical location of a particular community. The other crucial regional event that has introduced another contender to the nation's geographic space has been the creation of the state of Israel in 1948. Exiled Palestinians are now a notable part of the population of Lebanon, and their encampments around the country and in Beirut have also been sites of severe violence.

The city of Beirut was a microcosm of the country. Beirut was also similarly fragmented, with neighborhoods organized mostly around confessional identity such that the urban space of Beirut was mapped out along the various communities. Rue Damas, the road that ran from the port area on the western end of the Beirut coastline and across the city to its eastern reaches, was a prominent marker of territories. The neighborhoods to the east of this road were predominantly Christian. The Western neighborhoods were mostly Muslim. More than half of the urban population of Palestinians was in camps around the city. Druze quarters also dotted the city, mostly in the north and east. The sprawling Armenian quarter of Bourj Hammoud flanked the coastal road in the north. Most of these traditional quarters, as defined by their communities, were almost exclusive wholes complete with their own schools, hospitals, social clubs, political offices, and religious buildings. Newspapers and popular periodicals published from these places also had a distinct confessional character. In the situation where a sectarian identity marked one's place in society and mapped out an arena of social contact, the place one chose to live in was bound to be a reflection of these parameters. And again, in times of hostility, these became the sites in which respective militias could consolidate their own and exert their control in either offensive or defensive action, and they became "insular community ghettoes"[3] with armed policing of borders and territories. However, the exceptions to this rule of the city as a confessional collage were two localities, the downtown area and Ras Beirut, a Western district that had distinct cosmopolitan features. My ethnographic accounts of two neighborhoods in the city, described in the following, are set against the background of these two areas.

A description of the civil war of 1975–89 would be an account, episode by episode, of how the local power elite, in their struggles for supremacy in intragroup rivalries or intersectarian differences, gave ample opportunity to regional power brokers to play out their stakes. Also, it would be a document of a society trapped in a historicity of confrontation, which could not address differences in any way but by the ineluctable logic of violence. The ongoing border conflicts between the Hezbollah and Israeli forces are another development, more reflective of comparatively recent power dynamics, and the July–August 2006 war was an inevitable punctuation in that continuing hostility. Whatever the origins of hostility and confrontation in the political historiography of Lebanon or the parameters in which these can be analyzed, they have constructed a pattern of recurrence that cannot be removed from its spatial metaphor. In this spatial narrative of the effects of violence, my emphasis, once again, will be about how this afterlife locates a certain social relationality that these particular events of violence have engendered—one that emplaces identity into space by literally revealing the making of a geography of faith. Life and the social that is lived and experienced in this afterlife, then, comes into close negotiation with its location, with a sense of geography and, ultimately, the question of marked bodies in space.

HOSTILE IDENTITIES AND CITY SPACES

Emplaced violence, it would seem, is inevitable in racial conflict—geography (or territory, as the more appropriate term) intermeshes quite literally with violence. When reproduced within the densities of urban life, emplaced hostilities forefront a play between social formations that embed people in locations of the city and those quotidian practices that make up urban life. In another way, the friction of hostile bodies in city spaces, even outside the recognizable moments of violence, creates an abrasion between space and identities, whether that abrasion is real or speculated and imagined. This friction, however expected in Beirut, complicates a simplistic understanding of a heterogeneous, multicultural city driven to violence by politics. Nor is the involvement of place in such violence explained solely by the kind of phenomenon that the earlier discussions on Delhi and Gujarat showed, where targeted people are identified by their locations in city neighborhoods well recognized as community locales. Beirut's geographical history is a city mosaic etched with clear patterns of confessional living, where these places were not only about violently protected borders during episodes of hostility; they have also been spatial markers of cultural separation and difference, simultaneously creating spaces of belonging and identity.[4] When armed hostility envelops these spaces, these markers transform themselves into insulated boundaries. This movement between two kinds of experience of urban life lived in spatial metaphors of harmony or hostility seems to elicit a city poetics or, in keeping with my arguments, the pathos of a city witnessing its own suffering. This is a witnessing that takes place in the shadows of time past, where memory, or rather, nostalgia, comes to represent the real or imagined ideal of a harmonious city of cosmopolitan ideals, whether mundane or elite.[5] The afterlife in such city poetics weaves time with space, narrating nostalgic stories of places wrecked by violence, where personal biographies embody corporeal experience of such poetics of the past.

In Beirut, this embodiment of confessional geography is undeniably about life marked by faith—whether that faith is indeed a matter of private devout piety or of public sectarian identity. The parenthetical markers of both violent time and space interact with such embodiments to reveal nuances about how inscriptions of violence and hostility in urban space interact with faith-based identity, especially in an afterlife where violence seems to be in suspension rather than completed. My discussion here reads these experiences as those of emplaced affect that reveals personal and social negotiations of nostalgia;[6] as recognitions of dismantled everyday environments in the present; and as apprehensions of uncertain futures that pervade ongoing living in that urban horizon. In that sense, the afterlife of urban experiences of violence that involve faith-based identities is acutely about space, space that is deeply imbued by the enactment of identity in space.[7] This notion becomes sharpened because of the exact locations that my ethnography is anchored in. As mentioned earlier, my work was based in two neighborhoods, Saifi and Hamra. The former is a small neighborhood in the northeastern corner of Downtown Beirut, the latter a neighborhood in Western Ras Beirut. Both were places considered exceptional in their cosmopolitanism, especially in the patchworked environment of the city, however harmonious that horizon looked in peacetime. The suffering that is evident in these two places engulfs the social by exposing the scars of a social space that has been undone and made precarious by hostility, a suffering that mourns the loss of an urban ideal while exposing the contours of identity much too sharply.

These interwoven motifs of faith, identity, and place implicate three major patterns that I privilege in Beirut. First is the work of emotion in geographies that are imbued by social imaginaries of belonging or exclusion, whether externally imposed or internally assumed (however fractiously). This notion fuses with Richard Casey's words that I have used as an epigraph to this chapter, "container of experiences that contributes so powerfully to its intrinsic memorability," or the powerful presence of remembrance. Second is the nature of this emotional work when it is channeled through years of violence experienced in idioms of identity and then expressed as memories or longings of urban harmony in a damaged city. Third is the embodiment of these experiences in selves that negotiate not just the quotidian aspects of an afterlife in city space but also in acknowledgment of an environment of suffering that has engulfed a city. Reflecting on the first two, "reputational geographies"[8] is an apt phrase that sets in place the pathos that I anchor here:

This emotional work involves the construction, reproduction and contestation of what we term here reputational geographies. These are social imaginaries defining an area as "good" or "bad," safe or volatile, "no-go" or peaceful. Reputational geographies refer to the symbolic and material boundaries drawn around places as indicators of social status, sites of memories and repositories of affect that can have profound socio-economic as well as emotional consequences for local residents. Our focus is on the everyday practices that create and dispute these reputational geographies.

The work of acknowledging a city's corporeal suffering in war and prolonged armed violence is one of spatial witnessing and participation. The participation in that pathos is by bodies that mediate faith and identity into constructions of self/selves, which are then experienced as presences in places dismantled and inscribed by violence. Together they underline how faith underscores the emplacement of an afterlife, creating in its stead a singular sense of life in the social.

The temporal dimension of this afterlife suggests an analytical complexity that I anchor through Paul Ricoeur's *thesis of a threefold present*. When the "location for future and past things insofar as they are recounted and predicted appears untenable as temporal experiences that are firmly fixed in discrete categories of the past and the future, the past and future appear to be dimensions of time whose possibility of consciousness remains inherent in an acknowledged present." Finding a solution in the "present," he states, "by entrusting to memory the fate of things past, and to expectation that of things to come, we can include memory and expectation in an extended and dialectical present."[9] As a grounding notion, I suggest that the temporality of this afterlife is one that is manifest in such a mediating threefold present. It is a phase that is resolutely engendered in the present because of a critical past; similarly, the speculations of the future are stimulated because of the resonance of a particular past.[10] The spatial anchors are based on the notion of *social space* that Henri Lefebvre proposes—it is a fecund and fluid conceptualizing of space and its experience as a combination of three meanings. These include, first, Spatial Practices, spatiality that "produces and reproduces" social formations where space becomes the mediation between social formations and their material forms, which are open to a degree of mappability and measurement.

Second are Representations of Space—a conceptually produced spatiality through the use of signs and codes and principles of design that are used to produce regimes of order or control by the mental spaces, for example, of planners, urbanists, technocrats, creative artistic imagination. Third are Spaces of Representation, denoting primarily a "lived" spatiality that encompasses either of the preceding but also surpasses them to include those unseen sites and places, sometimes marginal, at other times peripheral, manifested by "users and inhabitants" in moments of change, appropriation, or resistance.[11] The afterlife that I seek to pursue in the narratives from the two neighborhoods that I base my writing on, Hamra and Saifi, gets its theoretical scaffolding in a combination of Ricoeur's threefold present (the temporal frame) and Lefebvre's Spaces of Representation (the spatial scale). A further qualification texturizes Hamra and Saifi as "places" that remain embedded in the larger dynamics of space and its representations that violence engenders. The words *space* and *place* and their distinction follow from Yi-Fu Tuan, where space is a fluid, amorphous notion as compared to the stable fixity of place.[12] The question, then, that guides the discussion is, what form of afterlife gets expressed in this crux of time and space/place, and in that, what are the bios that find emplacement in this pathos?

EMPLACED AFFECT AND NOSTALGIA NARRATIVES

The narratives and representations from Saifi and Hamra that are described here were collected more than a decade ago—they are located in that present.[13] Since then, as can be expected, these neighborhoods have undergone substantial transformation. Saifi, as part of the new Central Business District (the erstwhile downtown), is in fact spectacularly different in both visual and social terms. More striking is the way in which these neighborhoods or the spaces they represent have been "used" and experienced in recent times. The reconstructed Downtown Beirut has become the new public arena where the tumultuous political pulse of the nation finds expression just as it comes into being as a slick, newly sculpted, globally contoured business district.[14] Hamra seeks to find its place in a rapidly changing, competitive commercial city, and at the same time, its residents transform or make subtle accommodations for a changing social profile. In rapidly changing environments, ethnographic representations always feel the charge of uncertainty, of being able to find the right balance between the time and space of location versus the changes that have overcome those contexts. In the following depiction, I have chosen to leave the vignettes as witness to a time that is now no longer decipherable—yet it's these transitory, fleeting moments of change and uncertainty, of remembrance and apprehension, that shape an ongoing afterlife in Beirut. Collected during 1997–98, the representations from Hamra and Saifi articulate experiences that lie in the shadow of a city trying to cope with the first prolonged violent disruption mentioned here, the Lebanese Civil Wars of 1975–89.[15] They are spatial narratives expressed by people at a time when their lives were closely intertwined with a transitory moment, a moment in which a turbulent past still seemed to linger, the future appeared to be alienating, and the present was at best ambiguous. I read these narratives here as spatial experiences of an afterlife, that is, life in the social that articulates a coming to terms with changed socialities and topographies.

In Beirut, to start with, a basic spatial organization that had resulted from the war was the division between Christian East Beirut and Muslim West Beirut, marked off by the Green Line running through Downtown Beirut. On April 13, 1975, a shooting incident between Palestinian guerrillas and Kata'ib militiamen (the Kata'ib were the leading Christian coalition in Lebanon) in an eastern neighborhood in the city led to an outbreak of armed confrontations between Christian and Muslim militias in various parts of the city. Violence escalated quickly and began to encompass the entire country. In the same year, by the beginning of September, the Kata'ib bombarded the Souks in the city center, destroying this area almost entirely. To some analysts, the political message of the time was symbolic and clear—the Souks were the melting ground for the Christians and the Muslims who worked side by side here, as a common economic and social community.[16] The Kata'ib, representing Christian interests, were announcing their rejection of coexistence, and their attack on the Souks eloquently established their goal of political survival at the cost of coexistence. This was perhaps one of the first divisive strokes that would eventually establish the most lasting of hostile boundaries and the most generic division in the city, the Rue Damas front line or the Green Line between Christian East Beirut and Muslim West Beirut.

By the end of 1975, it was becoming increasingly clear that the conflict was no longer between the Palestinians and the Christians alone but was escalating rapidly into a civil war. Armed clashes between militia groups became more pronounced in the city center and the area around. For the ordinary citizens of Beirut, Downtown Beirut represented an arena of fear, the Green Line marking the most dangerous of all lines of confrontation. Following December 1975, militias on both sides of the city, East and West, in a continued cycle of attack and retaliation, expelled or killed those "different" from their own, gradually creating homogenous territories on either side. In the city center, the Mourabitoun were able to drive the last Christian strongholds out of the strategic Hotels District that lay to the northwest corner of the city center, on the Muslim side of the demarcation line. This was the final and most definitive act to establish the dividing line as a zone of militant activity as well as a rigidified boundary frontier between community territories.

In Beirut, those lines that had previously served to trace the social map of the cityscape now became formalized as antagonistic boundaries. Throughout the war until 1989, violence organized itself around the city in typical sections of inside–outside formations and across various front lines. During the time of my fieldwork, although the Green Line no longer existed as an armed barrier, the habit-forming remembrance of hostile mappings lingered in the everyday experiences of the city's spaces. Saifi and Hamra lie on either side of the erstwhile Green Line. Saifi[17] is on the eastern side, located within the expanse of Downtown Beirut, and Hamra is on the Western side, a little over a mile away from Saifi. These sites were not chosen as opposing locales in a divided city; rather, there is a compelling link between them. In a city where confessional communities were and still are vigorously sustained in personal, political, and professional lives,[18] these locales laid a shared claim, during the prewar era, to mixed living that supported and encouraged a shared common ground for all sects and communities. These two places suggest a kind of subversion in a city that has been discursively framed around geographical mapping of sectarian identity and, for my argument here, compelling illustrations of changed topographies.

The neighborhood called Hamra is roughly distinguished as a residential/commercial quarter that surrounds the main Hamra Street. Before the war, Hamra Street was perhaps the most vibrant of city spots, with its range of entertainment and leisure spots, shopping avenues, important business concerns, embassies, schools, and universities. As part of the wider area of Ras Beirut, Hamra traces its development and its character to the American University of Beirut, which, since its establishment in 1866, has come to be one of Lebanon's premier universities, well known across the region. The combination of local city folk, expatriates and tourists, intellectuals and students, tradesmen and professionals, made Hamra into a quintessential cosmopolitan urban locality. In fact, in the years before the war, Hamra stood out as an iconoclastic space, unusual not only in the city but in the surrounding Arab world, cherished for its open tolerance and engagement with people identified not by their sectarian markers but by their diversity of interests and proclivities.

The war changed Hamra—like the rest of West Beirut, Hamra fast became reterritorialized as a Muslim zone, receiving large waves of people relocated either from other parts of the city or from the volatile south, who began to move into the abandoned homes of Christians or others who were moving out. Like in the rest of the city, a rhythm of everyday shelling and regular gunfights measured the years; however, serious warfare, in a concentrated manner, started in Hamra after the Israeli invasion of Lebanon and their subsequent siege of West Beirut during 1982. Bombarded by shelling from both land and sea, Hamra became more of a focused target because the Palestine Liberation Organization (which had by then established its base in West Beirut), in a somewhat misplaced attempt at retaliation, pulled their guns, anti-aircraft missiles, and rocket launchers out of their camps and placed them around the residential blocks of Hamra. Following a monthlong episode of such attacks, life in Hamra deteriorated immensely; the area gradually lost its erstwhile profile, losing out to several other centers in the city that emerged in tandem with the many insular neighborhood pockets.

Since the end of the war, Hamra has not been the focus of any formal reconstruction plans; however, the prominent trading community here has been active in refurbishing the area with an intention of revitalizing the area's commerce and regaining its former place in the city. Hamra has a new look—the main street has been attractively cobbled and converted into a partial pedestrian zone. Many new business concerns, cafés, restaurants, and chic shopping options, alongside renovated older establishments, have given Hamra a new gloss and perhaps a new atmosphere as well. The imperceptible changes are those that lie behind these surfaces, changes that come to light when ongoing experiences of the neighborhood through the phases of the past, present, and future are documented. The issues that constitute the postwar phase here are, of course, different from those that are seen in the city center. Given the past resonance of the neighborhood, the aftermath here has been a combination of resilience and adaptation to a changing situation rather than actual reconstitution, as in Saifi. At the end of the war, Hamra retained very little of its earlier character, but it did manage to hold on to a fairly tenacious group of residents and businessmen, including a fair number of Christians, who, either by choice or by force, refused to abandon their work and homes. The social character, though, had changed perceptibly, the various facets of which are expressed in the following narratives.

In our[19] meetings with a variety of Hamra people, one outstanding feature emerged from every remembrance—the past in Hamra is encapsulated as a quality of life, of an environment, an ambience, and an atmosphere. In various ways, this quality stood for the best kind of urban living possible—worldly, cosmopolitan, prosperous, and vibrant. The name "Hamra" collapsed the place, a quality and an experience such that, frequently, they became interchangeable, particularly at a time after a critical phase when remembrance demanded the recalling of a lost experience. Not unlike Downtown Beirut, Hamra was also talked about as a meeting point where people from all over the world converged to share in an urban experience. However, whereas Downtown Beirut was a "popular" center, Hamra was known more as a place for a sophisticated experience, laying out its own criteria of inclusion and exclusion. Once again, the comparison with the golden past underlined recollections of the war. A Christian Hamra resident who had been in the area for about forty years said,

The war came along and of course it changed a lot of things. This particular area came under the control of groups that were not of the area . . . people who perhaps used to dream that one day I would go and walk down Hamra Street, all of a sudden became masters of the region. The militia groups, they did not have the educational, cultural background that in any way was compatible with what Hamra used to be. They came primarily from areas far out of the capital. Their educational standards were very low and they had no real relationship with this part. And under the gradual religious polarization where basically Christians living in West Beirut fled to the east or left the country. So . . . all of a sudden it plunged to the point perhaps where it was 90 percent Muslim and the 10 percent Christian who were here were tamed, were docile. They didn't dare say anything.

Gradually this area was de-Westernized and de-Christianized to at least a certain extent. I remember someone saying that you walk down the street and you wouldn't see a man wearing a suit. They were all wearing these black leather jackets. . . . I know people who deliberately wouldn't dress up nicely for fear [that] they would be conspicuous on the street. The place just went downhill. Nice shops closed out because there were no customers anymore, and we saw all kinds of vendors selling cheap shoes and cheap clothes and simple food—shawarma and falafel[20] and this kind of stuff. The image is like that—it became very unclean, to put it very simply, dirty, garbage everywhere. All these people—they were coming from a nonurban background, far off. It's got nothing to do with religion, but I think it's to do with culture.

Embedded in the preceding quotation is the initiation of a distinct divide between an "us" against a "them," which clearly sets the tone of a social "othering." Almost all of our informants underscore this—the people who came to control Hamra "did not have any relations with the area"; they came from outside, they came in with a subversive, almost polluting influence of lower education, lack of discipline, hygiene, and cleanliness, and, most of all, a "culture," all of which contributed to the deterioration of Hamra's quality. The resentment against the invading influences appears to require a naming, and here the "other" becomes the nonurban, people from "faraway" places, far removed from "our place" here, in other words, a spatial distancing. Another feature that is implied is the sensual experience of a neighborhood—the sights, sounds, and scenes that create a spatial circumscription, an experience that comes to the fore when it is contrasted with a change. Clothes, language, food, and even quality of goods in shops are mentioned as markers that define an area and their subsequent subversion with the coming of an external influence. This sense of a particular pristine environment deteriorating into a chaotic undesirable mess envelops another transitory experience, that of the familiar turning into the unfamiliar, as is articulated in the following by a member of a prominent Christian Hamra family who continued to live in his imposing early-twentieth-century mansion off Hamra Street:

> I'll talk about myself personally and it reflects the way a lot of people feel. In this area, before the war when you walked in Hamra Street or any street around, I used to know practically everybody, even the owners of shops and everything. Walk, stop, and ask something, but after the war, there were strangers. Occasionally I see some people that I know, but you don't see them much out anymore. They prefer to stay at home and many of them who could afford it just left the country. Really, the sidewalk of Hamra in the high days of Hamra was straight and nice and it was like walking in any city in Europe . . . and now you can't even walk. But the influx of foreigners, I wouldn't say foreigners I would say Lebanese "after the war," and they came with a totally different mentality from the people in this section of Beirut and these people ruined Hamra. They came out of nowhere, unfortunately they had money, they thought with money they can do anything, but money is not everything. . . . They changed the society of this part of Beirut.

The remarks about the invasive outsiders in Hamra take on a literal sense because of the occupation of houses. Apart from the gunmen and their cohorts from various militias or political groups, the "outsiders" that the preceding narratives mention are Shia Muslim families displaced from southern Lebanon.[21] These families, either through personal contacts or simply by walking into empty homes, or through bargain deals from Christians pushed to distress selling, came to occupy many homes in Hamra. The change in the occupation of homes in Hamra has a double meaning. First, their physical occupation implied the replacement of an earlier neighborhood, a somewhat palpable substitution of an alternate community with whom conviviality, at best, was strained. On the other hand, the emptying out of homes—the exodus of the "usual" Hamra residents—implied the gradual dissipation of the "authentic" Hamra community. Despite the gradual exodus of a large number of Christians under conditions of threat, some still held on steadfast to their homes and, more significantly, to their sense of sanctity in their neighborhood, often offering somewhat mundane explanations of a fairly overwhelming situation. As we were told by one such resident,

> I am a Christian, nobody touched me—and many other Christians live here—nobody touched them. They turned it into a war between sects to scare the people, so that they would run away elsewhere and buy their buildings on the other side. This was another business. The ones who wanted to buy/sell these buildings made threatening calls at night, perhaps... this is how you make money in the war... they pick up the phone book look at the names and call and say this and that. So people get scared—they have kids and daughters etc. and they have to run away, many of my friends had to go away.

In another conversation, it was said,

> People leaving, they were very few, they went for their businesses. But the people of Ras Beirut, be they Christians, Muslims or Druze were never bothered, were never subjects of any discrimination, believe me, at all. So anybody who moved out did not move out because of discrimination at all, people moved out because there was so much rubbish around the place, garbage collection was minimum, water supply was minimum, power supply was lacking so they had one reason or another, they moved out to comfortable areas—but not, believe me, because of discrimination... none of the Ras Beirutis moved out because of that.

The experience of the hostile environment in Hamra has been mediated through a very strong recognition and reiteration of a community/neighborhood quality that is resistant or not amenable to disruptive fissures. Many noted that even though the wars were ostensibly a deadly conflict between Christians and Muslims, their experience of the war years crystallized relations and created relationships that clearly subverted the dominant preconceptions of hostility. As the following vignette of a conversation with the first Christian resident quoted earlier indicates, the presence of militias and persistent violence in the everyday brought about a somewhat new equation in neighborhood relationships. For these people, it was clearly a reflection of the character of the neighborhood that mirrored itself even in their most trying times:

> Yes, it's true, it was different, but we never talked about religion or nationalities or anything. Some people are still the same in this building. With the

PSP—there was a very, very short period of time when we were short of food, we would share. The PSP, they were not against religion. . . . In their party they had Christians, Druze, Muslims, . . . here we could hear them calling each other . . . Muhammad, Ayatollah, George, Khalilullah, Robert. . . . It was amazing for those who understand this it is really something . . . this is really what kept this area.[22]

For some the area and its "quality," despite all the other problems, offered a better option than other places that could have given them a sense of community security. I was repeatedly told that it was only in Hamra where the experience of living together created the cherished ambience of secular living. Therefore the potential safety of the "other side" to the apparently threatened Christians of Hamra also implied a cloistered, insular community life that would have endangered something that is held at a higher premium—their own brand of Hamra cosmopolitanism. The negotiation of Hamra in the present is thus a coping with a fragile sense of belonging. Second, it is also a reordering of one's social mapping of the neighborhood. The present, then, brings about a peculiar juncture between the remembrances of a double-sided past and the gradual unfolding of a barely comprehended but somehow wary future in Hamra. A pastor in a church told us,

I do think there is much less tolerance, not only across the Muslim Christian line but also across the sectarian lines within the religion. The wars had polarized into two religions but also into sectarian groups, Shias and Sunnis are less friendly with each other than they used to be. More antagonistic, any way you look at it. And also among the various Christian groups—I will just give you an example—we used to have a lot of children from some of these churches for what we call Sunday schools or something for the children. We had a neighbor here, a priest, Mr. X. We used to joke—you are taking my children, and I would say I am picking them up from the street for you and so on. But now, oh, no, the man who has taken his place is very, very insistent on not allowing his children to come here even though they don't provide anything for them . . . you see. We used have a lot of non-Christians, in other words, Muslims, coming to our Sunday school, children . . . nobody anymore, you used to be able to go and visit people and knock on the door and say I am from the church here, we would like to invite you to come and visit our services . . . you don't feel at all that you have the same reception [now]. . . . Certainly there has been a hardening along the religious divide. Or the sectarian divide and this is one thing. Another thing is this area never did regain its mix.

As these changes are consciously talked about and recognized, there is clear movement toward the experience of a future, of the coming times. The evaluation of a potential future in or of Hamra is a clear refraction of the evaluation of the vista available in the present—if the present environment is alienating and, at best, simply unfamiliar, the coming times are going to be the same. At the same time, the expectation of the future takes on a subtle nuance. The inherent change in Hamra's character has been attributed to the influx of another people with another culture, but at the same time, as is quoted subsequently, it is also the change in a generation of people, not only in the type of people. Such an observation draws attention to the conditions of disruption when it encompasses more than episodic spurts but blends into a changeover in generations. The memory of violence is not only about a place but is also differently embedded in separated biographies:

> This is a generation of war. A boy who was five years in 1976 . . . when it finished in 1990, how old is he . . . twenty . . . this boy, he did not see the good old days, he did not see the prosperity of Lebanon. He has seen only destruction and killing. His way of thinking is completely different from our way of thinking. These are the majority of people now. Most of the people who were thirty or forty before the war are now gone, dead or emigrated. So this is a new type of generation, a new type of people . . . a new type of thinking. They don't know . . . they have seen the fear, the killing . . . now they want to continue living . . . always in their mind there is going to be war. There is going to be killing. They have seen the bad times . . . they have worked and worked, standing in line for bread, now they want to enjoy. These new generations of people have seen only war . . . it's in their blood, in their soul.

The lived past of the generation growing up during the war is overwhelmingly one of fear, hostility, violence—a recollection that creates a time frame of remembrance completely different from that of the older generation. The sense of recuperation, of healing, as it were, between the two generations will have to address two different kinds of movement from the past to a present and on to the future. The elders are able to connect with a past of "how things actually were" before an era of disruption and garner a memory that enables the possibility of a return. The war generation, conversely, concentrates on the viability of the present, a present that is informed by their biographies of the past. Although this is not necessarily an experience that is limited to a single neighborhood alone, it may not be a mistaken speculation to note that some of these biographies may have translated into cognitive mapping of a social geography (over neighborhoods and groups of people) that translates into possible borders or even frontiers that the younger generation could be limited by or perhaps transcend. Hamra's transformations are upheavals of social geographies brought about in a hostile city, and as the preceding vignettes show, remembrance continues to mediate the experience of space and that of identity. Saifi, conversely, has another kind of transformation, one that records similar upheavals as in Hamra, but the social geographies here are now erased for newer inscriptions of how identity may yet be experienced, as I describe in the following.

A simple description of Saifi in its prewar years suggests that, like the general ambience of the city's core, the downtown district of which it is a part, it was a concentrated hub of commerce, entertainment, and government and packed residential pockets that directed an ebb and flow of all Lebanese groups and others. Close to Saifi was the Martyr's Square, one of the city's most prominent historic sites and a popular public arena. The city's transport terminal and the central taxi station were a few minutes' walk away, making the neighborhood a place of lively comings and goings. Saifi was also well known for a carpenter's market called Souk Najjareen. Architecturally, it was a quintessential segment of Downtown Beirut—an eclectic mix of the modern and traditional. Business establishments covered most of the street level, and the higher levels were usually residential apartments. By all accounts, Saifi was a vibrant neighborhood of homes and shops, reverberating the pulse of a Mediterranean city that had grown from antiquity to modern times.

Between 1975 and 1977, when the cycle of the wars began, the forefront of warfare was manifest in Downtown Beirut, as described earlier, with the Green Line as the main front line between the Christian East and the Muslim West. Saifi, lying close to the Green Line, came to be surrounded by militia bases ferociously engaged in the protection of their "territory." After the first two years, when warfare gradually moved out to engulf the city and country, leaving the center devastated and apparently "silent," except for the remaining hazards of sniping and occasional gunfire, the indelible marks of war damage began to show. Business died or moved out; the cinemas, restaurants, and shops closed down; most damaged buildings deteriorated beyond recognition, turning further into the squalor of squatter homes for those fleeing from other parts of the country or city. Many of the original residents who could relocate their homes did, while others managed to cling to a precarious existence—the situation in Saifi echoed its surroundings.

From 1995, one of the world's largest rebuilding projects had been launched in Downtown Beirut under the aegis of a state-supported private real estate company called SOLIDERE.[23] During 1997–98, the time when the narratives I describe here were collected, the area was going through the entire gamut of rebuilding activities—demolitions and new constructions, infrastructural makeovers, restoration and conservation, and so on. Currently, after more than a decade of reconstruction, the new city center is slick, glossy, and spectacular, with sweeping avenues, gardens, and landscaping; pristinely renovated historic buildings; impressive business real estate; and trendy entertainment and leisure spots—the "Ancient City of the Future" that SOLIDERE envisioned. Against this backdrop, Saifi finds place as a "traditional urban village," a high-end residential block renovated meticulously with Mediterranean facades, attractive landscaping, antique detailing, and cobbled pathways.[24] Given Saifi's location in the "new" city center, these refurbished apartments are sold for upward of a million dollars each, making Saifi one of the most exclusive residential addresses in the city. The narratives of recovery, of "coming to terms," are framed in a present that was negotiating with the impending totalizing changes that are visible in today's Saifi. They were about lived everyday experiences of reconstruction, ones that mapped a separate, cognitive space distinct from the formal instrumentality of the planned exercise of spatial recovery.[25]

During 1997–98, as we[26] made our queries about experiences in postwar Saifi, most articulations started with a recollection of the war years. They speak about how the early episodes of warfare and the subsequent sniping gradually imposed a sense of closure and bounding off from the Downtown Beirut area and the city at large. Some said that the war itself was an incomprehensible situation made real only through their experiences of violent incursion and threat in their physical proximity. Once the physical threats of warfare established its regimes of access and exit from the area, the first engravings of a divided city began to take shape for the people in the area. The sense of hostile difference among communities seemed to have been a later consciousness; rather, it was the actual physical acts of violence and their accompanying effects on physical mobility that transformed the area into one of physical borders and frontiers. In addition, it is important to mention that during the time of our fieldwork, questions regarding religious denomination or other identity-related queries had become cause for suspicion, and we refrained from insisting—not unpredictable in a precarious neighborhood and in light of the fact that no formal census had been taken in the nation since 1935. Also, Saifi was a place too close to the Green Line: many residents had abandoned their homes and returned over different periods; some occupants that we met may not have been original owners but could have been squatters; some others were businessmen who owned commercial properties there but lived elsewhere, and so on. A businessman in Saifi who had returned to reopen his enterprise told us,

> There was only a physical separation, it was an artificial separation. The proof to that is that I used to have employees from the other side coming to this side and there are employees on this side they love each other, they are still working with us—we never had that problem and if ever a Christian employee has trouble in the Western side it is always the Muslim who helps him out and vice versa. Once we had a problem here [and] it was called the Black September, when they started killing, we had a Muslim employee—the militiamen kidnapped him, the Christian employees came and negotiated with the militiamen—they [the employees] did not accept what was happening. And of course, they saved the guy who was about to be shot. For me, I don't consider it to be a problem. In terms of the Lebanese there is small minority on both sides who are extremists. It exists. And for me everything what happened was externally imposed—it's outside—it's political, it's foreign, it was created. All of this has been created—it's not the Lebanese as Lebanese.

The persistent idea from many in Saifi is about an imposed condition in which the "Lebanese," far from participating, had actually denied hostility in their everyday negotiations even under duress. It suggests an idea that Saifi, as an immediate place of reference for these people as a mixed space, included a sense of social sanctity, one that has been transgressed by violence externally generated and imposed. However, when the narratives move to another temporal level, that of "after the war," the separation or division is no longer imposed; rather, it is a matured remembrance that informs experience in the present. One Saifi resident remarked when we asked her how she felt about going to Hamra now, a place she had frequented before the war, "I feel the difference, whenever I go there, the atmosphere, the people, they are different. We have our own customs, we have our own insides.[27] They are different."

Even when the division between East Beirut and West Beirut is often endorsed as imposed sectarian territorialism, it is not always removed from a self-conscious reflection of one's own reactions, impressions, and voluntary/involuntary disposition to difference and suspicion. Before the war, Beirut had been a city of distinct community localities, but the borders that circumscribed neighbors were not combative frontiers or insulated territories. The "other side," through the dynamic of the Green Line, had also become a spatial metaphor for the "other." The other side is about people who are now strangers, people not from our own neighborhood, and eventually they do take on sectarian labels as the "Western" Muslims against the "Eastern" Christians, and vice versa. However, there are attempts to transcend, through a going back to remembrances that can nurture and sustain the comfortable notion of "normal" relations, as the following quotation from another resident states, where she notes her opinion about the ostensible end of hostility:

> We feel the enmity much less now. Our souls have changed—our way of thinking. I am a social worker, all my life I used to work with Muslims. I am a Christian and I have never in my life looked down upon the Muslims. I used to work with them all the time, value them, we used to work a lot together. Now when things went back to normal again, my heart opened to them. These are normal people—like you and me—I don't find any difference at all. On the contrary, Lebanon is one, we have to live. The young people in

our family—in fact, we are pushing them to go to the Western side, we are calling it the Western side but we should not be doing it. We should call it Hamra, Ras Beirut. These are words that are stuck in our heads.

Embedded in the preceding is the sense of the spatial, an aspect that continues to divide, despite no obvious acceptance of social fissures. For instance, another resident, commenting on the difference between the Eastern and Western sides, said,

> I don't feel the differences anymore. But I find the distance far now. I was not used to and did not know Achrafiyeh nor its roads or anything as I used to shop in the Ras Beirut area—Hamra. I used to go and shop in Hamra—on foot—now it is more difficult for me. You see, now I got used to Achrafiyeh— I just don't know—it's either habit or it's closer.[28]

It is as if the experience of territorialized hostility has translated itself into rendering the known into a distant and inaccessible physical distance, on one hand, and on the other, it has rendered the unfamiliar but safer places, places protected within community boundaries, closer.

Alongside these experiences of division lay another compelling aspect of the present—the remembrance of Saifi before the war. The metaphor that appeared to capture best how Saifi was remembered among my informants was the notion of a *foyer,* one that resonates the sense of a core, a hub, and the heart from which the city and its life emanated. For instance, we were told in a conversation with a mother and her daughter, both of whom had lived through the wars in Saifi, escaping only for brief periods when the fighting became too much to cope with,

> There used to be much more people then—services[29] used to come and go. Our house here used to be like [a] station, people we knew used to stop by for a drink . . . wait here if they have to go somewhere else . . . have a coffee . . . go shopping during breaks—*ahlan wa sahlan* and *maa al salame* [welcome and good-bye].

It is significant that for the residents of Saifi, when recalling their experience before the war, their remembrance of Saifi as a place always merges into the wider milieu of Downtown Beirut—the bustling, busy ambience, the crowds and incessant movement. The remembrance of an ambience and its subsequent loss also carries with it, as the following impressions show, a retrospective reflection of the quality of community and urban life that is determinedly anchored to a place. One owner of a popular motel in Saifi, who was at the time closing his establishment and moving out, as he could not afford to continue in Saifi, said,

> Here it was full of life—you couldn't say day from night—all categories of people were here. All nationalities—if you are walking on the street, if you brushed shoulders with the passersby, you would get all languages—now, things have really changed. Life was really nice here. At 3:00 A.M., we would go and have breakfast—we would find shops open, people would be walking on the streets.

In another instance, a car garage owner who also had to abandon work in Saifi said, "It was the *ruh al wataniya* [spirit of a nation]—people mixing together from all religions, involved together in work. What more can I tell you . . . there used to be true 'national spirit.'" These kinds of remembrances became more vivid in Saifi when, alongside the past, the future instituted by SOLIDERE appeared as a clearly discernible horizon. As the preceding respondent said,

> With the creation of SOLIDERE we have to see what it will give us—we have to wait—but I hope it will be the way it used to be before. Like it used to be in the past, the meeting point of all Lebanese. The new plan has some flavor from the past and some modern ideas for the future. We will never have the old Beirut. The spirit is lost. It was historical. If it had stayed, it would have been a historic base—now Beirut is a new city. Even though we are trying to make it look like the way it was with the restoration, it is becoming a new, an extramodern city. They are building a new city while still considering it as an old one. For me things have changed. And I don't think we will ever go back to the old way. There are many reasons for that—it will still remain the center—but this time it is going to be the business center; it won't be the *centre de rencontre* [center for meeting] for the Lebanese.[30]

Although there are a variety of ways in which SOLIDERE or the processes of reconstruction permeate "experience" in Saifi, the impression of the rebuilt new city center as one that cannot replace or substitute for the old one is an opinion that is echoed by most. This is a perception that is clearly linked with the sociality that the area provided, something that has disappeared with its destruction and that a newly built environment cannot really achieve. One of the issues that the preceding quotation implies is the loss of the old city not just by the destruction attributed to the wars but also by the reconstruction operations themselves. Some people in Saifi were persuaded by our queries to verbally trace a memory map in Saifi and its surroundings, and most often it was about locating buildings that were once there but seem to have disappeared. But, once again, the memory map that sustains the remembrance is a spatial temperament: the intangible sensation of a built environment that does not always get identified by the structures themselves but rather an overall image of a space that has been embraced and nurtured by a remembrance. It is this sensation that appears to inform the experience of self, of the performance of that self with an identity in that space.

Following the spatial transformations of the city through these sorts of experiences, the subsequent bout of work in Beirut during 2004 took me toward those people and experiences that were related to relocations made as a result of the transformed neighborhoods. It was clear that, although it would be impossible to trace the movements of the thousands who had left their homes and businesses during the war years or even later, some tangible networks could be traced in the movements out of the Downtown Beirut area. These networks revealed, once again, the experience of identity in space, especially in the way people chose or were compelled to choose safer or more secure, and significantly more affordable, housing. I have written about this subsequent bit of my work in Beirut with an emphasis on how geography, once again, literally mapped an afterlife in Beirut, with futures that held a more tragic meeting of warfare with identity spaces than what my apprehension would have acknowledged at the time.[31] My work with those moving out of Downtown Beirut to the southern suburbs at the time mentioned some of the insularity that these suburbs invoked. Religious codes of social life were overwhelmingly maintained and not always appreciated by the few whom I met. Their compulsion to move there was partly to be close to family but more because of the unaffordability of housing elsewhere. The Hezbollah were also very active in aiding relocation efforts, especially when SOLIDERE was clearly using methods far less than fair in evacuating these people from their real estate investment project.[32] The Hezbollah-dominated, -protected, and -maintained southern suburbs of Beirut were a geographical entity that revealed the peculiar relationship of violence and the experience of a city. During the July–August 2006 war, the southern suburbs, clearly recognized as enemy targets, were under direct attack by Israel and were reduced to rubble. Even within the density of a cityscape, the clear demarcation of hostile territory did not distinguish unarmed civilians from armed participants. The indelible embedding of people as marked bodies results in a place that is etched thickly with identity—implying that spatialities can provoke a violent recognition, in a sense shaping geographies of attack and defense that merged faith-based identity into city space. But the 2006 war was too drastic a fate—too stark an endorsement of how identity spaces interface with urban violence, emplacing a potential of impending destruction and prefiguring the spatialized affective lives of those who had to move in the pathways literally coerced by this afterlife.

SPATIAL SUFFERING AND THE SCARRED URBAN

In the representations of Beirut that I have described, I have attempted a teasing out of the sense that when a city witnesses the loss, not only of innumerable lives, socialities, homes, and familiar environments that years of war could claim, but also of an idealized urban future of a convivial multireligious society, it expresses the pathos of that suffering in the everyday corporeal experiences of its people. There is an evident irony here—Beirut is a city, as I said, that could be called a microcosm of the nation; that is to say, it was a patchwork of confessional territories that kept sustained violence in some abeyance, but sectarian violence was clearly present, however localized and minimal. At the same time, the ideal of a multiethnic/religious society cohabiting in a national territory, with some sense of a common identity, was certainly a notion, embraced and nurtured, it would seem.[33] My intention behind choosing two ethnographic locations, which were neighborhoods in Beirut, manifesting a sense of cosmopolitanism that was at odds with a city inherently mapped by confessional space, was to explore this seemingly contradictory condition.

After the wars, the sense of loss of that cosmopolitan ideal, one that seemingly stood in resistance against identity hostilities, had another aspect—cosmopolitan space gave way to sharper contours of confessionalized space where secular identity acquiesced to confessional identity or faith-based urban living. Public life, as much as personal life, in these neighborhoods gets superimposed on locational experiences in ways that sociality is acutely spatialized and clearly identified with paradigms of identity. Life led in this afterlife is intensely about marked bodies in space and about marking bodies with place. This is a condition that speaks of two vectors, each symbiotically making the other—on one hand, there is the experience of space being dismantled on account of identity inscriptions and, on the other, identity experiences begin to produce emergent spaces. The sharpening of confessional geography in Beirut is amply visible in the mentioned southern suburbs (as one instance among others), which have now become Shia neighborhoods largely under the political control and "protection" of the Hezbollah. In the second span of violence that I mentioned, the attacks were a clear exposition of Israel's strategy of targeting and attacking specific bodies in Hezbollah space. Without belaboring the point, the notion of bios in these lives/bodies embedded into confessional space simply accompanies the pathos, and all that it invokes, of living identity in space. Life and the social here is about recognizing physical space as an incontrovertible condition of an afterlife, a condition that prolongs the emplacement of embodied experiences of violence in the social narratives of suffering beyond recognizable limits of violent events. In drawing out that afterlife, my emphasis in the vignettes and moments of conversation herein has been to illuminate a fleeting "present" that my ethnographic involvement in Beirut documented, so as to listen carefully to how remembrance recognizes transformation. The affect that seemed to be predominant in those moments echoed Edward S. Casey's proposition on nostalgia.[34] I find that nostalgia is indeed a part of the tragic poetics that the ways of life in Beirut could suggest in its afterlife. In Casey's words,

> one of the most eloquent testimonies to place's extraordinary memorability is found in nostalgia. We are nostalgic primarily about particular places that have been emotionally significant to us and which we now miss: we are in pain [algos] about a return home [nostos] that is not presently possible. . . . All that we need to notice is the poignant power of the phenomenon . . . has everything to do with the memory of place. That the place in question is normally

that special place called "home"—"there is no place like home," according to nostalgia's primary axiom—testifies emphatically to the strength of the internal bond between "place" and memory.[35]

While this nostalgic longing of places past is central to the experiences I have described, an underlying feature is that these spaces are ones that make the sense of belonging a troubling one insomuch as they are spaces marked by confessional mapping—a mapping that has had the capacity to locate threat as much as it provided a "home." Home here is about a possible sanctuary located in a landscape of hostility, and indeed, homes that have been found in such "safe" environments seem to trouble contentment or security. It is as if this is a home displaced from its aspired harmony with its social environment. Time and space become incommensurate with actuality, with the present. I am tempted to make the discussion a little further nuanced by referring to something Susan Stewart seeks to emphasize.[36] The meaning of nostalgia, as she states, lies in a loss, yet there is a confusing double-speak in Beirut. On one hand, there is a lost ideal of cosmopolitanism in the places I have worked in. On the other, there is a subterranean but certain knowledge of a fragile society, buffered by an always-extant militia attached to confessional identity. I would suggest that violence in ways not clear makes a sense of loss possible, one that may yet be unmoored in "reality"—and in that afterlife, the loss assumes a presence that might well be tenuous in the actual past.

The nostalgic is enamored of distance, not of the reference itself. Nostalgia cannot be sustained without loss. For the nostalgic to reach his or her goal of closing the gap between re-semblance and identity, lived experience would have to take place, an erasure of the gap between sign and signified, an experience that would cancel out the desire that is nostalgia's reason for existence.

Thus, while a sense of nostalgia (the bringing together of past-present-future) and its representations (lived spatialities) cohere the strands that Ricoeur and Lefebvre provide for my arguments, the question of confessional identity in urban space still remains as a tangle of several other strands that inform the sense of life in the social—a few of which I try to sketch in the following pages.

Although religion in space is not an unknown aspect of urban living in multireligious environments, scholarship focusing on the exact contours of how space and religion etch themselves into urban experience is fairly recent. The overarching orientation I privilege in Beirut's afterlife is faith-based identity and space, and in that, the interfacing of sectarian or ascriptive identity with space could find an easy fit among perspectives in human geography where the analytics of space and place with identity is a widely investigated terrain. Race, class, gender, and sexuality, among other categories of conventionally recognized identity, have been explored in spatial terms, where the mediation of space in the experience of these identities is found to be formative in social life. The question of faith- or confession-based identity in space, however, is a complex of factors that has to begin with a larger and far more recent problematic that has found due place as a "geography of religion." Brace, Bailey, and Harvey, using that phrase, carefully unpack two constructs—first, the usual conflation of sacred space with the understanding of religion in space, and second, the artificial separation of the sacred from the secular. With a base in these parameters, they say,

> We argue that, in order to understand the construction and meaning of society and space, it is vital to acknowledge that religious practices, in terms of both institutional organization and of personal experience, are central not only to the spiritual life of society but also to the constitution and reconstitution of society.
> . . . Indeed, most geographers would acknowledge that aspects of religion—of faith, sacredness and spirituality—intersect with geography at each turn: from understanding the construction of identity or the meaning of bodily practices at a personal level, to unpacking the complex relationships and politics of institutional space and place at a regional or national level.[37]

Clearly not just the construction of identity but its performance and its corporeal expression, especially in the religious idiom, whether spontaneous or imposed, have a literal implication of *where* they happen. This relationship of geography and religion takes on a sharper contouring when the space in question is that of hostile factions of a city.[38] Particularly significant here are those discussions that analyze violence among religious groups in different urban locations. However, not all aspects of religious violence in the city offer a similar template of analysis, and I hesitate in using any common parameters.[39] A "geography of religion" or an orientation of "reputational geographies" does initiate the experiences, the representations, I have described; however, a further calibration between space and religion is useful. I do not want to overwhelm the urban experience of Beirut as one that is mediated only by the experience of violence, whether past or continuous. The quotidian practices of living in Beirut, in its various registers of time and place, incorporate much more than the confines of violence.[40] In this articulation of life and the social after violence in Beirut, then, I privilege space and suggest an emplacement of bodies, made legible by faith-based identity in violently mapped space.

The frame that I place on the formation of an afterlife in Beirut highlights a topographical perspective—one in which corporeal living in a city, marked by violence and identity, brings into sharper relief a spatial texture of an afterlife, where the social is a sphere of relationalities lived in an acute, embodied experience of space, whether from an internal subjective sense or from the exteriority of subjectification captured in faith-based identity. The social experience of the city of Beirut has been and is undeniably about confessional space—from everyday sights and sounds of a cultural and symbolic environment, community, and religious rituals to kin networks, institutional affiliations, livelihood practices, emplaced histories, political negotiations, and more. Violence, whether as protracted events or as ongoing sporadic events of continued hostility, blankets this social spatial experience with a blending of pasts, presents, and futures that appears clearly in the representations that I have described from the locations in Beirut. Hiba Bou Akar suggests significantly that the geographies of war in Beirut, the impacts on urban planning and real estate development (especially in Saifi), the rise of the Hezbollah, and other related factors play out a spatiality of political difference in the city in ways that, she says, keep a "war yet to come" at bay.[41] Her view endorses mine insofar as the experience of identity that I discuss here is an overwhelming aspect of this afterlife, which deals with more than an episodic moment of violence to a prolonged duration.

These intertwinings of time and space invoke a poetics of urban space where memory and nostalgia inflict upon the sense of present and future living in a city—a living that is undeniably ensconced in the embodiment of faith-based identity. It is an embodiment that extends itself to a sphere of social encompassing, where the sense of belonging to an identity also implies belonging to a spatialized location and together; that is, the inscription of faith into space marks out a potent combination of vulnerability and security. So long as violence expresses itself through hostilities of politicized identities, marked people in marked spaces will be vulnerable to threat. In an irony of belonging, the same community and confessional space that can offer refuge can and has also been the target of concerted hostility or can also be experienced as spaces constraining an urban ideal of cosmopolitanism. When these experiences are recounted through the yearnings or recollections of an alleged benign past, a pathos of suffering engulfs the city—where all mourn the passing of an urban ideal (whether imagined or real) and also share in the vulnerability of urban ideals fractured by faith-based living. The fact of some of these identities being more vulnerable than others speaks of a differential embodiment, to be sure. The social suffering here finds its expression in a spatial encapsulation. The everyday experience of faith merges with the experience of the urban, making city life an articulation of faith-based identity. Participating in or witnessing and communicating the pathos of a violated city locates a geography of religion in the texture of the urban. Whether that texture becomes visible through events in time or through an ongoing duration of sporadic or suspended hostility, the pathos here is one that weaves a social through a narration of time in space—thus the prevalence of nostalgic invocations with which to understand the present or the future.

To reiterate, the narratives from Saifi and Hamra clearly articulate a remembrance of a benign past—even though both have different constituents of the past. The Saifi narratives have emerged as negotiations with transformations brought about both by war and formal plans of reconstruction—in addition, these are transformations that provoke a sense of one's identity and place in the narrative of a place that moves a sense of everyday cosmopolitanism to one of conscious faith-based identity. Hamra has had to bear the brunt of transformations of economic decline, social divisions, confessional difference, and so on. Remembrance in both situations touches on a sense of the nostalgic. The nostalgic paradigm in Hamra parenthesizes a splendid past of the area coming into being as an urban center that celebrated a cosmopolitan way of life. It marked a golden age of authenticity where genuine participants of this place sustained spontaneous social relations that made belonging a matter of pride. The subsequent collapse of Hamra and the changes in the social fabric attributed to the influx of "inferior" others create an atmosphere of estrangement and alienation. The paradigm here distills the range of remembered values into a symbolic reification, one that operates as a social metaphor for meaning. In Hamra, this metaphor is that of the "Hamra quality" expressed through the parameters of an identity assigned to the vehicles of that quality, namely, the members of a religiously defined community. Once this construction is in place, it also serves as a unit in which a kind of boundary maintenance can work to seal off authenticity and genuineness from the polluting penetration of the inauthentic or "inferior" social codes.[42] These symbolic constructions clearly work with a geographical mapping, where place becomes the physical encapsulation of identity.

A quick overview of the narratives emerging from Saifi resonates with those from Hamra in a few ways, for instance, in the sense of a lost community, a quality of life, and so on. However, experience in Saifi is expressed through a very pronounced consciousness of the material environment. As the narratives trace the transformations brought about by the war, the remembrances begin to take cognizance of the sense of irreversibility in the surrounding ruins, and this sense was primarily encapsulated as one of disappearance of the visually familiar—the built environment. It was as if, with the gradual fading, deterioration, and disappearance of the buildings, squares, and popular places, the vibrancy of cosmopolitan life that these places sustained had also been drained out. Like Hamra, Saifi faces a kind of invasion—that of pervasive erasure that traces a metonymic connection between the material and affective, the sensory and the emotional.[43] For the people in Saifi, it is the complete subversion of their "foyer"—a foyer they experienced as a contained space in which a sense of intimate interaction is sustained. The commonality of the public arena over which such social bonds take place contributes to the idea of a shared identification with place and, thereby, a common social grouping.

In Saifi, the contact was one among the familiar and the recognizable, not necessarily because most of these meetings were among the known and the familiar (like those of one's own community) but because the *place* of meeting rendered them known and trustworthy. In this sense, the foyer functions as a circumscribed space that permits and sustains a kind of social domesticity—one that extends beyond the private space to a public domain. This circumscription did not imply a boundary around an insulated core of emplaced identity; rather, it implied the heart of a city, to and from which the life of the city flowed. Once the possibility of such a tangible sociality is lost, the sense of a disappearing neighborhood is acute—the places that nurtured such public contact lost their social appeal and became alienated and alienating spaces. The present/future in Saifi has seen a dismantling of a foyer into estranged spaces.

The stories from Beirut and Saifi that I sketch in this chapter are mundane articulations of everyday negotiations and impressions, uttered reflectively and retrospectively, or speculatively and apprehensively, about and in reference to dramatic events that have ostensibly passed and in cognizance of an extant environment. I have tried to fathom the sense of the ongoing, one that is fleeting and transitory in a constantly shifting and changing spatial and temporal environment, yet one that also reflects the gradual congealing of that same environment. Drawing this discussion to a close, the parameters of a bios and a pathos that I have used in varying significations across different contexts are reaffirmed here again—their articulation in the context of Beirut has been about the entanglement of identity in space. The sense of life in the social that emerges in this environment of a long afterlife is the adherence of bodies to faith-based identity and their further attachment to specific place. In Beirut, this is a historical condition, yet their relevance becomes differently expressed when long episodes of devastating violence and the expectation of more to come disfigure a city's aspirational and corporeal horizon. It is not too trite an observation that a city bears its scars of suffering too—in its bullet-ridden surfaces, its erased buildings, its dismantled neighborhoods, and its transformed urban surfaces. This is a suffering that communicates its pathos as much in visual and corporeal public experience as it does in the intimacies of private experience. Whether in nostalgia or in passionate recounting of a past, the social relationality of a lost cosmopolitanism, especially in the places that I have described, becomes a loss—and, in terms of a pathos, also implicates a rhetoric of emplaced suffering. When faith-based identity becomes a particularly emphasized nuance of this experience, the individuated experience of that urban horizon embodies itself in bodies that are constructed by an exteriority as much as they are experienced in interiority. Life, and its urban embedding here, emerges as a fusion of bios in space, where the meaning of lived experience identifies bodies as labeled (as vehicles of faith) in space. Individuations work with the label of identity and in faith rather than as *city*-zens, undoing, as it were, the very core of what urbanism seemed to have implied. Bios here populates and transforms urban space from an originary meaning of anonymous heterogeneity (however aspirational) to a spatiality that urbanism is unable to grasp, unless it is consumed under hyphenated nomenclatures like the "multi-sectarian" city of bodies with ascriptive identity. It is difficult to say whether such aspirations are more acute in a city that has a subterranean consciousness of fragile ethnic relations that come to the surface much too often, even in the span of an allegedly benign history. Notwithstanding, the social relationalities that emerge are built on the network of these embodiments in space—where everyday experience of urban social life refracts imagined or real pasts into a scarred and reconfigured present, moving toward a future that can only be reconciled to the overarching allocation of faith onto space.

Emplacing suffering as I have here calls forth a special configuration of the frames of bios and pathos invoked in the afterlives of violence I have explored. It is difficult to make a definitive statement on how identity endures violence when violence becomes a force that envelops one's presence in a physical environment that is entirely encapsulated by such markings of identity. Undoubtedly, violence becomes the oppressor, in the brutal machinations of which the pathos of suffering communicates the claustrophobia of identity enclosures that defeat the ideals of a city meant for all—if we are to follow the originary ideas of urbanism. Finding one's self as much enclosed by identity as by the place that that enclosure demands, the form of life or bios here is an expression of embodied space. The aporia of belonging here would be the subtle trauma of having a home but remembering it to be someplace else. The tragedy here (if tragedy may be another metonym for pathos), and the bodies that it communicates through, echoes in the words of Richard Sennet when he reads the experiences of Modena, the extraordinary seventeenth-century cosmopolite and rabbi who lived in the Venetian Jewish ghetto and to lament the weight of place: "A group identity forged by oppression remains in the hands of the oppressor. The geography of identity means the outsider always appears as an unreal human being in the landscape—like the Icarus who fell unremarked and unmourned to his death."[44] This chapter closes with these words by Sennet, which, in the best way that poetics can do, capture the tragic sensorium of oppressive violence in city life.

5

Bios, Pathos, and Life Emergent

A life.... No one has described what a life is better than Charles Dickens, if we take the indefinite article as an index of the transcendental. A disreputable man, a rogue, held in contempt by everyone, is found as he lies dying. Suddenly, those taking care of him manifest an eagerness, respect, even love, for his slightest sign of life. Everybody bustles about to save him, to the point where, in his deepest coma, this wicked man himself senses something soft and sweet penetrating him. But, to the degree that he comes back to life, his saviors turn colder, and he becomes once again mean and crude. Between his life and his death, there is a moment that is only of life playing with death.

—Gilles Deleuze, *Pure Immanence: Essays on a Life*

FRAMES OF AFTERLIFE

Deleuze takes a vignette out of Dickens *(Our Mutual Friend)* to find a remarkable allusion to life between life and death, when a sense of life pervades and overwhelms any sense of good or bad.[1] Before or after, it would seem, a surrounding, an environment, objectivity or subjectivity, internality or externality, would take over and make it a social presence (with its "goodness" and "badness"). But, in between, it is a pure sense of life, a belief, a common, which I have suggested as a belief morphed into knowledge, that overwhelms and blurs all else. My explorations here have started in this in-between sensation of life, but in a peculiar form of reversal rather than the in-between of life–death, it is the in-between of death–life. Given my milieu of violent events, when lives are destroyed by violence, death is prior to the life that now remains to be saved, protected, remembered, and survived. In this duration of death playing with life, this sensation of life is prodigious; it sparks off an intent, which then invokes and incites a social world into being that begins to recognize forms of life—life that will be restored, protected, and saved, life that will be coped with, dispensed with, concealed, remembered, or forgotten.

I have pursued both the formation of a social universe and the forms of life that it constitutes in a variety of contexts of violence, such as the civil wars of Sierra Leone and Lebanon and the episodes of communal violence in Delhi and Gujarat, India. In each context, I have followed the path that life traces, with a conscious focus on the idea of "making live," where I suggest not just the powers of governmentality or statecraft in wielding power *over* life but also the intervention of the social in construing a "making live." In this favoring of the social, I explore the possibility of an affirmative biopolitics that speaks of the power *of* and *in* life. This focus has been a response to a specific problem—when a query of life is posed at realms of killing in the contemporary, the biopolitical response or the politics of letting die becomes an indispensable orientation. It then becomes important to ask if it is enough to let the "letting die" of biopower seize the imagination, to make thanatopolitics the predominant dispensation in the biopolitical surge.

How does a query of life find an answer outside thanatopolitics—how does it find an answer in the social that allegedly does not kill but makes live or lets live? What is the play of "making live" in the social rather than in the biological? This book has explored that query in contexts where, I have suggested, violence creates a threshold across which emerges both a transformed social and the lives embedded in it—this transformed expanse is what I encapsulate in the idea of an afterlife that grasps a sensation of life when death plays with life. The sense of life that is framed in this afterlife articulates the powers, the economies, the cultures, the politics, the discourses, and the practices that come together to "let live." In that framing, it would appear that affirmative biopolitics becomes the other to thanatopolitics—but, while I have retained a kernel of meaning from that notion, I do not do so to endorse a radical, emancipatory politics. Rather, I have tried to find a way through to what indeed is the "making live" inhered in biopolitics, to what comes into play when life, and not death, is the analytical focus. Or how, through a socioanthropocentric lens, the social comes to actualize as life, or in another way, how life comes to actualize the social. In finding some answers in this terrain of making live, life does not appear as something that stays apart from death—I have suggested that death shadows life as another form of life, so to speak, around those living after a violent, transformative event. Life transacts with these shadows in formulations, and recapitulating from the preceding essays here, first, as those standing as custodians to a sense of humanity violated by atrocious death, that is, the International Criminal Court and the persecution of crimes against humanity; second, as those bearing witness and burden in a misshapen nation haunted by those shadows, that is, the Hindu–Muslim communal violence that shows as episodic bursts under a majoritarian nation; third, as the "I" living and dying in a community of those surviving the dead of a beleaguered "we," that is, the Sikh survivors of targeted attacks and the seeming splinters within their community; or, last, as those emplaced in visceral spaces marked by the persistent presence of those killed, infringed, or potentially targeted, that is, the literal living of faith-based identity in the overinscribed spaces and places of past, present, and suspended warfare in Beirut. Life's disavowal is also a response to how the question of life finds actualization in the social—and in these supplementary worlds of life and death, ultimately, life and its politics seem to be released. This remaining problem of politics of and in life is what I dwell on in this concluding chapter, not with an attempt to posit a resolute answer but to mark this book as a stepping-stone to others.

Just as it is feasible to argue that political violence shares discursive conditions across contexts, I have suggested that violent contexts and their transformative conditions can also be posed as a shared paradigm—that of an afterlife, as I argued throughout. The paradigm is shaped, at its very inception, by recognizing the ubiquity of suffering in violence and by posing social suffering as the given ground on which it finds form. At the same time, its unique expression in each of the locations of mass violence is equally recognized. I have dwelt on social suffering as something that is experienced and communicated in the manner of rhetoric, where participation also provokes a persuasion and a response, which includes those directly involved in the event and then goes beyond to assemble those who choose to witness and react. It is this assembly of those who experience and those who participate in the suffering that generates the ideas, the affects, the practices, the economies, the politics, and the cultures of how life and the social will be addressed, once it has been transformed by an event of violence. Harnessing the idea of suffering as a tragic rhetoric, one that insists on a communication and provokes a participation, I find that aftermaths of violence are about the making of a pathos—an affective assembly of participants and responses that bring about relationalities, connections, emotions among people, institutions, mechanisms, discourses, and practices, creating a sense of a social in an afterlife. Through this pathos, subjects, subjectivities, or even subjectifications emerge embodied as forms of life that are now constituted in the afterlife. To these forms of life, I suggest the figuration of the idea of bios. Bios and pathos, or forms of life and the social relationalities in which those forms emerge, respectively, become the double realms that inhabit the paradigm of an afterlife. Finding their combined emergence in each afterlife of violent damage that I explore, an answer to how life as that which is actualized from the sensation of immanent, pure life into social figurations of life finds some shape. As a subterranean impulse, it also underlines how the life query is a vector of multiplicity, of a plurality, where every context explored offers the potential for understanding a new configuration of life—leaving, as it were, the meaning of life always incomplete, always a virtual that each rendition or each historical arrangement, though always real, can only explain a version of. Violence, in that same way, seems to replicate that incompleteness, that yet unexhausted repertoire of devastation that continually actualizes a virtual; more on this later.

Four themes cohered the discussion in each location—law, justice, community, and identity. These themes, as they took shape in each of the listed contexts, addressed a fundamental query: when life and the social are actualized in the realms of making live, what theories, practices, and discourses come into play? What affects, experiences, and representations articulate those plays of theory and practice? These themes are the ways in which the answers found integration and focus—not as insulated and distinct features specific and limited to each location but rather as threads taken apart and laid out from an intertwined pattern, in which every one of the preceding, and more, were interwoven. In addition, a sense of scale has guided the organization of the chapters, starting with what can be seen as the largest rubric under which a life and a social finds form, that is, international law and its application in Sierra Leone in the first chapter. Following from that, the second chapter draws the boundaries of a national space (India) and the questions of citizenship and legal justice inside those borders. Third, the focus moves to a formation smaller in question than a national space, a particular ethnic/religious community (Sikh) within the borders of a nation, in particular, the fragmentation of that community in the duration of survival. Fourth, I have literally grounded a sense of life and the social in a material intimacy, in the proximity of violence to space and its reverberations into an afterlife where a city scarred by violence (Beirut) emplaces identity. Each chapter channels the basic conceptual formulation of bios and pathos. Each harvests a local formation associated with the context itself and adheres together a set of notions that allow an approach to the question of making live in that specific social contouring.

The preceding sketches the intended table of contents; however, these are not chapters that remain in their own pages. Clearly every one of the themes (and more, certainly) could apply in each. What I have said in terms of pathos in international law could well apply, with its own nuances, to the question of legal redress among all of the other contexts. Similarly, the question of bodies emplaced in the emotional spaces of violence will find resonance in all the contexts. My intention in assembling a heterogeneous catalog of life and the social in the afterlife, as they appear in the interstices of pathos and bios, is to draw attention to the ability of life to slip away from any firm grasp, from any one formulation, from any one living, from any one politics.

In framing this book as a document on life and a social, as it appears in multiple frames and contexts of the afterlife, in other words, in varied events and episodes spanning different durations of time, location, and specificity; the need to outline an epistemology, a method that creates a coherent object that is accessible, seems indispensable. The following section outlines that epistemology, and finally, in the last section, I return to the query of what politics of and in life these interpretations prompt toward.

EVENT–AFTERLIFE

Agamben, when writing on method, says, "Anyone familiar with the human sciences knows that, contrary to common opinion, a reflection on method usually follows practical application, rather than preceding it."[2] In some resonance with that, I add this section at the end of this book, rather than at the outset, to underline my bewilderment in finding the immense heterogeneity that life offers, in situations, some would argue, of commensurate devastation. I have tried to address that plurality by offering both a scalar organization and a thematic one under the theoretical anchors of bios and pathos. Even within that organization, life and the social did not allow a neatening, a tidying of theory or interpretation that can follow through from one context to the other. Rather, each context showed its uniqueness, and on the whole, the "jagged incommensurability"[3] of life remains much too vivid to sweep under a blanket interpretation. The following argues for a method that approaches that incommensurability, at the same time underscoring the implied intent of understanding an afterlife—first, as laying out a form, and second, as the content and substance that fill that form.

The events that I explore here are large-scale disruptive episodes of violence that transformed the ordinary lives of those who experienced them in ways that life led after the event came to be formulated in the overlapping arenas of private and public realms—state practices, legal universes, policies and institutional structures, community responses, and individual subjectivities. Approaching violent catastrophic events seems to be one of the most unsettling pursuits in social research. Massive disruptions and damage, sudden or continuing violence, appear in almost every location on the globe and in every sphere of human life. Jostling for space are events as diverse as military interventions, genocides, massacres, terrorisms, and civil wars, as well as famines, gas leaks, air crashes, hurricanes, earthquakes, tsunamis, market crashes, the HIV/AIDS pandemic—making up a list that can never quite be complete, yet they suggest a shared understanding, a common impact. In varying calibrations, each implies great losses in life and property; they transform the lives of those who experience them and often the societies that they occur in. Their apparent translatability from one sphere of existence to another and their ubiquitous presence around the globe in these comparable ways seem to suggest two possible explanations—calling an event a catastrophe is a "glib invocation" that has no meaning outside its own instrumentality, or in effect, there is a possible other "underlying logic," a "shared form and function" that connects these various apparently similar but arguably different occurrences.[4] The challenge lies in seeking the possibility of conceptualizing this shared underlying logic, not so much with the intent of defining catastrophes better as categorical events but rather of situating them as occurrences that can cohere larger social formations. The movement, then, is a step back from the variegated mass of catastrophic events, to decipher the possible connective tissue, without simply providing a generic form that could pass by as a glib invocation but attempting a formulation that provides for both virtual and actual, real and potential.

In my arguments, however, I do not use the term *catastrophe,* nor do I make possible the identification of *a* violent event per se; rather, I propose the ensemble *event-afterlife.* In pursuing a problem of recovery, it stands to reason that violent events are *not* seen as events per se, in terms of their manifestation, their agents, or the effects of their occurrence, but rather in the combined complex of the *event* with the unfolding of an *afterlife*; thus *event-afterlife,* where the combinatorial meaning includes both the "event" of the violent catastrophe itself and the concurrent discourses, practices, and experiences of recovery or reclamation that bear with the event. In lexical semantics, the Greek *katastrophe* suggests an overturning, a ruining, or a conclusion.[5] A catastrophe is an occurrence that overturns an existing state of affairs, often effecting ruin and ending sustained ways of life. The event–afterlife complex is the meaning ensemble that contains within it a threshold (not as a point in linear time but as a duration, a temporality that inheres within)[6] at which life gets constituted—at the very moment of its destruction. It is a phrase where the word *event* recognizes the occurrence in its substantive content and, *simultaneously,* recognizes the occurrence of an afterlife, where the *after* to life is a committed recognition that thrusts consciousness in a moment of concurrence, to the past, the present, and the future. In a methodological point of order, this formulation thus includes, in its temporal and spatial and cognitive reach, the overall discourses, institutions, practices, and experiences that accompany the form—the "state of affairs" that will generate the relationalities that will cohere a life-social.[7] In other words, the analytic of the formed object also appears concurrently with it.

The event–afterlife paradigm, in the sense that I apply here, connects back to the notion of an apparatus/*dispositif* that was mentioned earlier in the first outline of what the afterlife implies.[8] To start with, Agamben reads the concept of apparatus as closely related to Foucault's use of that idea, particularly through the notion of a *dispositif*. As Agamben writes,

> further expanding the already large class of Foucauldian apparatuses, I will call an apparatus literally anything that has in some way the capacity to capture, orient, determine, intercept, model, control, or secure the gestures, behaviors, opinions, or discourses of living beings.[9]

He derives the preceding from Foucault's *dispositif,* both as similar terms/ concepts and through Foucault's basic outline of the *dispositif*:

> It is, firstly, a thoroughly heterogeneous ensemble consisting of discourses, institutions, architectural forms, regulatory decisions, laws, administrative measures, scientific statements, philosophical, moral and philanthropic propositions,—in short, the said as much as the unsaid. . . . The apparatus itself is the system of relations that can be established between these elements. Secondly, what I am trying to identify in this apparatus is precisely the nature of the connection that can exist between these heterogeneous elements. . . . Thirdly, I understand by the term "apparatus" a sort of formation which has as its major function at a given historical moment that of responding to an *urgent need*. The apparatus thus has a dominant strategic function.
> . . . I said that the nature of an apparatus is essentially strategic, which means that we are speaking about a certain manipulation of relations of forces, of a rational and concrete intervention in the relations of forces, either so as to develop them in a particular direction, or to block them, to stabilize them, and to utilize them. The apparatus is thus always inscribed into a play of power, but it is also always linked to certain limits of knowledge that arise from it and, to an equal degree, condition it. The apparatus is precisely this: a set of strategies of the relations of forces supporting, and supported by, certain types of knowledge.[10]

First, weaving together the Foucauldian essentials of power and knowledge, the apparatus appears as a network of relations that brings into recognizable relief "the said and the unsaid," where the connections are made possible through a response to a need. I will suggest that the apparatus that I delve into here is that of the social, one that appears in the relationalities, both audible and silent, specific to the conditions of an afterlife, in other words, a historical moment that responds to the "urgent" need of attending to the business of damaged, vulnerable life. Second, drawing on another Foucauldian essential, I suggest that this apparatus involves relations of power, which implicate themselves in the making of subjects (often subjectivities as well) and subjectifications. I have read this apparatus to be an ensemble of affective realms, where affect certainly does not exhaust the interpretive potential of these relations but guides an understanding of these realms. More so, it is about their connections among and between knowledges, discourses, institutions, laws, administrative measures, philosophies, moralities—and their coherence around the idea of pathos. I suggested that this pathos finds its subjects, subjectivities, and subjectifications in certain forms of life (and its living) that I have called bios, which are emergent in the networks of relations.

In understanding the episodes of mass violence here, I read them as paradigms of event–afterlife, which carry with them the epistemological instrumentality of a *dispositif* or an apparatus. The *dispositif* inherent in the event–afterlife paradigm is thus the state of affairs at which social life sits at the threshold between damage–denial and reclamation–recovery, in either individuated or collective lives, revealing at the same time the peculiar churn of knowledge, power, technique, agentiality, and subjectivity that influences that social life. In excavating each location, each context where I place the event–afterlife paradigm, I attempt to understand the *dispositif* that creates possibilities of a particular pathos and its contingent bios. Deleuze, in his reflections on Foucault's understanding of the *dispositif,* says,

> We belong to social apparatuses *(dispositifs)* and act within them. The newness of an apparatus in relation to those which have gone before is what we call its actuality, our actuality. The new is the current. The current is not what we are but what we are in the process of becoming.... In each apparatus *(dispositif)* it is necessary to distinguish what we are (what we are already no longer), and what we are in the process of becoming: the historical and the current past. History is the archive, the drawing of what we are and what

we are ceasing to be, whilst the current is the sketch of what we are becoming. . . . In each apparatus we have to untangle the lines of the recent past and those of the near future: that which belongs to the archive and that which belongs to the present; that which belongs to history and that which belongs to the process of becoming; *that which belongs to the analytic and that which belongs to the diagnostic.*[11]

As a *dispositif* that allies with the analytic rather than the diagnostic alone, I propose event–afterlife as a paradigm to underscore a social theoretical framing of violent occurrences as aspects of a human condition that can allow an analytic of life and the social. Finding a resonance between this notion of a *dispositif*/apparatus and that of a paradigm, I start the making of a method through a Deleuzian schema. In that, I suggest a relationship between the *pure or virtual event* of event–afterlife, on one hand, and its expressions—the representations, the lived actualizations, the located occurrences—as *incarnations or actualizations* of the pure or virtual event, on the other. These incarnations can be read as impure events that repeat the original concept, the original form, in ways that reverberate its eternal interiority in multiple surface incarnations, in the historical contingencies of time and space. I lay out this relationship as the necessary frame with which to find analytical access to the meaning ensemble event–afterlife and also to propose that this approach is, in effect, both a method and the analytic itself. The formulation that I argue for and use in every context (the chapters here) is that the event–afterlife meaning ensemble suggests the architectural blueprint of a form through which I approach each context, which secures the methodological uniformity of approach. In that context, in "each" incarnation of the event–afterlife, I attempt to locate the *dispositif* that can inform how my propositions of pathos and bios come to be constituted. As I reason, this epistemological approach allows me to propose that neither the event–afterlife paradigm nor the notions of pathos or bios are exhausted by the temporal narrative of history or by the locational specificity of geography. Their content, their actualizations (their surface incarnations), remain anchored in the chronology of time and in the geopolitics of space, each time and location capturing *a* meaning but yet not exhausting the meaning of the paradigm.[12]

Following from this methodological outline, the fact remains that the episodes that I work with, in this set of essays, are events of violence that remain identified as such; in other words, I have worked with episodes that have found discursive and historical acknowledgment. But then, my query of life and the social could well be placed in those realms where damage to life goes unacknowledged. However, by stating that separation, I emphasize the next epistemological ground, which is that the identification of a violent catastrophic event seems to be intricately tied to the ways in which it can be or does get represented in the course of its occurrence (or in retellings of past events or in potentials of future events), particularly through the mechanisms of the visual or textual. Both visual and textual representation, each of which is likely to follow some apprehension of its experience (direct or indirect), relies on tropes of recognizability and iterability—each, though, in substantive content, is always new.[13] Linear time does not allow the "same" but similar and singular. For instance, the contestations on whether some episodes of ethnic violence are to be labeled a genocide underline the *dispositif* that produces the conditions of recognizability or iterability. A genocide is enunciated or claimed as one because of the double functions of recognition and iterability—pushing the past into the future, as it were.

In the cultures of representation in the contemporary, though, one of the most powerful ways in which catastrophic events register on common consciousness is undoubtedly their mediatization, or simply their visual or textual representation in the media. It stands to evidence that the worldwide proliferation of images, visuals, and media reports ranging from immediate to ongoing reportage is indeed one of the first ways in which a catastrophic episode attains representation. The impact of the visual or textual in catastrophic events has definitely not gone unnoticed—the media apparatus and the depiction of events of crisis have been unraveled in terms of the politics of image making; the technologies of producing different kinds of imagings, from still photography to moving images; the economy of circulation; the interactiveness with textualities; the functions of disaster imagery, and so on.[14] I use the problem of representation (often visual), in the following, as a quick illustration to clarify the Deleuzian relationship of pure event to incarnated event, in other words, laying out the event–afterlife paradigm and its articulation of the pathos and bios as both method and analytic.

Hayden White prefaces his discussion of the "modernist event" with a quotation from Walter Benjamin, that "history does not break down into stories but into images," just to appropriately point toward his argument about how one of the pressing critiques of modernist literature or art has been the dissolution of the "realist" story—the trinity of event, character, plot—and thus the breakdown in the complicated relation between "fact" and "fiction" in contemporary representations of the historical event. In his argument, this relationship becomes more tenuous when the form is visual—especially in the genres of docudrama, faction, infotainment, and so on, to other forms of what he terms "post-modernist, para-historical representation."[15] Stating categorically the meaninglessness of belaboring the point of historical, factual, or objective accuracy, he maintains that these events of the past serve as "contents" of bodies of information— "the only thing that can be said about them is that they *occurred* at particular times and places."[16] It is only this singularity that gives them the label of an *event,* to which all inconsistencies, contradictions, and gaps relate as the common referent.

In his view, this unstable relationship between fact and event is a clear expression of two connected developments in the historical imagination: first, the occurrence of events in the last century (and undoubtedly continuing into this one) of such scope, scale, and depth that they challenge any historian's ability to construe them as objects of scientific objective knowledge (his reference here is the Holocaust). Second, what echoes through this observation is the entangled challenge of comprehending not just the nature of events unprecedented in discursive (or practical) consciousness but also the fractured traces and imprints that they produce in the representative practice dominant in our age. Spinning off uncontrollably from the incredible interplay of media technology and economies— auditory, visual, or textual—with the explosive moment in the real time of occurrence of such episodes, their representations become entities that defy the very event they have captured. The cognitive disorientation that White writes about is the continuing process of evanescence, but a paradox of evanescence where there is, in the first instance, the loss into infinity of the moment of occurrence—no moment in time is repeated in its linearity. Yet, there is the infinite recurrent possibility of its appearance, which could also imply the endless possibilities of re-seeing the story or of retelling the story.

For White, the modernist rendition of these events strives to maintain them as *stories,* ones that, however close they are to the truth, do not disclaim the identity of a story, just so to avoid claiming any intellectual mastery on the event itself. By keeping the notion of a story, these representations also mark their distance from other kinds of knowable historical events and their narratives, perhaps to convey the sense that representation of these events is not always comprehension but rather recognition of tragedy which has happened and will continue to occur, into the future. Comprehension could suggest a closure that could also preempt mourning, but noncomprehension, or almost real, but not quite so, representations keep alive the possibility of the need to understand, to mourn, so that newer tragedies do not get mastered but rather get perceived better. Perhaps, we could add, they could even reach a newer politics.

The impossibility of finding meaning in the geometrics of hyper mediatization or the escape from narrative fetishism seem to indicate one thing for certain, the tenuous grasp of "representation" on certain kinds of events, especially in the events I explore. Beyond White's arguments, another nuance can be argued for—the fixing of interpretation and meaning, in any one moment, while it seems to defy factual fixity because of White's non-objectivity, yet it does occur in a located and specified political economy. In effect, in both arguments, the only certainty seems to be the agreement that something has occurred, often also the knowledge about where and when it has occurred, but once the attempt to represent is made, we are back to the dilemma of losing the moment of occurrence forever but still remain in the need to recognize its occurrence by retelling the story as many times as needed or possible or in as many interpretations as discourse, practice, and politics will allow.

How does this tension between nonrepresentability, yet coherent recognizability, on one hand, and, on the other, the specificity of meaning and the particularity of substance appear in the event–afterlife complex? This repeating, apparently because of both the inability to capture the meaning of what the event is and the possibility of infinite representations, lies at the core of the potential of the event–afterlife paradigm. I would propose that all repetitions or rereadings of any one event, or reading several events under the paradigm, suggest the methodological and analytical potential of accruing meaning to concept—in this case, the concepts of life and the social. In another way, there is a production of a new catastrophe, a disruption, a tragedy, every time there is a new reading of it in the presence of emerging institutional, practical, or political practices. For instance, as I have discussed, can a "new" crime against humanity be considered a discursive element that can change the way in which humanity or life comes to be constituted? Can the moment of this new humanity exhaust the idea of humanity, or does it anchor a historical "now," a "current need," a moment in a *dispositif,* which captures a meaning in the infinite progression of its knowing? But at the same time, I have to hasten to add, the newness does not obliterate the old, the past representations, because it is through drawing from the past that generalities are recognized in which new specificities are found. Let me recall Deleuze's comment on Foucault's *dispositif* here: "History is the archive, the drawing of what we are and what we are ceasing to be, whilst the current is the sketch of what we are becoming. . . . In each apparatus we have to untangle the lines of the recent past and those of the near future: that which belongs to the archive and that which belongs to the present."[17]

In emphasizing the analytic here (rather than the diagnostic)[18] and tightening the methodological grip on how that analytic can be reached, no reading of an event can possibly exhaust the meanings that it can offer. Moreover, reading events, that are recognized as similar does not indicate a need for reductive reasoning but rather underlines the need to explore meaning across contexts. Exploring violent events in this manner is not simply to point to the almost simple observation that they are repeatedly occurring and that their repetition is a function of the differing representations or their new descriptions; rather, it is to explore an arguably more powerful aspect of what these repeated understandings lead to in the realm of their philosophical import and their political consequence. And it is the repetition of this combination that requires attention, because it tells us about the *dispositif* or, in other words, what the terrains of political action have been, or what the discursive movements have been in extending the comprehension of the event in understanding the potential or destruction of life. This is where the eventedness of any violent catastrophe invites deliberation, because it signals the actualization of interpretation and action and tells us how they have marked newness in the tension between the forces that continue life or those that deny and thwart it. Embedded within these tensions, these newer singularities, is the articulation of the life-social, that is, the generation of relationships that trace the networks of power, the rhetoric of policy, the obfuscations peddled by cognitive sureties—and even the hope for politics, the will to knowing. This is what the event–afterlife *dispositif* is meant to reveal.

I take my cues from Deleuze and Guattari's constant reiteration of the importance of the event, in making progress not just in philosophical thought but also in critical, political thought and action.[19] This is not an intent that indulges in extracting some elusive, "true" metaphysical meaning of catastrophic violent events; rather, it is an attempt that is about their continual reading of meaning for "a new earth and people that do not yet exist."[20] Utopian vocations aside, the intent to understand the paradigm of event–afterlife and its relationship to its multitude of incarnations, its expressions in the variety of spaces and times, is to seek a new assemblage, another *epistēmē*, so to speak, so that received wisdom does not limit the potential of knowing more to understand more. At the very outset, then, my analytical foundation of this book is to read through Deleuze and Guattari the relationship between the pure event of event–afterlife, on one hand, and its expressions—the representations, the lived actualizations, the located occurrences—as impure events that relate to the original. They repeat in singularities, but differentially, and they reverberate its eternal interiority in its multiple surface incarnations. What then could be said is that each of these incarnations/representations captures something that is essentially present in each but assumes different forms in all—the underlying logic or shared form and function that Eric Cazdyn refers to—that which appears translatable to all spheres. The loss of life, the disruptions of sustained "normality," the imperative to recover, take different forms in the different spatiohistorical contingencies of a given occurrence. What then could be this essence whose sense can never be fully grasped but yet apprehended in multiple forms; what is it in violent catastrophes that is repeatedly experienced but differently represented?

Event–afterlife as paradigm and its articulation of life and the social, each of which mutually constitutes the other, resonate with Deleuze's idea of the pure event. Their expressions in the various different kinds of wars, genocides, or other humanitarian emergencies arising out of violence are the surface incarnations—the impure events that bear an eternal relation to the pure event. To use ready illustrations, the Holocaust, the Partition of India, or 9/11, each can be expressed as propositions of violent catastrophes, each in its own category of paradigmatic historical violence. But a catastrophe does not become the Holocaust, the Partition, or 9/11, yet their being is profoundly bound with the state of affairs each denotes. It is the *sense* of the proposition;

> sense is both the expressible or the expressed of the proposition, and the attribute of the state of affairs. . . . But it does not merge with the proposition which expresses it any more than with the state of affairs, or the quality which the proposition denotes. . . . It is this *aliquid* at once extra-being and inherence, that is, this minimum of being which befits inherence. It is in this sense that it is an "event": *on the condition that the event is not confused with its spatio-temporal realization in a state of affairs.* We will therefore not ask what is the sense of the event: the event is sense itself.[21]

My suggestion that the paradigm of event–afterlife be apprehended as a pure event is to indicate a principal dimension that has emerged through this book. There is a sense inherent in the concept of event–afterlife that is not exhausted by any of the episodes I have associated with in the thematic chapters, nor is the life-social by any of its spatiotemporal dimensions of relationalities and connections. In another fundamental instance, this nonexhaustion of the concept is a reflection of a condition of life, a continuing cycle of damage–recovery in which neither damage nor recovery stands alone as cause or effect, or as precondition and aftermath, but coheres an undifferentiated principle that repeats itself infinitely. The continual occurrence of catastrophic episodes is not just the coming together of a set of conditions in a given point in space and time but rather an actualization of the pure event, wherein each episode marks its present occurrence, repeats a past episode, and precludes a future episode—each of which reverberates the infinite sense of the mutuality of the life and the social.

This confounds Marx's statement a little—all great events occur, as it were, twice, the first time as tragedy, the second time as farce. If indeed a catastrophe is what we comprehend it to be, a "great" event of disorder, the first occurrence is all that would have been needed to appropriately comprehend the second. The second would have had the impact of a farce because we would have known it to be a mere copy, yet this kind of sequencing of events is the work of history, not the work of historiography or of comprehension. The method and analytic, then, that I arrive at is this: the pure event of "event–afterlife" encapsulates within itself the emerging pattern of connectivities of the life and its social. The surface incarnations, occurring at any given space and location, erupting out of the existing strata of the social apparatus, presents a possibility of understanding and interpreting the potential of knowing and political action, in that particular singularity of incarnation. At the same time, it opens up the possibility of recognizing the relationalities that will form the social around the giving and taking of life. Thus we return to the idea of life itself but approach it through the contingent and ongoing economy of constitution and creation or destruction and denial within the frames of contemporary pathos and bios. Thus what remains to be done is to *revisit* the surface incarnations of violent crisis and show how their limits cannot be found in their descriptions (hence the insufficiency of representation) of occurrence but rather in seeking the singularity embedded in their repeated interiority, in their reach to the pure event. The irony of farce or the inevitability of tragedy will still, perhaps, elude meaning.

POLITICS OF AND IN LIFE

The learning that this book has led me to, limited as it is, is a provocation of a philosophy, the crafting of an epistemology and a theorizing impulse toward a sociological–anthropological grasping of life. In this concluding reflection, I suggest an opening up of frontiers and a flagging of directions that need yet to be explored. Weaving a pattern from Esposito's work and Campbell's interlocution, I am led to propose that what sociology and social anthropology deliberate as a sense of contemporary life must find an affinity with the sense of life and social that Esposito's work seems to imply—especially when a politics of and in life becomes inevitable.[22]

In delving into the actual time-space of certain events (i.e., the parenthesized afterlife, the parameters of bios and pathos, and the separate vectors that I have explored in each context/event of afterlife), the concern has been to understand what life is and what a politics of and in life could be, when culled from an apprehension of the social. This implies a contraindication to the surge of the biological in the contemporary understanding of life, which, following Timothy Campbell, leads to an inevitable implosion of thanatopolitics.[23] While seeing an other or alterity to biology in the politics of life, I have attempted a sense of affirmative biopolitics that has its basis in Esposito's rendition of forms of life individuated as bios. Endorsing an idea of affirmative biopolitics, I have kept this fragment, bios, of Esposito's larger philosophical argument and have added the motif, pathos, to delve into a sense of the social. My affirmative biopolitics, so to speak, develops from these two tropes to understand a power of and in life that emerges from the social rather than the power over life that biology suggests in the biopolitical realm of things. However, Esposito's argument follows other tropes, of which I attempt, perhaps, an ill-advised summary here. His affirmative biopolitics speaks against the extreme immunization of the individual that personalized politics today seems to have achieved.[24] To put it bluntly, he asks why it is that, despite arriving at a place where we have inculcated human rights into our consciousness, politics, and practice, these are the very rights that are under the greatest threat today. His proposal is that

> the problem we face—that is, the absolute impractibility of the rights of man as such—arises not because we haven't completely moved into the regime of the person but rather because [. . .] we haven't yet left it behind.[25]

Developing a reasoning that finds efficiency in the impersonal rather than the personal, thereby removing the extreme individuality that leads to devastating autoimmune conditions in community (society, as such), he asks for the impersonal to envelop a sense of life that goes beyond the human, to animal life or more. It is impersonal insomuch as it does not rely on the individual, the person, as much as it relies on a sense of expanding life, leading to an affirmative biopolitics that preserves the community through impersonal politics. I draw from this, but in the realm of human life and in the context of violence and the *dispositif* of an afterlife. Under this rubric, if I am to read a politics of and in life, I am led to find in the afterlives that I have explored a sense of life that supports an affirmation rather than a denial or a letting die—thus a movement away from thanatopolitics. A question forms itself—what in the contemporary realms of the social sustains life, and what disallows it? If I can follow the logic of the impersonal, what is its location in the social?

Reiterating, then: in the symbiotic relationship between bios–pathos or life–social and the social that I pose here, I have not intended to judge the social nor evaluate the forms life, the individuations, that that social in an afterlife has created. As I have said, I have interpreted Esposito's sense of individuated life as bios, as the conceptual hold for the forms of life that are created within the social relationalities of an afterlife, where ascendant pathos circumscribes the emotional sphere in which suffering is witnessed, experienced, judged, and participated in. The social here, in addition, creates a ground for what I propose makes this sensing, this forming of life, possible, and that is a presumption, a belief, an instinct, a proximity that life exists as a value for all—much akin to the singularity of life (as opposed to the individuality) that, for Deleuze, the Dickensian wicked man seemed to attract and repel when he moved from individuality to singularity and then back again to individuality, in the moments between life and death. In the afterlife, the social I sense coheres an assembly of affective relationalities, at once constitutive of and constituted by affect. This assembly grasps at a sensation of this life, when it appears in its most unadorned, rendered so at the moment of its threat and transformation, when it stays suspended between life and death in a milieu of mass violence when a threshold separates the moment of change. The belief that life is a shared value, one that moves around and across others, is an effect of affect, so to speak.[26]

Or in another way, the pathos here is that membrane, that emotionally chafing surface, that touches one to another, that draws and attracts an insistent adhesive that reiterates a belief which, in the ultimate knowing, makes possible the sense that while it is my individual life, it is a singular life, it is a life that I hold in custody, in trust, and that in turn requires a protection, both in the name of life. This is also the life I transact with death if I am to separate from the "we" and, perhaps, even from the "I," or in another circumstance, give my "I" to the "we." This connection that life establishes between a "we" and an "I," which seems more about Deleuze's "a life" and about a shared-ness than about an individual-ness, is the presumption that makes possible the affective relationalities of pathos, which then returns to enclose the sense of life in an embodied form of life. Thus it is the ressentiment or the solidarity that I feel with my community or society, when I find my life a shared common with those of my own. My individuality, my proper name, "I" is not what makes me belong but is the commonness I share. I feel the sharing of my life, but I feel it in the embodiment of my gayness, my Dalit-ness, my Muslim-ness, my Sikh-ness. This is the social movement of individuality to singularity, where "I" or "we" will no longer matter or cannot matter; rather, a life—a form of life, or bios—will appear that includes, but surpasses, both.

At the same time, it is impossible to suppress the equal alterity of this—that it is the reckoning of that same social emotion which makes belief a knowledge of life that can also make possible a reversal that leads to ignoring and neglecting or targeting and destroying life by establishing a separation, a ripping apart of the singular life from individual life, returning to an "I" or to Esposito's "person" and not to a sense of common life. Once again, thus, when my politics is that of an identity—Dalit-ness, Muslim-ness, Sikh-ness—it is the emergence of that as a form of life that makes that politics possible at all, not my individual life. But then, when I am affectively targeted or when my pathos makes me choose to target, it is a personal life that will come into the fray. A name will be killed, an individuality will be disavowed—life will return from singular life to individual life. The converse, too, as Esposito says, in relation to human rights, is also possible—whatever be the community of my ressentiment, of my politics, the right I demand can only be given, by law, to the "I" that I am. Between the singular "life" and the individual "I" lies situated the politics between the impersonal and the personal—how does this play out in the contexts I have explored?

To recapitulate, the individual terrains in each essay spoke of the following—starting first with law. The Special Court of Sierra Leone made a historic contribution to international humanitarian law by passing convictions in three new crimes against humanity. This court was established in 2002, under the mandate of the International Criminal Court, as one of the first mechanisms of its kind in international justice, and it was intended to negotiate crimes related to the decade-long civil wars in the nation. One of these new crimes was child conscription, which meant that the use of children aged fifteen years or younger in armed warfare was an atrocity committed against humanity at large. I suggest here the making of an international social, one that represents the affective impulses of a global moral community of humanitarian discourses and actors, which make for the pathos here. This pathos trains its effects on Sierra Leone to legally codify the protected child as an embodied sign of saved life, which is the bios that finds embodiment here. In this I suggest that in the failed pursuit of the meaning of humanity, life appears as a site of its transgression, or it appears as a child *individuated* out of the myriad individual young lives, a figure that law creates.

Second, justice: after months of statewide violence directed at the Muslim community in Gujarat during 2002 in India, which was triggered by the burning of two train compartments carrying Hindu pilgrims, a movement called Nyayagrah was launched in Gujarat to pursue justice for the unaccounted killings. Inspired by Gandhian ideals, but adapted to the present, the movement seeks a pursuit of justice that promotes conscious citizenship in place of ascriptive identity in a nation scarred by episodic communal violence. I pursue this movement as a combination of compassion as a political force (the pathos here) and the understanding of legal citizenship as a reconciliatory goal, which, in their processes, brings together a community of empathy constituted of Muslim survivors, civil society, and some Hindu participants as well. In the intention to imbibe citizenship, or be political subjects that affirm life acknowledged rather than life denied, the form of life or bios here appears in the embodiment of citizen life.

Third, in the twenty-five years after the 1984 Sikh Carnage in Delhi, India (when, after the assassination of the prime minister by her Sikh bodyguards, the menfolk of the Sikh community were slaughtered over three days in the city), the Sikh community has moved along in disparate registers. From abject conditions leading to self-killing or "successful" coping, the narration of the aftermath in this event reveals a community fragmented by the work of survival. Working against the grain of how beleaguered communities find their succor in "wounded attachments," I show how domains of affect (the pathos here) inscribe the work of survival separately for separate groups of people. The negotiations between the "we" of a community and the "I" of suffering reveal the embodied subjectivities in this afterlife—which, in turn, measure the fragmentation of wounded attachments. These embodied fragmentations become the bios here, where it etches a range from extreme individuality (or, as I argue, subjectivity) of suicide to the emblematic social contours of the survivor collective.

Fourth, the ongoing cycles of militancy, warfare, or repeated incidents of violence since 1975 in Beirut, the capital city of Lebanon (a year that marks the beginning of a fifteen-year cycle of the Lebanese civil wars but can now be said to continue in different configurations), speak of mass violence as a duration that inscribes the very landscape of the city. The "ongoing" aftermath here, as it were, texturizes life and embeds it in the space of the city in ways that make the spirit of urban cosmopolitanism a lost ideal, especially in a city where the multiplicity of faith groups has engraved an uncertain narrative of coexistence. Instead, sustained life or its vulnerability is about identity-in-space, a condition that permeates a city living under the shadow of imminent violence. The emotional city experiences works as an emplaced pathos here, which captures the experiences of violence marked in space and, in that sense, draws out the subjectifications and subjectivities of space as a mediation of violent damage. Individual lives move into the terrain of individuated identity, where life shadows the embodiment of social faith-based identity—they, then, are the bios in this description.

When I assemble these horizons and see them in relation to each other, what seems to come to relief is an unevenness in the texture of the social. It may even be the appearance of a palimpsest, a seeming overwriting of the social, the collective, and its politics that invokes Esposito's interventions. Those interventions do not agitate, rather they persuade a clarity, in fact, an evaluation of what indeed is the politics of the forms of life that lie embedded in a social—and how that clinches an argument for the social in the letting live of contemporary life, as contrapuntal to the biological. To start this explanation, let me attempt a tentative mapping of connections and resonances that establish this. Esposito's affirmative biopolitics as the impersonal and the impolitical is achieved by moving away from the individual to a politics of life that is not "enthralled," as Timothy Campbell reads it, by the concept of the personal.[27] I employ Campbell's succinct rendition where he states that Esposito finds that the continual rebirth of guises of life makes possible political forms that do not rely on the personal. He further understands Esposito to say that the subject, rather than the personal, moves across a threshold when it transforms into a form of life, a form that now not only escapes the "scriptures of the personal, but in doing so can now relate impersonally with other forms of life, as they too have crossed the same threshold."[28] Clearly, this process is not about the ontology of the individual; rather, it is about the characteristic of individuation through which emergent life-forms are recognizable.

The resonance of subjects moving across the threshold of violence, and assuming the form of life as bios, in my making of an afterlife is obvious, and it underlines the process of life-becoming. But the resonance that reverberates between Deleuze's "becoming-animal" and Esposito's impersonal requires that I emphasize one particular nuance. Deleuze's becoming-animal is similar to Esposito's impersonal in that they both establish "zones of proximity" and put "in relation completely heterogeneous terms like human, animals, plants and microorganisms."[29] For Esposito, becoming-animal and the impersonal is about this—"even before the relation with the animal, is above all the becoming of a life that is individuated only by breaking the chains and the prohibitions, the barriers and the borders that humankind has constructed."[30] His impolitical impersonal is a complex that explains life in what may yet be an expansion of the concept of life to animals, organisms, plants, and so on, one that achieves its formulation beyond the human and the social and, indeed, is about life as such.

But my explorations are anthropocentric, and they seek a *human* social in the politics of life, which needs to emerge from an individuation, from an impolitical and an impersonal. However, by claiming a human declension, I do not suggest that the notion of life as such be limited. Rather, the problem is about this query—what is the potential for the impersonal or the impolitical *within* the social, especially in the context of Esposito's reflections on Weil, who holds the social as the terrain of impossibility for the impersonal or the impolitical. As Campbell interlocutes,

> for Esposito reading Weil, no category more than the Social enacts what theology has historically done, namely to confuse the Good with power. Why? Where precisely does the social confuse power with the good? The answer will be found if we consider that nowhere more than in the social are relations with what is outside of the social limited.
> ... The idolatrous tendency of the social therefore is to incorporate every relation within itself as belonging to it, as being precisely a manifestation of itself, of the social.[31]

This overwhelming understanding of the social as good makes the confirmation of it idolatrous—a deification of the social.[32] In this reasoning, then, the sense of life remaining within the relationalities of the social tends to be personal and political, whereas the impolitical and the impersonal extend relationalities beyond the social, to life itself: to animal, to bacteria, to plants, to the nonhuman constituents of life. Yet there is a hesitation in this logical minimalism. This hesitation emerges from my inability or reluctance, on one hand, to argue for a classification of all the forms of life I have listed in my Borgesian listing of afterlives here, as either one of the two—impersonal and impolitical or political and personal. And on the other, it becomes equally difficult to consider each form of life, each bios, as being on par with others in their contribution to the impolitical or the political, respectively. Let me formulate an argument why: in each vector, whether law, justice, community, or identity, I have argued for an individuation, an emergence of a form of life that occurs at the transformative threshold of violence, where a pathos of affectivity finds expression in a social and which then releases individual, personal life into individuated forms of life, into bios as part of the eternal rebirthing and, more so, as an accretion (and not an evaluation of good and bad life) to the concept of life, as it were. If I were to be faithful to Esposito's construction of this life as impersonal, as impolitical, I would have to find a similarity in the way that the threshold behaves in each situation (and the social, for that matter), such that forms of life that appear after the crossing are the individuations of the impersonal and impolitical. That is, for him, it is in the breaking of the social barrier and constraint that the impersonal and the impolitical take place.

But what if I delve deeper into the social, the assembly of pathos that I propose in each—do all forms of life, all bios, for instance, the figure of the child in law, the status of the citizen, the inhabitant of a community, or the carrier of an identity-in-space, cross the same threshold of violent transformation to merge with the same sense of impolitical life. I fear, and literally so, that there is a declension between them—more specifically, those produced in the thresholds of ascriptive identity as against those produced in the realms of law and justice. The fear is in the nature of this declension, about what place the social as sacred has in any or all of these forms of life. In my limited explorations, I suggest that there is the occultation of the subjective, the personal in all my conditions and contexts of afterlife, so that there is indeed an individuation and singularization in each, but there appear to be two itineraries that they follow. To begin the explanation of these two itineraries, I return to how Esposito's sense of the constraining social evolves out of the accord he finds with Simone Weil's idolatry of the social.[33] Weil, as Esposito reads in his "Categories of the Impolitical," suggests that the social, in its very nature, is understood as providential, fated, and guided toward the sustenance of a good life. My reading of declension seems to be along the two movements that the social seems to bifurcate into. Can the first be shown in the contexts of law and citizenship (as in chapters 1 and 2), and the second, the more troubling one, in the latter two of ascriptive identity (as in chapters 3 and 4)? I do not serve a conclusion here but rather leave the following argument as an interrogatory one, a query that my exploration of violence in its afterlife leads to.

The individuated life that finds form in bios in the contexts of faith-based identity seems to remain trapped in the subjectifications of the social. It would seem that the forms of life that these two tropes—both communities of ascriptive identity—release are those that remain trapped in the social of violence. They are rebirthings that carry within them the trace of this idolatry of the social. They are the markings of those relationships that do not empty out of the social in which the violence found itself, thereby making them marks of the personalized, politicized, individual, subjective carriers of their identity. They make a movement out of the personal to the collective of identity but cannot become impolitical, as these embodiments do not and cannot go beyond the social (and, perhaps, the human). One could claim that the inability of identity to allow for impersonality, to always count on the "I" and the "we," leads to forms of life that are precarious. They are so because they are reborn from the diabolical relationships that violence created, but their rebirth is a return to those socialities. Will it be possible here, then, to say that if I have suggested that an afterlife situates a recognition of populations by affect, then these are recognitions of ascriptive identity—because there is no biology possible there unless we are in the realm of conventional biological racism. Once ascriptive identity becomes the object of politics, there seems to be an inevitable result. Reading a few lines from Vanessa Lem's introduction to Esposito's *Terms of the Political,* "once the life of the human species becomes the object of political preservation and thus of immunization, one conclusion—which is typically thanatopolitical—becomes inevitable: that life can be preserved only at the cost of killing other life."[34] A logic seems to follow—can ascriptive identity be preserved only at the cost of other ascriptive identities? The fear then that returns here is that this relationship of ascriptive identity is indeed the creation of a violent social.

However, law, rights, citizenship, and justice—are they then forms that allow for a potential nonsocial and thereby an impersonal relationship? Can they, here, be found as the impolitical, the impersonal? My answer would have to echo some of Frédéric Neyrat's arguments where he introduces Esposito's notion of immunization, which hinges on modernity as the historical moment of the production of the individual, in both concept and reality. This, Neyrat is correct in saying, is a treacherous suggestion, especially when he says we have in front of us "an individual constructed by philosophy and liberal practice, armed to the teeth with subjective rights instituted to protect it against the attack of the Other and of others."[35] Ascriptive identity seems to arm one to one's teeth, in self-affirmation and self-assertion, and proceeds to immunize to the extent where neither the collective nor the individual survives in the onslaught of violence, or survives only when another such collective or individual is annihilated. I have to retain Neyrat's words here:

> Immunization does not only affect individuals, it also concerns collectives. Historically, this has been the case since the birth of nationalism. And today, we see how so-called "national" "identities," even though they have had their day and are no longer capable of "imagining" themselves, replace the impossible imaginary institution of society by the reality of walls, camps, of fortress Europe, of control and spatio-temporal surveillance. But should societies stop, then, to immunize, against themselves? Through a sort of immunization of community that would mark the bio-political destiny of modernity?[36]

But law, justice, and citizenship—how can they be considered as not so much about the collective or the individual of ascriptive identity as about the individuated, the singular, or as about a life? I am only too aware that when I propose law and citizenship, I do not find a solution, nor do I resolve a tension between law and human rights. Consider the following statement by Esposito:

> the association, which the modern legal notion has made for some time now, between the category of the person and the subject of law, tying them together in such a way as to make of the former a condition for conceiving of the latter and vice versa. In order to be able to assert what we call subjective rights—to life, to well-being, to dignity—we must first enter into the enclosed space of the person. Conversely, in a similar fashion, to be a person means to enjoy these rights in and of themselves. . . . What we have here is the increasingly widespread idea that the category of the person has the conceptual (and therefore, sooner or later, also practical) function of bridging the still dramatically gaping chasm between the concept of human rights and that of Citizen, set out so starkly by Hannah Arendt at the close of the second World War.[37]

The appearance of this chasm, the irreconcilability between law and humanity, seems to lie in the recourse of human rights to the personal. But what if the intervention is life with law, or life-rights, without forgetting that rights are accompanied by duties—the duty here is the regulation of affect. If life is a belief sustained by affect, then affect can also turn that belief, as we well know, into a force against life. Identities that are immune, that are committed to the idea that my life shared in proximity with self, individual, or community (under the guise of the good social) can only be sustained when no other kind of identity exists, are an affect that is against life rather than for life. How can that notion of the social be imagined when we are considering the contemporary as a simultaneity of time and geographical space and not an ahistorical or aspatial "social"? I would understand simultaneity of space and time (history and geography) as a factor that makes difference of identity in society around us as immediate and present and, in fact, the only way the social can even be imagined. The imagination of a good social without difference seems to be a-temporal as much as a-spatial. How a good, providential social can be one that affirms only "a" kind of ascribed identity (however extended it is—even the nation-state as no larger ascribed identity seems to exist) is a challenge to the imagination. That brings me to a notion of time, space, and ascriptive identity in the contemporary that I cannot meaningfully expand here without making too burdened the line of reasoning. To be sure, another opening to future deliberation.

The affect that can commit to the belief, the instinct, that the killing of the other is killing of the self, because the other lies in that proximity of the self that makes my belief of life possible at all, makes the social possible at all, recognizes the simple fact that life without the social is no life at all, just as language without a community of speakers and listeners is no language at all. Killing another in a social is killing the self, because persons against persons, individuals against individuals, cannot make a social (in the contemporary, ranging from the international to the intimate), which makes emergent the belief of life one that relies on that affect that recognizes perpetuation of life not through the death or nonexistence of the other but rather through the life of the other. Killing one life is killing all life, or rather killing singular life is killing the social. In this sense, life is separate from persons, individuals, nations, or citizens; rather, they are coterminous. If affect can understand life as belief—as that knowledge which is impossible without the social—can the affective membrane sustain life rather than destroy it?

How, then, can we reclaim that imaginary institution of society that can still make and let live so much that we can find an eternal rebirthing of life and not the replication of biopoliticized persons, individuals, or collectivities? The only impression I can suggest at this point is that, if we are to follow Simone Weil, she proposes the way of the mystic whose "whole effort" is "to become such that there is no part left in his soul to say 'I.' But the part of the soul that says 'We' is infinitely more dangerous still."[38] This is where life, in my interpretation, becomes belief and the effort of the mystic becomes the experience of the affective—where it takes from an "I" to a "we," but perhaps also beyond the "we" to a concept of life beyond the immunized human. Can affective proximities, thus, be the molecular proximities that Deleuze finds in the zone of becoming-animal? Can affect become the fluid that flows through the social membrane but flows out of the constraints of idolatrous, providential (and immunized) sociality to encounter life as a belief—a belief that works within the social and the human to give a concept of life that will no longer be trapped in an immunized, "political–personal" social, especially a social trapped in ineluctable violence? Could this be the return of the social in becoming-human, in addition to becoming-animal?[39] Can affect as the belief of life usher in a concept of life as a "haecceity" that Deleuze suggests, where life, much more than human, is "no longer of individuation but of singularization; a life of pure immanence, neutral beyond good and evil, for it was only the subject that incarnated in the midst of things that made it good or bad? The life of such individuality fades away in favor of the singular life immanent to man who no longer has a name, though he can be mistaken for no other, a singular essence, a life."[40] What the good and evil implies is my zone of uncertainty, especially when I understand too closely the danger (which Weil says earlier) in the affect that will inevitably create a "we" in law, justice, and citizenship.[41]

The urgency of these questions arises from that fundamental one—how do we reclaim a social, a benign social as much as a benign form of life, once it has been altered by the norms of violence? I must not claim an answer here but rather conclude this incomplete project with the hope that the ineluctability of violence, the repetitions of history, still lead to forms of life that can make sacred a value that we accord life and not accord value to the sacred that overwhelms life.

Acknowledgments

This first book is a long pause in an inexorable journey. Finding an infinitude of lives caught in the inescapable labyrinth of wars and violence, a single question has crafted itself over these many years and across those geographies, and that is a query of life. Those people, those lives, and those encounters have urged me to find a language and a grammar for an answer—this book begins that writing. My learning in this process, my gratitude and acknowledgment, are owed to many.

The University of Minnesota has been the ground where this book found its first contouring. My first year there was in a postdoctoral position with the Sawyer Seminar, led by Robert Duvall and Michael Barnett— to both of them I am grateful for a rewarding year that helped me find my way around the world of humanitarianisms. That year was also the beginning of my relationship with the Interdisciplinary Center for the Study of Global Change (ICGC)—one that I will cherish and nurture for a long time. My continuing years of interaction with the fine cohorts of interdisciplinary students have been another source of fascinating learning for this project. This book would not have been possible without the quiet, unquestioning support of Karen Brown, codirector of ICGC. For Allen Isaacman, as former codirector with Bud Duvall, my gratitude, for generosity beyond the call of ICGC.

The Institute for Advanced Study (IAS) at the University of Minnesota helped in giving this book concrete shape with long periods of hospitality. First, as part of the cohort that was awarded the Quadrant fellowship under the Global Cultures theme, I had the patient and unwavering support of the University of Minnesota Press, especially Jason Weidemann and Anne Carter. Jason has been the constant, patient reminder that demanded that this project be completed—my interaction with him has been a privilege. Ann Waltner and Susannah Smith have been part of this book from the very first tentative moments by giving me a confident place at the IAS from which to interact with a stunning range of scholars and to spend uninterrupted time with my reading and writing. This is another relationship with the University of Minnesota that I hope I will sustain. To many others at the university and the press, I owe deeply felt warmth that will undoubtedly thaw the memories of those cold and icy winters.

No book can be written without the presence of caring teachers. My years at the Department of Sociology, Delhi School of Economics, University of Delhi, first as a student and now as faculty, have accompanied me in this effort. Deepak Mehta, as thesis supervisor, colleague, and friend, has been constant with his confidence that I have something to offer to the profession. Veena Das has taught me the value of unwavering commitment to this pursuit—her generosity, her work, and her support are indelible here. Roma Chatterji and J. P. S. Uberoi are teachers at the department who have not hesitated in their attempts to make me work as I should.

Over many years and many places, I have found a special place for others whose presences in my endeavors are deeply etched. Samir Khalaf and his welcoming Center for Behavioral Research (CBR) at the American University of Beirut helped me find my feet and friends in the bewildering environment of that haunting city. At the University of California, Los Angeles, Edward Soja's infectious passion for the urban always reminds me of how much more I would like to be involved in understanding the city. The newly minted Department of Anthropology/Sociology at the Graduate Institute in Geneva, Switzerland, led me, during my fellowship there, to students who have reinforced my commitment to the classroom. Riccardo Bocco, Alessandro Monsutti, Isabelle Schulte-Tenckhoff, and Isabelle Milbert have been caring colleagues who have gone beyond mere collegiality to provide help and encouragement in my work. Most of all, my work on international law finds its inception in that environment.

The Sephis Program at the International Institute of Social History, the Netherlands, sponsored by the Dutch government, funded my doctoral work in Beirut, some of which finds its place in this book as a chapter. Ulbe Bosma from Sephis was unstinting in his help during tough moments in my fieldwork year. The Ford Foundation also funded a subsequent research stay in Beirut, a part of which work also appears in this volume. The Institute for Socio-Economic Research and Democracy (ISERDD), with the Indo-Dutch Program for Alternatives in Development (IDPAD), funded my work in Delhi among the Sikh Carnage survivors. My research appointments at the University of Minnesota–Twin Cities have been funded by the Andrew W. Mellon Foundation. ICGC supported my teaching appointments at the university. The Fulbright–Nehru Senior Research Fellowship (India) funded the academic year that I spent at the University of Minnesota and brought this book to completion.

Friends, sometimes at work and sometimes outside, occupy a place that is irreplaceable. Pratiksha Baxi and Janaki Abraham always find time to cajole a ruffled brow. Michelle Obeid, Zeina Misk, Anna Cjaska, May Haddad, and Jens Hanssen in Beirut were endlessly supportive at a time when I could barely find my wits about me. Govind Nayak, Joe Wangerin, Catherine Preus, and Adil Hasan Khan have been faithful companions who have listened to much rambling. Upendra Baxi has long been a strength I have been reassured by. William Beeman, Michael Goldman, Helena Pohland McCormick, Donald Johnson, and T. N. Madan always had a kind word when the clouds were dark. Kurt Campbell and Therona Moodley are special people—their presence in that room at ICGC was crucial for the final push for this book. Amishi Panwar's assistance in the initial moments of this book was indispensable, as was Mohammed Sayeed's in the culminating moments. This book could not have found its final form without Anirudh Raghavan's careful scrutiny and cheerful, unstinting help. Unnamed but unmistakably present here are also students I am indebted to for allowing me to keep my commitment to the profession over the years.

Finally, my brother Nazeeb and his family, Farahnaz, Zeina, and Zehan, have offered a home when the one I knew faded away. They will perhaps never know the joy and hope their caring brings to the fraught world that my work leads me to. Jaivir Singh has been the shelter throughout all my efforts and where, unknowingly, I have found the threads to stitch together my frayed life. To Baba and Mai, you return eternally in each moment I cherish, one of which is this book, dedicated to you.

The anonymous reviewers of this manuscript were extraordinarily engaged and generous in their sensitive reading and, to say the least, all ineptitudes are mine. Every word in this book is owed to those people and lives I have known through this work and the opportunity they have given me to think of how life is led in broken worlds.

Notes

INTRODUCTION

1 Agamben (1995, 15). I will return to how the sense of an apparatus works, both as epistemology and as analytic, when I outline their implications in chapter 5.

2 This refers to the triptych edited by Veena Das and colleagues (Das, Kleinman, and Lock 1997; Das et al. 2000; Das, Kleinman, and Reynolds 2001) and the genre of work that has based itself on that ground.

3 Chapter 5 discusses the epistemological potential of the idea of an event in this book.

4 See Das et al. (2001, 1–30).

5 Das et al. (2001, 3).

6 Das et al. (2001, 3).

7 In social anthropology, Veena Das has written powerfully about the folding of violence into the everyday and about those gestures that mediate tumultuous ruptures into a normalcy attained in the everyday, where she underlines the philosophical transactions with language that expresses that living. See, for instance, her book aptly titled *Life and Words: Violence and the Descent into the Ordinary* (Das 2006). That reading remains implied in what I intend to say; however, my focus is not on the everyday nor on the question of language.

8 Choosing any of the preceding thematic emphases has not been entirely contingential—the chapters also track a continuum of scale. The exploration of law in chapter 1 through the workings of the Special Court at Freetown, Sierra Leone, is in effect the largest rubric under which I pose my problematic. The work of international law can arguably be considered an attempt at making *global* a notion of life retrieved after violence and codified in law. Understanding the constitution of an *international* moral community as the social through which that legal work is channeled also suggests a similar scale. The relationship of compassion to citizenship in chapter 2 moves on to locate the idea of life and the social in the *national* spaces of citizenship in India. Community and surviving among the Sikhs in Delhi further traces the movement into identity communities *within a*

nation, which leads on to individual, personal experience as well. Last, violence, space, and identity carry forward the personal motif in Beirut to understand how the *intimate* identities of faith are literally emplaced in urban space. Although this tracing does not necessarily suggest an analytic, it makes a basic suggestion that the problematic of life and the social certainly spans the spectrum of scalar representation, however that may be imagined.

9 Foucault (2003, 241).

10 Rabinow and Rose (2006, 196).

11 Foucault (1980).

12 Agamben (1995).

13 See Timothy Campbell (2011) for an intensive philosophical commentary on how, in contemporary theory and discourse, the biopolitical perspective has been enveloped in an overwhelming thanatopolitical cover. His deliberations privilege the notion of the technical, or *technē,* but are expansive enough to accommodate a speculation on how thanatopolitics reigns supreme.

14 For instance, when Rabinow and Rose (2006, 203) say that "central to the configurations of contemporary bio-power are all those endeavors, that have life, not death, as their telos—projects for 'making live.'" Agamben's (2013) recent explorations of "the happy life" or Foucault's (1994, 465–79) discussions in *Life: Experience and Science* clearly indicate a desire to find more in the concept of life than the clarity of death.

15 Hardt and Negri (2000; 2004).

16 See Timothy Campbell's introduction to *Bios* (Esposito 2008) for an understanding of how Roberto Esposito critiques both Agamben's and Hardt and Negri's formulations. Esposito's own endorsement of an affirmative biopolitics is a continued set of arguments that he provides through his notions of *communitas* and *immunitas.* Although I return to these in the last chapter, Esposito's nuanced arguments are more than what I can amplify here; however, I stay with his critical endorsement of an affirmative biopolitics in a way that underlines the politics of life in terms of a making live, as I will say later.

17 Elsewhere (Arif 2015), I have tried to impress an anthropological and sociological epistemological need to indeed recognize life as it is and not only in the categories of success and failure that predominant theories of resistance or resilience seem to imply. From Veena Das's fine inflections on the everyday I learn this the most.

18 To make this statement without mentioning the contests of structuralisms and poststructuralisms in sociology/social anthropology is difficult.

The tension between poststructuralisms and structuralism still remains enmeshed (among other things) in the quagmire, for instance, of authenticity and multiplicity—the attributes of culture, on one hand, and on the other, the universals of concept. Especially in this project, the universal of humanity, human suffering, and its particular contexts of survival and redress pose a particularly acute statement of this tension. Though I do not gloss over this tension, I attempt to pose it as a query with which to frame the emerging contours of afterlives in the contemporary.

19   Available at http://www2.hn.psu.edu/faculty/jmanis/aristotl/poetics.pdf.

20   Carson (2006, 9).

21   Buch (2010, "Introduction").

22   Aristotle (2013, 5, 9).

23   As indicative volumes of the time, like David Hume's (2003) *A Treatise of Human Nature* and Adam Smith's ([1865] 2000) *The Theory of Moral Sentiments.*

24   The number of titles published in the past decade and a half amply illustrates affect as a worthy analytical intervention in social science or humanities research. A good representation of current perspectives on affect theory is Gregg and Seigworth (2011) and the special issue on affect of the journal *Qui Parle*. Other important volumes that bear relevance here are Teresa Brennan's (2004) *The Transmission of Affect*; Martha Nussbaum's work in the area, including her *Political Emotions* (Nussbaum 2013); and John Protevi's (2009) important work in *Political Affect.*

25   Massumi (2002, 61).

26   Deleuze and Guattari (1987, xvi).

27   Massumi, in the following, draws this sense out of what affect, and its crystallization into socialized emotion, can bring about, and this sense is about connectedness: "In affect, we are never alone. That's because affects in Spinoza's definition are basically ways of connecting, to others and to other situations. They are our angle of participation in processes larger than ourselves. With intensified affect comes a stronger sense of embeddedness in a larger field of life—a heightened sense of belonging, with other people and to other places." http://archive.org/stream/InterviewWithBrianMassumi/intmassumi_djvu.txt.

28   Kleinman and Kleinman (1996).

29   Robert Buch (2010) interlocutes Alain Badiou's (2007) "passion of the real." I do not privilege that part of the argument here, except to note that Badiou's recognition of the last century's ambiguities of radical politics against recalcitrant tragedy indicates, perhaps, a pessimism that I would rather not endorse.

30 I will return to the notion of apparatus, following both Agamben and Foucault, in the final chapter. My arguments will make it apparent that I position both bios and pathos as elements of an apparatus that appears in the unfolding of an afterlife.

31 This sense of affirmative biopolitics is different from Hardt and Negri's formulations mentioned earlier, even though both summon a sense of the social. While Esposito's *Bios* is immediately relevant, my work relies on all his work currently available in English. I also rely on Timothy Campbell's translation and interpretation of Esposito's *Bios*.

32 Rose (2007).

33 Anidjar (2011, 698–99).

34 Arendt (1973, 316).

35 Anidjar (2011, 720).

36 I do suggest a small reading of how the sacred overwhelms the social in chapter 5. But that is an idea that I leave for future work.

37 Esposito (2008).

38 Campbell (2008, xxxiii).

39 Not far from this is Deleuze's (2005) "A Life," a singular life that I will return to in the last chapter in order to follow through my version of an affirmative biopolitics. Deleuze's singular life perhaps echoes, and here I take somewhat of a leap of trust in my own interpretation, his readings of Gilbert Simondon's initiations of the ideas of individuation. I quote from Deleuze's (2001b, 44) rare review of Simondon: "Singular without being individual, such is the state of pre-individual being. It is difference, disparity, *disparation*. Amongst the most beautiful passages of the book are those where Simondon shows how the first moment of being, disparity, as singular moment, is effectively presupposed by all other states, whether they be of unification, of integration, of tension, of opposition, of resolution, etc." What I depend on for the forms of life I propose is the movement from a preindividuation through individuation (across the threshold of transformative events) into a kind of postindividuation. Going further with my leap, can the affirmation of life here lie in delving into this form of individuation as a form of life-becoming?

40 Deleuze (2001a).

41 John Rajchman, in his introduction to Deleuze's (2005) *Pure Immanence: Essays on a Life,* says, paraphrasing, perhaps, "Hume suggests that God as well as the self be regarded as a fiction required by our nature. The problem of religion is no longer whether God exists, but whether we need the idea of God in order to exist, or, in terms of Pascal's wager, who has the better mode of existence, the believer or the non-believer" (17). I am tempted to

say, isn't the belief in life required for us to continue to exist, or would life have perpetuated if we did not have the affective social to make us believe that it exists and must exist? Perhaps this is a nod to the secular sacralization of life, where to lose that belief is a nihilism, whereas to believe is an endorsement of the potential of and in life.

42 This does not quite answer the question of immunity that Roberto Esposito poses (and that Timothy Campbell suggests in the preceding quote)—individuation as a strategy and effect of immunity is a query I address at the very end of this project, in chapter 6, not directly but rather in the guise of the politics that this kind of life formulation leads to.

43 In an insightful (and useful for my discussion) set of arguments, Cooter and Stein (2010, 118) review Nikolas Rose's (2007) *The Politics of Life Itself* and Roberto Esposito's (2008) *Bios,* both of which are the stances that I negotiate with here to endorse the social, to say, "Critics might worry, too, that so much of his [Rose's] discussion is on individual subjectivities, and scarce nothing on the social or communal forms of life that these new biologically enhanced individuals might or should entertain. His liberal openness and intellectual casualness in this regard are unsatisfactory. That the individual–subjective category spawned through the growth of technologies of the self now rules over previous social–structural ones in explaining and sustaining the political order tends to forget that individuation is itself a social phenomenon and, further, that, as Esposito has it, the individual 'is not definable outside of the political relationship with those that share the vital experience.' *Indeed, sociology itself is abandoned here—at least the sociology that was founded on certain notions of what 'the social' was about, and sought (always as an inherently moral enterprise) to explicate it*" (emphasis added).

44 Deleuze (2005, 45–46). In Deleuze's summary of Hume here, partialities can be the result of not error in knowledge (as conventional philosophy might understand it) but rather *illegitimate* beliefs arising out of delirium or illusion—of fictional causative chains or illegitimate rules of association. Passions can often be that delirium, that illusion that the affective effect also recognizes in my reading of the social, the pathos here. Deleuze's reading of Hume (especially in the chapter included in Deleuze's [2005] last publication, *Pure Immanence: Essays on a Life*) will trickle into many crevices of this book, many more than I can cite meaningfully.

1. THE INTERNATIONAL SOCIAL

1 See particularly volume 2, chapter 2 of the report (Sierra Leone Truth and Reconciliation Commission, n.d.).

2 Foucault (1991, 3–72).

3 Clearly this is too short a statement to make when scholars of international law have probed deeply into the inequities of international law, particularly as "civilized nations" is also another duplicitous name for the colonizing nations and imperial powers and the legacy they have perpetrated. The presence of this legacy and influence in the making of a global "moral" community is concurrently undoubtable. However, I am not sure if pointing out that nexus makes for any particular analytical intervention apart from documenting newer descriptions—I do not attempt this work as that kind of description.

4 United Nations Security Resolution 1270 (1999), http://www.un.org/en/peacekeeping/missions/past/unamsil/mandate.html.

5 Peace Agreement between the Government of Sierra Leone and the Revolutionary United Front of Sierra Leone, July 7, 1999, Article XXVI (1).

6 The Lomé Peace Accord, Article IX (1 and 2).

7 For a detailed discussion on the Sierra Leone TRC and its relationship to the ICC, see Schabas (2003, 1035–36; 2004, 1082–99). Evenson (2004, 730–67) discusses the relationship between the SCSL and the Sierra Leone TRC. Also see Kelsall (2005, 361–91) and James-Allen, Lahai, and O'Connell (2003), among others, for details on the workings of the Sierra Leone TRC.

8 Evenson (2004).

9 Special Court for Sierra Leone (n.d., para. 9).

10 Statute of the Special Court for Sierra Leone, Article 1(1), http://www.rscsl.org/Documents/scsl-statute.pdf. The crimes enumerated in the statute are derived from international law developed over several decades, some of which could be traced back to the Nuremberg Charter. Broadly, the crimes can be classified into two categories: war crimes and crimes against humanity.

11 Special Court for Sierra Leone (2002–3, 9).

12 Remaining activities of the court, such as witness protection, are now under the jurisdiction of the Residual SCSL, established in February 2012 and located in Amsterdam. http://www.rscsl.org/.

13 Because of serious concerns of security, the case against the then president of Liberia, Charles Taylor, was shifted to the Hague.

14 For a sense of the legal debate on the new crime of forced marriage, see, among others, Frulli (2008, 1033–42) and Goodfellow (2011, 831–67). On the other new crimes, generally, see Sivakumaran (2010, 1009–34).

15 For arguments in legal procedure in the application of this principle in the SCSL, see Wharton (2011, 217–39). For general discussions on the

nullum crimen principle, see Schabas (2006, 67), Cassese (2008, 38–40, 87), Gallant (2009), and Shahabuddin (2004).

16 See, e.g., Broomhall (1999).

17 This court established two other new crimes: forced marriage and intentional killing of peacekeepers. Owing to space constraints, it is impossible to discuss each new crime and the legal reasoning accompanying it to make the basic argument. Briefly, in convicting under the crime of forced marriage, its inclusion under "other inhumane acts" listed within crimes against humanity (Article 2i) is reasoned by a process that recognizes the "special" and "distinct" suffering caused by such an act, which includes the harm caused by crimes of inescapable rape, torture, forced pregnancy, and other crimes of a sexual nature but exceeds and extends to questions of distress, dignity, social ostracization, and stigma, among other related concerns, thereby justifying its categorization as something outside of sexual crimes, which are already fairly widely acknowledged in the listings of crimes against humanity.

The intentional targeting of peacekeepers, in this case, largely members of the UNAMSIL, as a new crime comes within Article 4g under "Other Serious Violations of International Humanitarian Law." It was first specifically listed under Articles 8(2)(b)(iii) and 8(2)(c)(iii) of the Rome Statute of the ICC, and the accused of this crime were tried for the first time at the SCSL. The judgment in the RUF case convicted those most responsible with the view that peacekeepers are protected as civilians so long as they are not involved in the conflict themselves, and if they were to use arms, they would do so in self-defense, as is the case with civilians as well. For both of these new crimes, academic legal analyses have elaborately argued that none of these judgments violated the *nullum crimen* principle (see note 14). At the time of writing, there is less work on child conscription than on the other two new crimes relevant to the SCSL. However, some arguments are in Kelsall (2009, 146–70) and Sivakumaran (2010). An overall legal perspective on the war crime of child soldiers, reflecting on the SCSL, is in McBride (2014).

18 *Lex ferenda* is a Latin expression that means "future law," used in the sense of "what the law should be" (as opposed to *lex lata,* "current law"). The derivative expression *de lege ferenda* means "with a view to the future law." The expressions are generally used in the context of proposals for legislative improvements, especially in the academic literature, both in the Anglo-American and continental legal systems.

19 Lamb (2002, 746).

20 Meron (1987, 361).

21 The Rome Statute of 1998 ensured its inclusion in the list assigned to the ICC. There is a genealogy of international treaties and agreements that lead up to this inclusion. The Geneva Convention and its additional Protocols had proscribed the use of children in hostilities early on, in 1949, and again later in 1977. The Convention on the Rights of the Child was created in 1989.

22 Prosecutor v. Sesay, Kallon, Gbao (SCSL-04-15-A), paras. 1614, 482–519. All SCSL court records are available at http://www.rscsl.org/.

23 Ibid., para. 1619.

24 Ibid., para. 1640.

25 Ibid., para 1649. TFI-093 refers to the number of the witness testifying during trial.

26 Ibid., para 1623.

27 The witness was called as TFI-199 and was examined by Ms. Sharan Parmar on July 20, 2004. The record states that because this witness was given special protection, he testified via video link (case SCSL-04-15-T, Tuesday, July 20, 2004). The sketch here is taken from pp. 22–30. The transcript, at the time of writing, was available at http://www.scsl.org/SCSL/public /Transcripts/RUF/RUF_20JUL04_REDACTED.pdf. However, subsequent to the closing down of the SCSL (and its website) and the transference of all records to the Residual SCSL website, transcripts before 2006 are not online.

28 Available at http://www.unicef.org/slcrisis.

29 Justice Robertson's dissent note is available at http://www.sierralii.org/sl /judgment/special-court/2004/1117.

30 Legal scholarship on the issue, particularly from the international law perspective, has been prolific; however, I forge my arguments here from a few illuminating discussions that have been offered from a political philosophy or a general social theoretical perspective. In this regard, Vernon (2012; 2013), Luban (2004), May (2005), and Geras (2011) have been the most emphasized here.

31 Geras (2011, 38–74).

32 Geras (2011, 39). I use his exact phrases with the expectation that the words themselves convey the sense that he indicates, albeit in much more detail.

33 At this point, I have to make clear that *humanity* as a historical phrase covers much more than what is implied here in the narrow sense of crimes against it—and that narrow area remains my focus here. Without belaboring the point, it is easy to see how humanity quite easily develops proximity to the civilized, thereby opening the critical window to how the term itself creates

the categories of the savage, in other words, the inhuman. Within critical appraisals of international law at large, the term would imply a connected line of reasoning; however, here, I keep my analytical focus away from that, given the prolific nature of that critique in any postcolonial reading.

34 Lacan's (1977, 146–78) formulation of the signifier and signified, where the signifier stays above the signified, marked by a bar between them, is a part of his essay "The Agency of the Letter in the Unconscious." Changing Saussure's classical formulation of the sign as being made up of the components of signifier and signified, where the signifier and the signified are depicted with the former on top of the latter with a bar running between them, Lacan suggests that the signifier, in fact, slides above the signified, only occasionally crossing the bar to grip a signified, thereby producing meaning in the system of a sign. The movement of the signifiers above the bar, so to speak, is Lacan's understanding of the metonymic chain of signifiers—each pursuing the desire for meaning by endless associations and displacement of more and more words (in language). The movement across the bar is a metaphoric movement when meaning is grasped at by a replacement and a substitution. The poetic imagination, he would suggest, is metaphoric.

35 Geras (2011, 62–63, emphasis added).

36 Vernon (2002, 232).

37 The idea of belief here is a continuation of what I discussed in the introduction to this volume, as part of the conceptual framing of how I intend to understand life socially. See the section "Bios or the Affective Forms of Life."

38 I emphasize human life here: however, the appeal of this notion seems more inclusive especially when it can accommodate all that is constitutive of the posthuman, nonhuman life. I do not attempt a broader explanation of life, which understandably is quite outside of any single project; I have used the notion here in a specific emplacement.

39 I use this point to distinguish this sense of life from that associated with a "pro-life/pro-choice" kind of contestation. I suggest the idea of life that forms the basic ground on which zones of contestation can be inscribed.

40 Lacquer (2009, 31).

41 The reference is to Rorty's (1993, 111–34) "Oxford Amnesty Lecture."

42 Lacquer (2009, 32).

43 There are enough discussions about the world powers and their involvement in these strategies of who and what gets prioritized in the arena of international justice. My arguments through this essay do not privilege that approach mostly because there is hardly any surprise left there or

anything that cannot be predicted in the realm of the usual suspects of imperial power and its allies. I do not undermine the role of that power; in fact, I underline the importance of understanding how that power finds new ways of legitimation and articulation.

44 See Boltanski (1999) for an insightful argument about how pity, especially when it travels a distance between those who feel it and for whom it is felt, as is the case with a lot of formal humanitarian activity, achieves a political purchase. As he says, "to be a politics it must convey at the same time a plurality of situations of misfortune, to constitute a kind of procession or imaginary demonstration of unfortunates brought together on the basis of both their singularity and what they have in common. . . . They therefore must be hypersingularized through the accumulation of the details of suffering and, at the same time, under qualified: it is he, but it could be someone else; it is that child there that makes us cry, but any other child could have done the same" (11–12).

45 Foucault (1991).

46 This is also the place to mark this sacred–profane duality (produced by ritual) as somewhat different in application, but similar in resonance, from the sacrality of life suggested by Gil Anidjar (see the section "Bios or the Affective Forms of Life" in the introduction), an idea that triggered the sense of how life comes to be a supreme value in my arguments here.

47 The debate on childhood—whether African childhood need have a different culturally explained criterion—to me is a bad use of culture that ignores the viscerality, the ubiquity, and, eventually, the ineffaceable power of brutality and does not strike much of a chord in my arguments. There is some merit in "universalizing" brutality as much as it is important to understand life as a metaphor—using contextual metonyms to understand what extreme brutality is only leads to similar conundrums that "humanity" leads us to.

2. COMPASSIONATE CITIZENSHIP

1 Agamben (1995). I am avoiding here any reference to those who lose citizenship status for various conditions of statelessness, war, or transnational displacement. The context that I will proceed to discuss here involves the place of *citizens,* with alleged legitimacy in a nation-state.

2 Communal violence in India has received substantial scholarly attention; the following references are more in context and do not cover the range of interpretations. For a reading of how Hindu–Muslim violence in colonial India was constructed as communalism, see Pandey (1990a). For an understanding of Hindu–Muslim violence in postindependence India, with

some discussion of state involvement, see Brass (2003). For an approach that suggests an institutionalized conflict or "riot" mechanism, see Brass (1996). Mehta and Chatterji's (2007) specific attention to riot discourses compiles a set of issues that address a broader range of concerns arising out of the question of communal violence.

3 See Kapur (2006) for a discussion on the political and religious discursive constructs of the Hindu Right, which, she argues, normalizes the violence against the Muslim community. For an anthropological account of the violence in Gujarat and its connections with Hindu nationalism and how cultural practices, for example, vegetarianism, played their part in anti-Muslim sentiment, see Ghassem-Fachandi (2012).

4 See Weber's ([1919] 1946) essay "Politics as a Vocation."

5 As Baxi (2002, 3520) reads Shklar (1990) in the Gujarat situation.

6 Vernon (2010, 240).

7 The Sikh Carnage followed the assassination of then prime minister Indira Gandhi, ruling leader of the Congress Party. She was shot dead by her Sikh bodyguards at a time when Sikh militancy was a matter of immense concern and turbulence in India. The next chapter deals with the Sikh Carnage.

8 Baxi (2013, xii n.6).

9 In the case of Sierra Leone discussed in chapter 1, the state and its functionaries were in place when "political" pressure from "international sources" was influential enough to urge the Sierra Leonean government to request intervention, which resulted in the hybrid SCSL. Although the question of undue influence is not an unimportant one when misused influence is well known, the possibility of international attention in some situations has to be considered seriously when sovereign immunity/impunity becomes distorted.

10 See Baxi (2002).

11 Baxi (2002).

12 I use quotation marks around the term *minor* to signal that the terminology itself marks an unequal ontology in Indian citizenship. I leave this for further reflection, however, some of that intention is found in the following arguments about Gandhi's treatment of the same.

13 A vast and expertly argued literature has been cataloged—describing and tracing the various commissions, their shortfalls and their successes; or carefully discerning the critical points of discourse like that of memory, forgiveness, and vengeance; or evaluating what their efficacy could be as compared to the processes of criminal prosecution, especially in enabling the reconstitution of a healed society; or critically examining what actually remains undone despite public acknowledgment. Just as mere indications

of this literature, some well-read work is Hayner (2011), Minow (1998), and Minow and Rosenblum (2002).

14 At the time of writing, several new episodes across the nation, namely, in Muzaffarnagar, a town in the state of Uttar Pradesh, or in relation to the Bodoland and Bengali Muslim issues, in the state of Assam, have been reported.

15 See, e.g., Brass (2003).

16 A brief biography of Harsh Mander can be outlined as follows: he was a member of the Indian Administrative Services (IAS, the premier bureaucratic rank in India), a position in which he served for more than two decades in a few states. During this time, he was a responsible officer when riots against Sikhs broke out in Indore in 1984, where he effectively brought the violence under control. This experience has been the foundation of his conviction that no event of "rioting" in any area need last longer than a few hours, given the required deployment of state resources. This conviction led him to resign from the IAS in 2002, when he found his service colleagues unwilling to perform their duties regarding the mayhem raging in Gujarat. Prior to his resignation, Mander was also deputed as country director of Action Aid, a role he carried forth into relief activities in Gujarat in 2002.

In the years since, Mander has worked with many nongovernmental organizations and has also held positions in state commissions that involved work with social justice and human rights issues, including food security, poverty, and reconciliation and rehabilitation. His own trajectory of social activism has led him to be involved in and also establish a variety of organizations, one of which he currently holds the directorship of—the Center for Equity Studies. The work that is relevant to my descriptions here is most associated with the Aman Biradari (Peace Brotherhood, http://www.amanbiradari.org/), a network of volunteers who work with different initiatives aimed at secular ideals of peace and justice. Nyayagrah is an initiative of Aman Biradari.

17 See Mander (2004; 2008; 2009) for his work in Gujarat. I draw most of my descriptions from these. He has also written on other issues, such as poverty and right to food.

18 Mander (2008, 53).

19 Mander (2008, 61).

20 For a description of one of these omnibus FIRs, see Narrain (2004, 217–18).

21 See Jaffrelot (2012) for a description of the many kinds of communalized operations of the police, the bureaucracy, and justice officials alongside the many investigative reports made by media or other citizen's groups.

22 See Concerned Citizens' Tribunal (2002). Also see Mander (2009, 141).

23 For a description of the initial stages of this case, see Dhawan (2003).

24 See Jaffrelot (2012) for more detail on this.

25 This is the larger nongovernmental organization through which Nyayagrah is operated.

26 Interim application filed by Harsh Mander in CRL.MP.no. 9236/2005, CRL.MP no. 3741 and 3742/2004 and Writ petition (CRL) no. 109/2003 in the matter of National Human Rights Commission v. State of Gujarat and others (Mander 2008, 51).

27 At the time of completing this writing, Nyayagrah had extended its activities beyond Gujarat to Assam and Uttar Pradesh, as mentioned earlier, in response to recent incidents of ethnic violence and similar problems of justice. The written records, however, are best available for the first couple of years or so, and I rely on these for this writing and on Mander's own writing as well as other available documents. One such record of the initial years of Nyayagrah is "Progress Report: The Fight for Justice" (Nyayagrah, n.d.).

28 See Jaffrelot (2012) and Dhawan (2003).

29 Apart from the Nyayagrah movement, a number of other social justice-oriented nongovernmental organizations have been involved in handling some of these few cases. However, Nyayagrah has adopted as one of its strategies a "mass prosecution" approach (Mander 2008, 67), which, it hopes, will generate enough pressure, in sheer numbers, at least, to make the authorities react and respond.

30 The stated aims of Nyayagrah as well as the ethical rules, the cases, the kinds of investigations and procedures, and the duties of the Nyayapathiks are available as a *Mini Legal Information Manual* (Aman Biradari, n.d.).

31 Some Nyayapathiks, who work full time, are paid a small monthly fellowship; others are volunteers (Mander 2008, 69).

32 Aman Biradari (n.d.).

33 These profiles have been summarized from interviews, contacts, and research in the field with Nyayapathiks in their environment, undertaken by a number of individuals acting on their own volition; volunteers associated with Aman Biradari and Nyayagrah as well as other NGO activity involved in this effort. My compilations are from published material or documents that are available in the public domain. One such source has been Akanksha Joshi's work, which is published alongside Mander's, as a photo essay in Mander (2008). Another detailed report on Nyayagraha that provides ground for the arguments I make is "Transformative Learning for Human Rights: Case of Nyayagrah (TLHR)" (People's Campaign

for Justice and Reconciliation in Gujarat India for Equal in Rights 2010). The summary and conclusions are my own but remain indebted to their sensitive portrayals.

34 As said to Akanksha Joshi (in Mander 2008, 150).

35 Mander (2008, 146).

36 People's Campaign for Justice and Reconciliation in Gujarat India for Equal in Rights (2010).

37 All of the excerpts are from Akanksha Joshi's photo essay in Mander (2008), mentioned in note 34.

38 There is no easy determination of how Gandhi's Hindu spirituality, his views on caste, or his stringent personal values (experiments) with chastity or poverty could commiserate with the virulent caste politics and oppression in everyday India, on one hand, or, on the other, a mundane public or private life of the everyday individual. However, to the extent that some of his political philosophy as such has a bearing on Nyayagrah and its motivation, the arguments here make a selective reference—thus, this is no measurement of Gandhi but a reflection on the potential that some of his values may have in the present-day context.

39 Skaria (2011, 203).

40 For a discussion on Gandhi's understanding of and reaction to European notions of democratic ideals, see Gandhi (2008).

41 Gandhi's reference to *dayadharma* in chapter 17 ("Passive Resistance") of the *Hind Swaraj* appears with an invocation of the poet Tulsidas: "The poet Tuslidas has said: 'Of religion, pity, or love *(daya)*, is the root, as egotism of the body. Therefore, we should not abandon pity so long as we are alive.' This appears to me to be a scientific truth, I believe in it as much as I believe in two and two being four. The force of love is the same as the force of the soul or truth. We have evidence of its working in every step. The universe would disappear without the existence of that force." *Hind Swaraj* in English is available online at http://www.mkgandhi.org/.

42 Skaria (2011, 205–6). *Ahimsa* is simply translated as "nonharm" or "noninjury" and is the basis of Gandhi's notions of nonviolence.

43 Abandonment here is used in clear resonance with Povinelli's (2011) "Economies of Abandonment."

44 Nussbaum (2013, 380). She has written extensively on emotions and their role in politics—a summary of some of her positions, particularly with regard to the inevitable connection between love and justice, is in her "Political Emotions" that I refer to here.

45 Nussbaum's (2013) own answers take her through the path of various festivals, both comic and tragic, or the cultivation of benign patriotism and

so forth—all of which nurture emotional experiences that understand and protect the idea of liberty.

3. WOUNDING ATTACHMENT

1 I draw this from Wendy Brown's (1993) seminal essay of the same name.
2 A good amount of the ethnographic material used in this essay has been analyzed under varying rubrics in some of my earlier writing on related issues. A combined reading of all of them gives some sense of how I have tried to understand the experiences of surviving in this community. See, e.g., Arif (2007; 2008a; 2008b; 2015).
3 The specific issues that arise out of this sense of a doubled subject have been discussed in more detail in Arif (2007).
4 See Arif (2015).
5 I use these anchoring tropes from Brown (1993) and will return to them later.
6 To recapitulate, the Sierra Leonean (chapter 1) discussion marked the pathos within the makings of international criminal law, and in that reading, a sense of the *international social* appears. In the Godhra episode (chapter 2), the negotiations of compassion and justice in the Nyayagrah movement lead to the mediation of pathos in the aspired and potential *nation space* of citizenship. Here the exploration of the Sikh episode leads to pathos within the *confines of a community,* within ascriptive identity.
7 See Amitav Ghosh's observations of the tense city, particularly of a fairly affluent neighborhood, in his "Ghosts of Mrs Gandhi" published first in *The New Yorker* on July 17, 1995.
8 See Lalita Ramdas's (2005) personal narrative of her experience and association with the Sikh event.
9 The report was a Joint Inquiry conducted by the People's Union for Democratic Rights, headed by Gobinda Mukhoty, and the People's Union for Civil Liberties, headed by Rajni Kothari, published in November 1984. http://www.unipune.ac.in/snc/cssh/HumanRights/04%20COMMUNAL %20RIOTS/B%20-%20ANTI%20-%20SIKH%20RIOTS/01%20-%20DELHI /a.pdf.
10 The ethnographic information in this essay is based on interviews I had conducted along with Simi Bajaj and Harpreet Kaur from the research team at the Institute of Socio-Economic Research on Democracy and Development (Delhi, India). Funds for this work were provided by the Indo-Dutch Program on Alternatives in Development (Netherlands), and this work was part of a larger project that explored communal violence in a few Indian cities.

11 Drawing from her direct involvement with the groups who were instrumental in working with the immediate relief activities during November 1984, she had gone on to document an ethnography and read it through an understanding of social suffering.

12 See Arif (2015, 160–61) for some more vignettes of these conversations.

13 A set of official committees were set up, and varying amounts were offered as official compensation for material damage, for example, an offer of Rs 5,000 (approximately US$85) per dwelling was recommended by the Dhillon committee—one of those up set up specifically for the task of compensation (see later). The same committee recommended that loans should be offered from nationalized banks, and a total of Rs 340 million was disbursed at the rate of 12.5 percent interest—this rate was subsequently reduced and eventually written off. In addition, the Rangannath Misra Commission recommended that businessmen who could procure insurance claims not be further compensated. No judicial intervention on compensation for material damage was reported in Delhi. However, after the Nanavati Commission (this commission was expected to look into the violence, its causes, and impacts of the 1984 episode) report was made public in August 2005, the government announced two further committees, one of which, the Sankaran Committee, was to look into the adequacy of relief and rehabilitation and provide details for further action. As per these committees, Rs 1,000 crore was to be allotted for additional compensation, out of which about Rs 600 crore was meant for traders who had lost their houses, shops, businesses, and so on. (See http://www.carnage84.com/ for the committee reports mentioned here. The PUDR Report of 1992 also summarizes some of these committee recommendations: http://www.pudr .org/sites/default/files/pdfs/1984_carnage.pdf.)

14 Most of the original allottees in the widow's colony came from two of the worst hit colonies in the city—Sultanpuri and Mongolpuri. There were others from various parts of the city. The variations among the families in economic status or social classification in terms of caste groups were significant. This is not a point that I can elaborate here; suffice it to note that apart from visible differences in material goods (although the overall colony could be loosely middle to lower middle class), there were internal social differences made apparent by our informants with reference to caste groups.

15 Figures quoted from information available at http://www.nishkam.org/.

16 Even the monetary compensation, which was initially about US$200, was raised to approximately US$7,000 only after legal intervention contested the adequacy of the initial amount. I have discussed this in Arif (2007).

17 It is difficult to trace the trial proceedings or the exact number of convictions for any given charge filed during the 1984 carnage (or most other case proceedings in India) given the incredibly long time span and wide geographical dispersal of cases. I have taken recourse to a specific report compiled by Vrinda Grover (2002) that investigated a sample of 126 from the 1984 cases to provide an adequate overview of the state of affairs. Only eight cases resulted in convictions, while the rest resulted in acquittals. Of these eight convictions, two were overturned by the High Court, while the Supreme Court reduced the death sentences awarded in three of the cases to life sentences. In this sample, ninety-nine of the Trial Court cases related to the offense of murder under section 302 IPC. An analysis of the judgment reveals a pattern—that a combination of grave lapses in investigation, inordinate delays, insufficient evidence, and procedural lacunae led to a majority of cases concluding in acquittals. See Arif (2007) for a detailed reading of justice and the widow's colony.

18 The seeming exile of this group of people from the discursive city suggests trajectories of recovery that I have discussed in Arif (2007). To reiterate that notion, community as a spatial entity within the city, especially one marked by violence, has compelling repercussions in recovery—the marked space works to congeal the circumscribing of a destiny to these residents, as if keeping their past and future eternally linked.

19 Butler (2004, 19–49).

20 Once again, names and other details are mentioned to maintain privacy.

21 B is referring here to Jagdish Tytler and Sajjan Kumar, both prominent congress politicians who had a number of cases filed against them. However, lack of evidence and other procedural irregularities have prevented any concrete outcomes. Fighting behind the gurudwara implies the internal politics within the religious authorities.

22 A lot of these women had been given jobs as a compensatory measure by the government. In a way, they understood this gesture of support as one that came with its own dark lining.

23 Das (1995, 344–74).

24 Das (1995, 347). The next morning the bodies had disappeared—as had the many others killed similarly. The inability to perform the last rites was another cause of relentless distress for Shanti, as it was for others.

25 Das (1995, 349).

26 Das (1995, 361).

27 Among several, two interrelated strands sit somewhat silently alongside my concerns with death in this essay. First, the sociological question of suicide and community, of course, can traverse arguments different from what I

emphasize in the suicide of Shanti. In a particularly vivid, sensitive, and poignant work, Stevenson (2014) understands the epidemiological proportions of suicide among Inuit youth and unravels the "psychic life of biopolitics" (see also Stevenson 2012) in that community, especially the connection between colonial "care"-giving regimes and its incommensurability with the Inuit way of life or its futures in death. Her work delves into a community cohered by suicide as a whole—I consider Shanti in her separation from the community through her suicide. Second, on the question of the dead among those surviving in communities marked by violence, for instance, the work of Heonik Kwon (2006) in Vietnam, where, when neither the state nor local rituals allow a sufficient resting together of the living and their dead, people and their refashioned cultures bring together the two in some semblance of a closure. Similar interventions can surely be made in the context that I deal with (in this essay and others), and I presuppose their possibility. However, like the preceding, my intention has been to draw attention to how death itself can appear as a form of life, insomuch as it "lives" as pathos, as emotional realms that constitute a community in the afterlife. In a sense, the dead live as another striation in a community of survivors in their afterlife.

28   This conceptual distinction is credited to Ferdinand Tönnies (2001) in his book *Community and Civil Society.*

29   Brown (1993).

30   See, e.g., Etzioni (1993) or Pearson (1995).

31   Brown (1993, 390).

32   Brown (1993, 391–92).

33   *Subjectivity* as a term has been used so far with varying connotations. Without making specific references to the vast literature that is available, I use the term *subjectivity* to suggest an understanding of individualized experience that is also generalized to groupings of individuals. See Biehl, Good, and Kleinman (2007, 1–17) for an overview of the issues involved in understanding subjectivity, especially in anthropological work. Subjectification, as said earlier (see the introduction to this volume), on the other hand, is the process by which these groupings are externally created, by a rationalized recognition of such experience. However, I do not read them as dual or dialectical opposites; rather, I see them as mutually constitutive.

34   Esposito (2010).

35   Esposito (2010, 5, emphasis original).

36   Esposito (2010, 6–7).

37   In his review of *Communitas,* Barder (2011, 29–30) makes a similar point when he says, "Community, as Esposito theorizes it with respect to its

intrinsic *munus* or obligation, thus involves a fundamental loss of boundaries among its members: 'That which everyone fear in the *munus*, which is both "hospitable" and "hostile," according to the troubling lexical proximity of *hospes-hostis*, is the violent loss of borders, which awarding identity to him, ensures his subsistence' (8). But it is this substantial lack, this gravitational effect without an object as such, the very Janus-faced possibility of hostility and hospitality, that constitutes the 'unreachable' origin of what binds a community."

38 I owe this nuance in this context to a reviewer's astute comment on this manuscript.

39 See Axel (2001), among others, for an overview of the Sikh militancy and its historical background.

40 It seems apt that Veena Das's (1990, 345–98) writing on these women's experiences at the time immediately after the Carnage was titled "Our Work to Cry, Your Work to Listen."

41 See Das (2004), "The Signature of the State," in *Anthropology in the Margins of the State,* and Arif (2007).

42 See Das (1990) for a discussion of how, in the months after the event, various male kinfolk took on significant roles in these women's lives, in terms of claiming compensation, making decisions about how the money need be spent, and other matters.

43 I am referring to the many events of communal violence that India has witnessed since 1984, including the Godhra event discussed in the last chapter. It is important to note that in the years following the Godhra episode, which has found more attention in many ways than the Sikh Carnage (which, I expect, is the result of a complex of factors ranging from global discursive formations of rights to media and civil society involvement), Sikh issues have found renewed vigor.

44 See Butler (2004, 19–49).

45 Arif (2007, 30).

46 See Arif (2015).

47 Das (1995, 29–31).

48 A simple Internet search of the "widows colony" in Delhi results in numerous hits, which include several films, journalistic pieces, public community archives, and all else that keeps the political presence of this group forceful. The ironical failure of that presence to break through into the portals of justice for the murders that haunt them is a frightening statement, once again of state impunity, like that in the Godhra incident discussed in the last chapter. It is also worthwhile to note that the three days of killing in Delhi add up to more than the number of deaths in the Godhra incident.

49 Arif (2007).

50 Das (1995).

51 Das (1990, 349) subtitles her description of Shanti with the words "I want *sukha* (peace)—won't you give me sukha?"—the words she hears from Shanti when she first meets her. The following account is a telling one, and I quote at length: "I remember these as almost the first words that Shanti uttered to me when I met her in her house . . . 'what do you mean?' I asked her, unsure of how to react. . . . 'She is asking to be given a medicine so that she can die,' explained her mother. 'I tell her again and again—daughter do not talk so. But does she listen? Does she care?' Almost on cue, Shanti responded: 'What is there to listen and why should I care? If my baby at least had been spared I would have hugged him to my bosom and somehow I would have gone on living.'" This was the point at which the neighbor, who was standing by the door, interjected. "She carries on as if she were the only one to suffer a loss. Look at the world around us. Everyone was affected. A storm came upon us and it destroyed everything in its way. Can we save anyone from such a storm?"

52 I do not make this statement without hesitation—clearly the importance of community cannot be undermined. Individual experience turns into a protective shield that turns on itself, or rather, in Esposito's reading (particularly his development of the idea of *immunitas*), immunity to the community can only be destructive of the social. His analysis, however, vectors in the question of an overly individual (-*istic*) orientation that dilutes the political potential of the community. I do not carry the fuller development of that argument that Esposito develops in his other texts, where he speaks of a more sustainable community through the involvement of difference. However, in my reading of what suffering entails in an afterlife, this is an exposition of subjectivity that needs some understanding.

53 Michel Foucault places suicide in relation to the biopolitical power over life. It resonates here insofar as it is posed as a claim to an individual right over life in relation to societal claims over life. As he says, "it is not surprising that suicide . . . became, in the course of the nineteenth century, one of the first conducts to enter into the sphere of sociological analysis; it testified to the individual and private right to die, at the borders and in the interstices of power that was exercised over life. This determination to die, strange and yet so persistent and constant in its manifestations, and consequently so difficult to explain as being due to particular circumstances or individual accidents, was one of the first astonishments of a society in which political power had assigned itself the task of administering life" (Foucault 1990, 138–39). See also Biehl et al. (2007, 2–3) for a brief discussion on how suicide

can be a phenomenon that makes explicit the transactions between socio-economic worlds, culture, and individual subjectivities. The increasing medicalization of suicide, as they suggest, could be state power coopting a particular expression of subjectivity—in an extension of biopower.

4. EMOTIONAL GEOGRAPHIES

1 The Dahiye is the name used to refer to the southern suburbs of the city of Beirut. A fairly clear-cut assembly of Shia neighborhoods had formed over decades of urban placements and displacements, some of which will be discussed in the following. Linked once to the growth of a sectarian neighborhood, not unlike other sectarian spaces in the city, the Dahiye have a particular current visibility because of their affiliation with a politically ascendant sect under the Hezbollah, the political party and militant group associated with the sect.

2 As I emphasize the cyclical nature of violence in Lebanon, I have chosen to preface this chapter with a small historical profile rather than describe the "event" alone, as in the other chapters.

3 Beyhum (1992).

4 Allen Feldman (1991) speaks about similar formations in Belfast in his masterful rendition of bodies, spaces, and violence in Northern Ireland. For instance, I could draw parallels between his notions of "sanctuary" or "interface" (17–45) with such inscriptions on space in Beirut. His work, however, deals with violence per se and, accordingly, with the "perfor-mance" of violence at the moment of its enactment. I make this observation here to reiterate that temporality in my work on Beirut is about an ongoing sense of the present where violence is allegedly in the past, yet expected in a future.

5 Samir Khalaf (1993) talks about this kind of interaction between a spatial past and future in Beirut in his explorations titled "Beirut Reclaimed." I have described the impossibility of cosmopolitan ideals in some places of the "present" in Beirut (see Arif 2008b).

6 Beirut and its wars are an eloquent call to an exploration of memory and violence unique to themselves. Some arguments in the literature in English mention how a seemingly formal adoption of amnesia for political memory (see Haugbolle 2005, 191–203) or the interest in maintaining a status quo (Khalaf 2002) prevents a direct dealing with the war years; rather, attention is directed toward a nostalgic past as the only resource of the past.

7 The afterlife of violent episodes in cities can take on specific spatial forms. In some contexts, for instance, recovery comes to be "located," whether in short-term conditions (like that of emergency relief camps) or in longer

durations, where camps turn into permanent settlements or, in another version of the same, become permanent neighborhoods like the widow's colony in Delhi discussed in chapter 3. See, e.g., Agier (2002) and Diken (2004, 83–106). See also my discussion comparing Beirut, Delhi, and Ahmedabad in terms of faith-based aid, rehabilitation operations, and spatial biopolitics (Arif 2008a; 2008b).

8   I use Parker and Karner's (2010, 1452) notion of reputational geographies here.

9   Ricoeur (1990, 10–11).

10 It can well be argued that this kind of a threefold present is indeed the temporality that is implied in all of the contexts in the preceding chapters. The distinction that needs underlining is the fact that violence here is a matter of suspension and not of abatement. While in both Delhi and Gujarat (India), or in Sierra Leone, the fear and anticipation toward similar episodes of violence are real, the same kind of event has not recurred (even though Hindu–Muslim violence continues unabated in other parts of India, as do occasions of political violence in Sierra Leone), keeping the sense of apprehension very different from in Lebanon, where violence between armed confessional militias is endemic, as are violent regional incursions into the nation. At the time of this writing (mid-2015), the IS crisis that started in Syria is fast spilling over into Lebanon, reaching Beirut as well.

11 Lefebvre (1990, 10–11). Lefebvre's project is an epistemological and ontological one that is embedded in a larger theoretical concern that posits a reassertion of space into critical theory. My brief allusion here to his sense of social space is not meant as an undue simplification but rather as a conceptual device to pose an argument and to indicate its presence in the spatial theoretical orientation in this afterlife.

12 Tuan (1977). There is a similar resonation in the distinction between space and place by Michel de Certeau (1984).

13 To the best of my knowledge, no academic work exists in English about Saifi of that time, a neighborhood that I document through some residents' experiences. It is likely that, in a few years after my field visits, since the neighborhood had so vastly changed, those with whom I met and interacted may have moved on to other areas, leaving very little trace, and may have even died. As such, their experiences remain erased, even in the scholarship, adding further depth to the question of erasure and memory here.

14 The Cedar Revolution was one such moment, when, after the assassination of Prime Minister Rafiq Hariri during February 2005, the nation, literally, stepped onto the avenues of Downtown Beirut, in apparent protest and

grief. Hariri, ironically, was also the main visionary behind the spectacular reconstruction of Downtown Beirut and, accordingly, was criticized widely as well. See Haugbolle (2010) for some discussion on these political moments in Beirut.

15   The fieldwork that this chapter draws on is based on my doctoral research that was funded by the SEPHIS Program, Amsterdam. The Ford Foundation funded my subsequent visit to Beirut in 2004.

16   E.g., Hanf (1993, 208).

17   The current location of Saifi is somewhat different from the Saifi that is identified in prewar or historical mappings, which indicate an area closer to the seafront. This "movement" is attributed to the comprehensive contours of the Master Plan that guided the recent reconstruction of the Downtown Beirut area.

18   See Khalaf (1987; 1993).

19   In Hamra, Michelle Obeid helped me with my interviews and meetings.

20   Lebanese street or fast food.

21   These opinions portray sentiments that have been expressed in reply to my queries and should be placed in context. At the same time, there is no denial of the fact that displaced families were some of the worst hit in the war tragedy.

22   The PSP is the Progressive Socialist Party, a party associated with the Lebanese left. Toward the later years of the wars, the PSP was a controlling political/militia presence in the area.

23   The use of private capital in a postwar reconstruction project is unusual. In fact, SOLIDERE has been given complete ownership and development rights to the entire square mile of Downtown Beirut, all of which is subject to a comprehensive Master Plan that is geared toward a complete makeover of the area. The making of SOLIDERE has been widely discussed as a singular controversial project engineered by a state–capital alliance that privileges private interests rather than other pressing needs of a devastated nation. For a range of interpretations on SOLIDERE and reconstruction in Beirut, see, among others, Khalaf and Khoury (1993), Makdisi (1996, 661–705), and Rowe and Sarkis (1998). Also see my semiotic reading of the reconstruction plans as landscapes of recovery (Arif 2009).

24   For the latest visual material on Saifi, see http://www.solidere.com/city -center/urban-overview/districts-main-axes/saifi.

25   Lefebvre's (1991) tripartite understanding of space that I briefly suggest is rather starkly available here.

26   In Saifi, Zeina Misk helped me in conducting my interviews and conversations. All our informants were Christian. I have refrained from using any

names or pseudonyms here. Also, for the sake of privacy, no biographical details are mentioned. Most of the quotations here are parts of long conversations sometimes extending over different meetings. The choice of particular sentences is a result of my editing aimed at illustrating specific points of the argument.

27 The word "insides" is a rough translation of the word *nafsiyye*—it could imply a sense like "character" or "mentality."

28 Achrafiyeh is on the Christian side, neighboring Saifi, roughly due southeast. Hamra is on the Western side, across the then Green Line. Both, in distance, are almost equal from Saifi.

29 "Services" refers to the shared taxi facility that operates across the city and to most parts of the country. Saifi was a few hundred yards away from the main taxi service center located in Downtown Beirut.

30 During February 2005, the shocking assassination of Rafiq Hariri, ex prime minister and one of Lebanon's most controversial and dynamic leaders of recent times, inspired a fascinating phenomenon in Beirut. One of the most vivid and powerful images televised across the world at the time was the coming together of thousands of Lebanese of all sectarian persuasions (with the exception of the Shia Hezbollah) in the rebuilt city center to express their united protest and anguish. In retrospection, the narratives that I quote here could not have predicted the irony of how Hariri's assassination actually inspired a reclaiming of the city's *center de rencontre*, as a genuine public space. Although I was not there in 2005 to document these events, my speculation at the time of my fieldwork in 1997–98 was and continues to be that the future energy that could be unleashed in the kind of spatial regeneration that Downtown Beirut was undergoing could take forms that sometimes vindicate, to some extent, the losses it had simultaneously produced. At the same time, I must reiterate that there can be no undermining of the experiences of loss and disappearance that I document in Saifi, nor can there be any erasing of the ways in which a sense of self and place—or the spatial experience of Saifi—was expressed.

31 Arif (2008a; 2008b).

32 The Hezbollah's role in the negotiations with SOLIDERE during the displacements and relocations induced by the reconstruction of Downtown Beirut is well documented. Hiba Bou Akar (2005) describes how these relocations happened, both during the initial phase of warfare and later, during the phase of reconstruction. Her description and analysis make it amply clear how homogenizing identity politics were dominant in all stages of these processes—finding appropriate empty homes in the abandoned houses of Downtown Beirut, eventually getting adequate compensation

during eviction, and so on, were situations where political parties or related militia groups had almost total influence. See Fawaz (2004).

33 Kamal Salibi's (2003) *A House of Many Mansions* is an illuminating historical rendition of this idea.

34 Casey's (2000) phenomenological interpretation, of course, links the agency of the lived body to the relationship between memory and place. Although the narratives I discuss indicate such connections, I do not intend a phenomenological analysis here; however, Casey's formulation of anchoring nostalgia to a fundamentally spatial experience is very significant for my discussion. A more classical interpretation is that of Bryan S. Turner (1987, 147–56), who identifies the nostalgic paradigm as an evolutionary "label" in social theory, one that represents, often metaphorically (e.g., in art and literature), a melancholic reaction, not necessarily always negative, to change.

35 Casey (2000, 201).

36 Stewart (1984, 145).

37 Brace, Bailey, and Harvey (2006, 29). Their arguments use the illustration of the Methodists in Cornwall during the period 1830–1930, particularly the ways in which the informal, quotidian practices of Methodists can help in understanding space and religion in ways removed from usual analyses of religion subsumed under a wider category of identities in space.

38 Scholarship in recent years has taken clear cognizance of the implications of this relationship, bringing into focus the discourses that seem to have a bearing. See, e.g., the special symposium in the *International Journal of Urban and Regional Research* 32, no. 3 (2008), titled "Spaces of Modernity: Embodiment, Religion, and the Urban in Asia and Africa" or the special issue of the *Journal of Urban History* 37, no. 6 (2011), called "God in the City: Religious Topographies in the Age of Urbanization." The Global Prayers project (based in Berlin) and its publications also deal with a similar set of queries posed in cities across the globe. See Becker et al. (2014). One significant strand of these discussions is the expression of such religiosity or faith as experiences of identity in city space—a dynamic that calls another discursive element into the fray: multicultural or ethnic existence in cities and its place in social cohesion or fragmentation. This is a large concern in urban studies; however, a good representation of sociological/anthropological perspectives is Amin (2002; 2007) and Parker and Karner (2010). At another level, while reading faith-based identity in space, I do not also undertake the question of private experiences of piety and spirituality— they may well be a part of them, but I have not explored that aspect in my ethnography or in my research queries.

39 For instance, in India, from where I write, "communal" violence has been studied in urban locations. I would make a distinction between the kind of violence among religious groups in Beirut and, say, that in Mumbai, especially in their spatial implications; illustratively, see Mehta and Chatterji (2007), Mehta (2006), and Hansen (2001). Violence marks space in enduring ways and creates frontiers and borders in almost all instances of urban conflict. However, the making and unmaking of such boundaries have much to do with the interplay of a few factors that I tentatively propose. First is the urban genealogies and histories of that violence and not just in terms of spatial factors alone. Second is the duration of such episodes, where longer durations or protracted fighting could establish near-permanent frontiers and where shorter episodes could make transitory ones. Third is the visceral density and spread of places in which such episodes occur. In particularly compact and dense places, violent borders by night may be thoroughfares by day. Or after some episodes, the intensity of use makes borders into bare traces of the past that only some remember. Closest to Beirut, as I have said, would be Allen Feldman's (1991) work in Belfast (different though his emphasis is), especially because of the common aspect of a long-duration violence.

40 In his work on everyday family life in Palestine, Christopher Harker (2011) makes an important point when he states that the dominant epistemology of Palestine, in geopolitical studies, as a space produced and represented by violence limits its understanding. Similarly, while my analytical intervention undertakes an understanding of Beirut as a cityscape marked by violence, I do not suggest that as the only epistemological possibility in understanding urban life in that city.

41 Akar (2012).

42 In Hamra, the nostalgic construction of an authentic community appears to follow A. P. Cohen's (1986) explanation of the community with reference to his work on Whalsay, a Shetland Island community. He looks at the way differentiated individuals in a collective make creative use of the symbolic form of a community, notwithstanding the internal variation that such symbolism might entail, to give themselves the means "whereby communities [can] contrive a sense of the collective self as a response or counterpunch to the subversion or penetration of their structural boundaries which had previously held at bay external cultural influences. . . . Thus we have come to regard 'community' as a masking symbol to which its various adherents input their own meanings. They can all use the word, all express co-membership of the 'same' community, yet all assimilate it to the idiosyncrasies of their own experience and personalities. . . . The community

boundary incorporates and encloses difference. . . . The boundary represents the mask presented by the community to the outside world; it is the community's public face" (9–13).

43 When such a recollection is being made, there is an additional burden of dealing with the disappearance affected by the reconstruction operations of SOLIDERE. Nostalgia in Saifi, therefore, seeks to recapture the imagination of a visual environment—a situation that leads to a speculation of the new environment that will replace the old one. The fear of material erasure has a sense of permanence to it, which makes the recalling of the earlier surroundings acutely physical.

44 Sennet (1994, 249).

5. BIOS, PATHOS, AND LIFE EMERGENT

1 Deleuze (2001a, 28).

2 Agamben (2009b, 7).

3 I owe this phrasing to a sensitive comment by a reviewer of this manuscript who underlines my interpretation of the heterogeneous and innovative claims that life makes in its multiple contexts of re-creation. How that heterogeneity can offer itself to an epistemology is the question I pursue in this section.

4 Cazdyn (2007).

5 Disaster, on the other hand, draws from the Greek *astron*, "from the stars," already removing agentiality from the human domain.

6 This leads me to draw a resemblance to the notion of the everyday, which sits so closely with the kind of anthropological work that I am attempting with these "events" of violence, especially in the way Veena Das has masterfully crafted it in her deliberations. In an earlier essay that established a reading anew of Das's ethnographic work in relation the Sikh Carnage, I had mentioned the possibility of event–afterlife as a heuristic device. I use her words to find the link (Das 2015, 383): "What Arif calls the event–afterlife might in fact be part of this continuing dynamic between event and everyday—something I conceptualized by saying that the social is constituted through unfinished stories." As the following discussion shows, my sense of the event develops from a Deleuzian perspective; however, it is not distant from the notion of the everyday—in effect, it offers a complementary epistemological perspective to the temporality that sits in the event–afterlife paradigm.

7 Following Deleuze (1990, 22).

8 See section "Frames of Life" in the introduction.

9 Agamben (2009a, 14).

10 Foucault (1980, 194–96).

11 Deleuze (1992, 164).

12 This methodological approach could be considered close to Agamben's (2009b) elaboration of paradigm in his *Signature of All Things: On Method,* where he says the paradigm, working with the rhythm of an analogy, "entails a movement that goes from singularity to singularity, and, without ever leaving the singularity, transforms every singular case into an *exemplar* of a general rule that can never be stated a priori" (20). I find this close to Deleuze's scheme I use here, but Agamben makes no reference to the same. The "general rule" could adhere to the sense of the pure-virtual event and the "singularity" to the incarnations.

13 As my reference is to large-scale violent events, which do find their place in public representation—however partial or circumspect—I have privileged the medium of the visual or the textual. At another level, as I mentioned, not all catastrophes are recorded in public or private experience by the visual or the textual. The loss of meaning in catastrophic life-worlds is often about the loss of words, of language. Similarly, the complicated terrain of private and public recollection and remembrance in traumatic conditions does not bear a simple relation to representation. However, at this point, I explore the iterability and recognizability of violent events, and that already precludes the tensions inherent in representation.

14 For the impact of the visual in capturing such events of disaster and their implications in eliciting "compassion" as an expected reaction (which undoubtedly carries its own complexities), see Moeller (1999), Berlant (2004), Boltanski (1999), Cartwright (2008), Spelman (1997), and Vitellone (2011, 579–96).

15 White (1996, 17–18).

16 White (1996, 22).

17 Deleuze (1992, 124).

18 My distinction here between the analytic and the diagnostic goes back to my initial propositions that I do not look for a philosophy that will fuel an emancipating potential in the ways that I try to understand life and the social. In that sense, I do seek an analytic that is tied to the finding of an epistemology but not a diagnosing of a good or a bad, so as to assume an ethical posture.

19 Deleuze (1990).

20 Deleuze and Guattari (1994, 108).

21 Deleuze (1990, 22).

22 It is not easy to point to any one text of Roberto Esposito to reference my use of his work—however, in addition to the *Bios* (Esposito 2008) and

Communitas (Esposito 2010) invoked in the earlier chapters, the combination of his *Terms of the Political* (Esposito 2012a), *Immunitas* (Esposito 2012b), and *Third Person* (Esposito 2011) suggests the interpretations I make here. I will also recall here my reading of Esposito's sense of individuation as a grounding for the notion of bios and connect to his development of the "impersonal." Timothy Campbell (2010), in his essay "Foucault Was Not a Person," also makes a combinatorial reading of Esposito's work mentioned here. At the time of writing, the explorations of Esposito's work in the English-speaking world still compose a small group, and among those, I have stayed with Campbell.

23 Campbell (2011).

24 Much of Esposito's work in English had been translated into English long after its Italian publication, and therefore we run the risk of mixing chronologies. Nonetheless, Esposito's work on the immunitarian paradigm is, of course, in his *Immmunitas,* but for a short explanation on personalized politics and immunization, see his *Terms of the Political* (Esposito 2012a) essay "Towards a Philosophy of the Impersonal." A resonance of the immunitarian paradigm is, in recent times, of course, in Derrida's (2003, 85–136) notion of autoimmunity. For a reading together of Esposito's and Derrida's sense of immunitarization, see Deutscher (2013).

25 Esposito (2013, 114).

26 See the section on "Bios or the Affective Forms of Life" in the introduction for an initial discussion of life as belief.

27 Campbell (2010, 142).

28 Campbell (2010, 143).

29 Deleuze and Guattari (2004, 302–4).

30 Esposito's words quoted by Campbell (2010, 145) from the 2007 Italian version of *Third Person: Politics of Life and Philosophy.*

31 Campbell (2010, 139–40).

32 Durkheim's ([1912] 2008) argument in *Elementary Forms of Religious Life* about collective consciousness and its symbolic encapsulation in the totem does not seem too far from this reasoning.

33 Weil ([1986] 2005).

34 Esposito (2013, 6–7).

35 Neyrat (2010, 34) writes this in his introduction to his French translation of Esposito's *Termini della political,* which is available in English as *Categories of the Political.*

36 Neyrat (2010, 34).

37 Esposito (2012, 2–3).

38 As quoted by Campbell (2010, 148).

39 This is a response, I would venture to propose, to Esposito's call to retain a community but purge it of individualism. See, e.g., Esposito (2013).

40 Deleuze (2005, 28–29).

41 One cannot pussyfoot around the question that is insistent here—does this line of reasoning lead us to say that a society of citizens and democracy is better able to allow the conceptualization of life which is impersonal and impolitical, insomuch as democratic rights and law need not be limited to the human only but may extend to the nonhuman that inhabits the concept of life? This would be a controversial problematic that Esposito (2013, 100–111) complicates by suggesting that democracy and totalitarianism are in effect much too close, with the latter literally born out of the "excess or surplus" of the former—"a democracy that is as radical, extreme, and absolute as it is full of egalitarian substance, so much so that it shatters its own formal limits and implodes into its opposite." Perhaps it would be worth taking stock of what the predominant impressions are about the failures of democracy in the social *epistēmē*. I leave this as a future point of departure.

Bibliography

Agamben, Giorgio. 1995. *Homo Sacer: Sovereign Power and Bare Life.* Stanford: Stanford University Press.

———. 2004. *The Open: Man and Animal.* Stanford: Stanford University Press.

———. 2009a. *What Is an Apparatus?* Translated by David Kishik and Stefan Pedatella. Stanford: Stanford University Press.

———. 2009b. *The Signature of All Things: On Method* .Translated by Luca D'lsanto, with Kevin Attel. London: Zone Books.

———. 2013. *The Highest Poverty: Monastic Rules and Forms of Life.* Translated by Adam Kotsko. Stanford: Stanford University Press.

Agier, Michel. 2002. "Between War and City: Towards an Urban Anthropology of Refugee Camps." Translated by Richard Nice and Loic Wacquant. *Ethnography* 3, no. 3: 317–41.

Akar, Hiba Bou. 2005. "Displacement, Politics, and Governance: Access to Low Income Housing in a Beirut Suburb." MA thesis, Massachusetts Institute of Technology, Cambridge.

———. 2012. "Contesting Beirut's Frontiers." *City and Society* 24, no. 2: 150–72.

Amin, Ash. 2002. "Ethnicity and the Multicultural City: Living with Diversity." *Environment and Planning A* 34, no. 6: 959–80.

———. 2007. "Local Community on Trial." *Economy and Society* 34, no. 4: 612–33.

Amin, Ash, and Nigel Thrift. 2002. *Cities: Reimagining the Urban.* Oxford: Wiley-Blackwell.

Anidjar, Gil. 2011. "The Meaning of Life." *Critical Inquiry* 37, no. 4: 697–723.

Arendt, Hannah. 1973. *The Human Condition.* Chicago: University of Chicago Press.

Arif, Yasmeen. 2007. "The Delhi Carnage of 1984: Afterlives of Loss and Grief." *Domains, the International Journal for Ethnic Studies* 3: 17–40.

———. 2008a. "Religion and Rehabilitation: Humanitarian Bio-politics, City Spaces, and Acts of Religion." *International Journal of Urban and Regional Research* 32, no. 3: 671–89.

———. 2008b. "'Impossible Cosmopolis': Locations and Relocations in Delhi and Beirut." In *The Other Global City,* edited by Shail Mayaram, 101–30. New York: Routledge.

———. 2009. "The Landscape of Recovery: The Polysemy of Spaces/Places in Downtown Beirut." In *Spaces of Urbanism: Comparative Citiscapes in the Middle East and South Asia,* edited by Martina Reiker and Kamran Asdar Ali, 274–302. Karachi: Oxford University Press.

———. 2015. "Communitas and Recovered Life." In *Wording the World: Veena Das and the Scenes of Inheritance,* edited by Roma Chatterji, 154–71. New York: Fordham University Press.

Aristotle. 1902. *Poetics.* 3rd rev. ed. Edited and translated by S. H. Butcher. London: Macmillan. https://www.stmarys-ca.edu/sites/default/files/attachments/files/Poetics.pdf.

———. 2013. *Rhetoric.* http://www.bocc.ubi.pt/pag/Aristotle-rhetoric.pdf.

Axel, Brian. 2001. *The Nation's Tortured Body: Violence, Representation, and the Formation of the Sikh Diaspora.* Durham, N.C.: Duke University Press.

Badiou, Alain. 2007. *The Century.* Cambridge: Polity Press.

Barnett, Michael, and Thomas G. Weiss. 2008. *Humanitarianism in Question: Politics, Power, and Global Humanitarianism.* Ithaca, N.Y.: Cornell University Press.

Baxi, Upendra. 2002. "The Second Gujarat Catastrophe." *Economic and Political Weekly* 37, no. 34: 3519–31.

———. 2010. "Revisiting Gujarat 2002 with Harsh Mander." *Economic and Political Weekly* 45, no. 14: 32–39.

———. 2013. Foreword to *Pursuing Elusive Justice: Mass Crimes in India and Relevance of International Standards,* edited by Vahida Nainar and Saumya Uma. New Delhi: Oxford University Press.

Becker, Jochen, Katrin Klingan, Stephan Lanz, and Kathrin Wildner, eds. 2014. *Global Prayers: Contemporary Manifestations of the Religious in the City.* Zurich: Haus der Kulturen der Welt, metro Zones, Europa-Universität Viadrina, and Lars Muller.

Benthall, Jonathan. 1993. *Disasters, Relief, and the Media.* London: I. B. Tauris.

Benthall, Jonathan, and Jerome Bellion-Jourdan. 2003. *The Charitable Crescent: Politics of Aid in the Muslim World.* London: I. B. Tauris.

Berlant, L. 2004. "Introduction: Compassion (and Withholding)." In *Compassion: The Culture and Politics of an Emotion,* edited by L. Berlant, 1–14. London: Routledge.

Beyhum, Nabil. 1992. "The Crisis of Urban Culture: The Three Reconstruction Plans for Beirut." *The Beirut Review,* no. 4 (Fall): 43–62.

Biehl, João. 2007. *Will to Live: AIDS Therapies and the Politics of Survival.* Princeton, N.J.: Princeton University Press.

Biehl, João, Byron J. Good, and Arthur Kleinman, ed. 2007. *Subjectivity: Ethnographic Investigations.* Berkeley: University of California Press.

Biradari, Aman. n.d. *Mini Legal Information Manual.* Reprinted in Mander, *Towards Healing?,* 83–89.

Boltanski, L. 1999. *Distant Suffering: Morality, Media, and Politics.* Cambridge: Cambridge University Press.

Brace, Catherine, Adrian R. Bailey, and David C. Harvey. 2006. "Religion, Place, and Space: A Framework for Investigating Historical Geographies of Religious Identities and Communities." *Progress in Human Geography* 31, no. 1: 28–43.

Brass, Paul, ed. 1996. *Riots and Pogroms.* New York: New York University Press.

——. 2003. *The Production of Hindu Muslim Violence in Contemporary India.* Seattle: University of Washington Press.

Brennan, Teresa. 2004. *The Transmission of Affect.* Ithaca, N.Y.: Cornell University Press.

Broomhall, B. 1999. "Nullum Crimen sine Lege." In *Commentary on the Rome Statute of the International Criminal Court,* edited by Otto Trifflerer, 679–94. Baden-Baden, Germany: Nomos Verlagegesellschaft.

Brown, Wendy. 1993. "Wounded Attachments." *Political Theory* 21, no. 3: 390–410.

Buch, Robert. 2008. "The Resistance to Pathos and the Pathos of Resistance: Peter Weiss." *The Germanic Review: Literature, Culture, Theory* 83, no. 3: 241–66.

——. 2010. *The Pathos of the Real: On the Aesthetics of Violence in the Twentieth Century.* Baltimore: Johns Hopkins University Press.

Butler, Judith. 2004. *Precarious Life: The Powers of Mourning and Violence.* London: Verso.

——. 2009. *Frames of War: When Is Life Grievable?* London: Verso.

Campbell, Timothy C. 2008. Translator's introduction to *Bios: Biopolitics and Philosophy, by Roberto Esposito,* vii–xlii. Minneapolis: University of Minnesota Press.

——. 2010. "'Foucault Was Not a Person': Idolatry and the Impersonal in Roberto Esposito's Third Person." *New Centennial Review* 10, no. 2: 135–50.

——. 2011. *Improper Life: Technology and Biopolitics from Heidegger to Agamben.* Minneapolis: University of Minnesota Press.

Cardozo, Benjamin. 1922. *The Nature of the Judicial Process.* New Haven, Conn.: Yale University Press.

Carson, Anne. 2006. *Grief Lessons: Four Plays by Euripides.* New York: New York Review of Books.

Cartwright, L. 2008. *Moral Spectatorship: Technologies of Voice and Affect in Postwar Representations of the Child.* Durham, N.C.: Duke University Press.

Casey, Edward S. 2000. *Remembering: A Phenomenological Study.* 2nd ed. Bloomington: Indiana University Press.

Cassese, Antonio. 2008. *International Criminal Law.* New York: Oxford University Press.

Cazdyn, Eric. 2007. "Disaster, Crisis, Revolution." *South Atlantic Quarterly* 106, no. 4: 647–62.

Clarke, Kamari Maxine. 2009. *Fictions of Justice: The International Criminal Court and the Challenge of Legal Pluralism in Sub-Saharan Africa.* New York: Cambridge University Press.

———. 2011. "The Rule of Law through Its Economies of Appearances: The Making of the African Warlord." *Indiana Journal of Global Legal Studies* 18, no. 1, Article 2.

Cohen, A. P. 1986. *Signifying Boundaries: Identity and Diversity in British Columbia.* Manchester: Manchester University Press.

Colwell, Colin. 1997. "Deleuze and Foucault: Series, Event, Genealogy." *Theory and Event* 1, no. 2.

Concerned Citizens' Tribunal. 2002. *An Inquiry into the Carnage in Gujarat— Findings and Recommendations.* 2 vols. Vol. 1 of *Crimes against Humanity.* http://coalitionagainstgenocide.org/reports/2002/cct.2002.report.vol1 .pdf, http://coalitionagainstgenocide.org/reports/2002/cct.2002.report .vol2.pdf.

Connolly, William E. 2011. "The Complexity of Intention." *Critical Inquiry* 37, no. 4: 791–98.

Cooter, Roger, and Claudia Stein. 2010. "Cracking Bio-power." *History of the Human Sciences* 23, no. 2: 109–28.

Cryer, Robert. 2005. *Prosecuting International Crimes: Selectivity and the International Criminal Law Regime.* Cambridge: Cambridge University Press.

Das, Veena, ed. 1990. *Mirrrors of Violence:Communities, Riots, and Survivors in South Asia.* Delhi: Oxford University Press.

———. 1995. *Critical Events: An Anthropological Perspective on Contemporary India.* Delhi: Oxford University Press.

———. 2004. "The Signature of the State: The Paradox of Illegibility." In *Anthropology in the Margins of the State,* edited by Veena Das and Deborah Poole, 225–52. Santa Fe, N.M.: School of Advanced Research Press.

———. 2006. *Life and Words: Violence and the Descent into the Ordinary.* New Delhi: Oxford University Press.

Das, Veena, Arthur Kleinman, and Margaret M. Lock, eds. 1997. *Social Suffering.* Los Angeles: University of California Press.

Das, Veena, Arthur Kleinman, Mamphela Ramphele, and Pamela Reynolds, eds. 2000. *Violence and Subjectivity.* Berkeley: University of California Press.

Das, Veena, Arthur Kleinman, and Pamela Reynolds. 2001. *Remaking a World:*

Violence, Social Suffering, and Recovery. Los Angeles: University of California Press.

Debrix, Francois, and Alexander Barder. 2011. "Agonal Sovereignty: Rethinking War and Politics with Schmitt, Arendt, and Foucault." *Philosophy and Social Criticism* 37, no. 7: 775–93.

de Certeau, Michel. 1984. *The Practice of Everyday Life.* Los Angeles: University of California Press.

Deleuze, G. 1990. *The Logic of Sense.* Edited by Constantin V. Boun. Translated by Mark Lester, with Charles Stivale. New York: Columbia University Press.

———. 1992. "What Is a Dispositif?" In *Michel Foucault: Philosopher,* translated by Timothy J. Armstrong, 159–68. New York: Harvester Wheatsheaf.

———. 1998. *Spinoza: Practical Philosophy.* Translated by Robert Hurley. San Francisco: City Light Books.

———. 2001a. *Empiricism and Subjectivity: An Essay on Hume's Theory of Human Nature.* Translated and with an introduction by Constantin V. Boundas. New York: Columbia University Press.

———. 2001b. "Review of Gilbert Simondon's *L'individu et sa genese physico-biologique* (1966)." *Pli* 12: 43–49.

———. 2005. *Pure Immanence: Essays on a Life.* Translated by Anne Boyman. New York: Zone Books.

Deleuze, G., and Félix Guattari. 1994. *What Is Philosophy?* Translated by Graham Burchell and Hugh Tomlinson. New York: Columbia University Press.

———. 2004. *Thousand Plateaus: Capitalism and Schizophrenia.* Translated by Brian Massumi. New York: Continuum.

Derrida, Jacques. 2003. "Autoimmunity: Real and Symbolic Suicides—a Dialogue with Jacques Derrida." In *Philosophy in a Time of Terror: Dialogues with Jürgen Habermas and Jacques Derrida,* edited by Giovanna Borradori, 85–136. Chicago: University of Chicago Press.

Deutscher, Penelope. 2013. "The Membrane and the Diaphragm: Derrida and Esposito on Immunity, Community, and Birth." *Angelaki* 18, no. 3: 49–68.

Dhawan, Rajeev. 2003. "Justice, Justice, and the Best Bakery Case." *India International Centre Quarterly* 30, no. 2: 1–11.

Diken, B. 2004. "From Refugee Camps to Gated Communities: Biopolitics and the End of the City." *Citizenship Studies* 8, no. 1: 83–106.

Durkheim, Emile. (1912) 2008. *Elementary Forms of Religious Life.* Translated by Carol Cosman. Oxford: Oxford University Press.

Esposito, Roberto. 2008. *Bios: Biopolitics and Philosophy.* Translated by Timothy C. Campbell. Minneapolis: University of Minnesota Press.

———. 2010. *Communitas: The Origin and Destiny of Community.* Stanford, Calif.: Stanford University Press.

———. 2011. *Immunitas: The Protection and Negation of Life.* Translated by Zakiya Hanafi. Malden, Mass.: Polity Press.

———. 2012a. *Terms of the Political: Community, Immunity, Biopolitics.* Translated by Rhiannon Noel Welch. Stanford, Calif.: Stanford University Press.

———. 2012b. *Third Person.* Translated by Zakiya Hanafi. Malden, Mass.: Polity Press.

———. 2013. "Community, Immunity, Biopolitics." Translated by Zakiya Hanafi. *Angelaki* 18: 83–90.

———. 2015. *Categories of the Impolitical.* Translated by Connal Parsley. New York: Fordham University Press.

Etzioni, Amitai. 1993. *The Spirit of Community: Rights, Responsibilities, and the Communitarian Agenda.* New York: Crown.

Evenson, Elizabeth M. 2004. "Truth and Justice in Sierra Leone: Coordination between Commission and Court." *Columbia Law Review* 104, no. 3: 730–67.

Farneti, Robert. 2011. "The Immunitary Turn in Current Talk on Biopolitics: On Roberto Esposito's *Bíos.*" *Philosophy and Social Criticism* 37, no. 8: 955–62.

Fassin, Didier. 2007. "Humanitarianism as a Politics of Life." *Public Culture* 19, no. 3: 499–520.

———. 2011. *Humanitarian Reason: A Moral History of the Present.* Berkeley: University of California Press.

———. 2012. *A Moral History of the Present.* Translated by Rachel Gomme. Los Angeles: University of California Press.

Fassin, Didier, and Mariella Pandolfi. 2010. *Contemporary States of Emergency.* New York: Zone Books.

Fassin, Didier, and Richard Rechtman. 2009. *The Empire of Trauma: An Enquiry into the Condition of Victimhood.* Princeton, N.J.: Princeton University Press.

Fawaz, Mona. 2000. "Agency and Ideology in the Service Provision of Islamic Organizations." Paper presented at UNESCO Conference on NGO and Governance in Arab Countries, March 29–31.

———. 2004. "Strategizing for Housing: An Investigation of the Production and Regulation of Low-Income Housing in the Suburbs of Beirut." PhD diss., Department of Urban Studies and Planning, Massachusetts Institute of Technology, Cambridge.

Feldman, Allen. 1991. *Formations of Violence: The Narrative of the Body and Political Terror in Northern Ireland.* Chicago: University of Chicago Press.

———. 2004. "Memory Theatres, Virtual Witnessing, and the Trauma-Aesthetic." *Biography* 27, no. 1: 163–202.

Feldman, Ilana, and Miriam Ticktin, eds. 2010. *In the Name of Humanity: The Government of Threat and Care.* Durham, N.C.: Duke University Press.

Fischer, M. J. 2003. *Emergent Forms of Life and the Anthropological Voice.* Durham, N.C.: Duke University Press.

Foucault, Michel. 1980. *Power/Knowledge: Selected Interviews and Other Writings 1972–1977.* Edited by Colin Gordon. New York: Pantheon Books.

———. 1990. *The History of Sexuality: An Introduction.* New York: Knopf Doubleday.

———. 1991. *Discipline and Punish: The Birth of the Prison.* Translated by Alan Sheridan. New York: Random House.

———. 1994. *Aesthetics: Essential Works of Foucault 1954–84.* Vol. 2. Edited by James D. Faubion. London: Penguin.

———. 2003. *Society Must Be Defended: Lectures at the College de France (1975–1976).* New York: Picador.

Frulli, Micaela. 2008. "Advancing International Criminal Law: The Special Court for Sierra Leone Recognizes Forced Marriage as a 'New Crime against Humanity.'" *Journal of International Criminal Justice* 6, no. 5: 1033–42.

Gallant, Kenneth. 2009. *The Principle of Legality in International and Comparative Criminal Law.* Cambridge: Cambridge University Press.

Gandhi, Leela. 2008. "Spirits of Non-violence: A Transnational Genealogy for Ahimsa." *Interventions: International Journal of Postcolonial Studies* 10, no. 2: 158–72.

Gandhi, M. K. 1969. "Hind Swaraj." In *Non-violent Resistance, Satyagraha,* 16–17. New York: Schocken Books.

Geras, Norman. 2011. *Crimes against Humanity: Birth of a Concept.* Manchester, U.K.: Manchester University Press.

Ghassem-Fachandi, Parvis. 2012. *Pogrom in Gujarat: Hindu Nationalism and Anti-Muslim Violence in India.* Princeton, N.J.: Princeton University Press.

Ghosh, Amitav. 1995. "Ghosts of Mrs Gandhi." *The New Yorker,* July 17, 35–41.

Goodfellow, Nicholas Azadi. 2011. "The Miscategorization of 'Forced Marriage' as a Crime against Humanity by the Special Court for Sierra Leone." *International Criminal Law Review* 11, no. 5: 831–67.

Gregg, Melissa, and Gregory J. Seigworth, eds. 2011. *The Affect Theory Reader.* Durham, N.C.: Duke University Press.

Grover, Vrinda. 2002. "Quest for Justice: 1984 Massacre of Sikh Citizens in Delhi." Mimeo.

Hanf, Theodor. 1993. *Co-existence in Wartime Lebanon.* London: I. B. Taurus.

Hansen, Thomas Blom. 2001. *Wages of Violence: Naming and Identity in Postcolonial Bombay.* Princeton, N.J.: Princeton University Press.

Hardt, Michael, and Antonio Negri. 2000. *Empire*. Boston: Harvard University Press.

——. 2004. *Multitude: War and Democracy in the Age of Empire*. New York: Penguin Books.

Harker, Christopher. 2011. "Geopolitics and Family in Palestine." *Geoforum* 42: 306–15.

Haugbolle, Sune. 2005. "Public and Private Memory of the Lebanese Civil War." *Comparative Studies of South Asia, Africa, and Middle East* 25, no. 1: 191–203.

Hayner, Priscilla B. 2011. *Unspeakable Truths: Transitional Justice and the Challenge of Truth Commissions*. New York: Routledge.

Hirsch, John L. 2001. *Sierra Leone: Diamonds and the Struggle for Democracy*. Denver, Colo.: Lynne Rienner.

Human Rights Watch, India. 2003. "'We Have No Order to Save You': State Participation and Complicity in Communal Violence in Gujarat." *Human Rights Watch* 14, no. 3.

Hume, David. 2003. *A Treatise of Human Nature*. New York: Dover.

Jaffrelot, Christophe. 2012. "Gujarat 2002: What Justice for the Victims? The Supreme Court, the SIT, the Police, and the State Judiciary." *Economic and Political Weekly* 47, no. 8: 77–89.

James-Allen, Paul, Sheku B. S. Lahai, and Jamie O'Connell. 2003. *Sierra Leone's Truth and Reconciliation Commission and Special Court: A Citizen's Handbook*. https://www.ictj.org/sites/default/files/ICTJ-SierraLeone-Handbook-TRC-2003-English.pdf.

Johnson, Michael. 1986. *Class and Client in Beirut: The Sunni Muslim Community in the Lebanese State 1840–1985*. London: Ithaca Press.

Kapur, Ratna. 2006. "Normalizing Violence: Transitional Justice and the Gujarat Riots." *Columbia Journal of Gender and Law* 15, no. 3: 885–927.

Kelsall, Tim. 2005. "Truth, Lies, Ritual: Preliminary Reflections on the Truth and Reconciliation Commission in Sierra Leone." *Human Rights Quarterly* 27, no. 2: 361–91.

——. 2009. *Culture under Cross Examination: International Justice and the Special Court for Sierra Leone*. Cambridge: Cambridge University Press.

Kennedy, David. 2004. *The Dark Side of Virtue: Reassessing International Humanitarianism*. Princeton, N.J.: Princeton University Press.

Khalaf, Samir. 1987. *Lebanon's Predicament*. New York: Columbia University Press.

——. 1993. *Beirut Reclaimed*. Beirut: Dar An-Nahar.

——. 2002. *Civil and Uncivil Violence in Lebanon: A History of the Internationalization of Communal Conflict*. New York: Columbia University Press.

Khalaf, Samir, and P. Khoury, eds. 1993. *Recovering Beirut: Urban Design and Post-war Reconstruction.* Leiden, Netherlands: E. J. Brill.

Khalidi, W. 1979. *Conflict and Violence in Lebanon.* Cambridge: Cambridge University Press.

Kleinman, Arthur. 1997. "'Everything That Really Matters': Social Suffering, Subjectivity, and the Remaking of Human Experience in a Disordering World." *Harvard Theological Review* 90, no. 3: 315–35.

Kleinman, Arthur, Veena Das, and Margaret Lock, eds. 1997. *Social Suffering.* Berkeley: University of California Press.

Kleinman, Arthur, Veena Das, and Pamela Locke. 1996. "Introduction: Social Suffering." *Daedalus* 125, no. 1: xi–xx.

Kleinman, Arthur, and Joan Kleinman. 1996. "The Appeal of Experience, the Dismay of Images: Cultural Appropriations of Suffering in Our Times." *Daedalus* 125, no. 1: 1–23.

Kwon, Heonik. 2006. *After the Massacre: Commemoration and Consolation in Ha My and My Lai.* Los Angeles: University of California Press.

Lacan, Jacques. 1977. "The Agency of the Letter in the Unconscious, or Reason since Freud." In *Écrits: A Selection,* translated by Alan Sheridan, 146–78. New York: W. W. Norton.

Lacquer, Thomas W. 2009. "Mourning, Pity, and the Work of Narrative in the Making of 'Humanity.'" In *Humanitarianism and Suffering: The Mobilization of Empathy,* edited by Richard Ashby Wilson and Richard D. Brown, 31–57. Cambridge: Cambridge University Press.

Lamb, Susan. 2002. "Nullum Crimen, Nulla Poena Sine Lege in International Criminal Law." In *The Rome Statute of the International Criminal Court: A Commentary,* edited by Antonio Cassese, Paola Gaeta, and John R. W. D. Jones et al., 733–66. New York: Oxford University Press.

Lefebvre, Henri. 1991. *The Production of Space.* Oxford: Blackwell.

Leys, Ruth. 2011. "The Turn to Affect: A Critique." *Critical Inquiry* 37, no. 3: 434–72.

———. 2012. "Facts and Moods: Reply to My Critics." *Critical Inquiry* 38, no. 4: 882–91.

Lifton, Robert Jay. 1968. *Death in Life: Survivors of Hiroshima.* New York: Random House.

Luban, David. 2004. "A Theory of Crimes against Humanity." *Yale Journal of International Law* 29, no. 1: 85–167.

Makdisi, Saree. 1997. "Laying Claim to Beirut: Urban Narrative and Spatial Identity in the Age of Solidere." *Critical Inquiry* 23, no. 3: 661–705.

Makdisi, Ussama. 1996. "Reconstructing the Nation-State: The Modernity of Sectarianism in Lebanon." *Middle East Report* 200. *Minorities in the*

Middle East: Power and the Politics of Difference, July–September, 23–26, 30.

———. 2000. "Corrupting the Sublime Sultanate: The Revolt of Tanyus Shahin in Nineteenth-Century Ottoman Lebanon." *Society for Comparative Studies in Society and History* 42, no. 1: 180–208.

Malkki, Liisa. 1996. "Speechless Emissaries: Refugees, Humanitarianism, and Dehistoricization." *Cultural Anthropology* 11, no. 3: 377–404.

Mander, Harsh. 2004. *Cry, My Beloved Country: Reflections on the Gujarat Carnage 2002 and Its Aftermath.* Noida, India: Rainbow.

———. 2008. *Towards Healing? Seeking Paths for Justice and Reconciliation in Gujarat.* New Delhi: WISCOMP, Foundation for Universal Responsibility.

———. 2009. *Fear and Forgiveness: The Aftermath of Massacre.* New Delhi: Penguin Books.

Massumi, Brian. 2002. *Parables for the Virtual: Movement, Affect, and Sensation.* Durham, N.C.: Duke University Press.

May, Larry. 2005. *Crimes against Humanity: A Normative Account.* Cambridge: Cambridge University Press.

McBride, Julie. 2014. *The War Crime of Child Soldier Recruitment.* The Hague: TMC Asser Press.

Mehta, Deepak. 2006. "Collective Violence, Public Spaces, and the Unmaking of Men." *Men and Masculinities* 29: 204–25.

Mehta, Deepak, and Roma Chatterji, ed. 2007. "Introduction: Riots Discourses." *Domains, the International Journal for Ethnic Studies* 3: 11–16.

Meron, Theodor. 1987. *Human Rights in Internal Strife: Their International Protection.* Cambridge: Grotius.

Minow, Martha. 1998. *Between Vengeance and Forgiveness: Facing History after Genocide and Mass Violence.* Boston: Beacon Press.

Minow, Martha, and Nancy L. Rosenblum. 2002. *Breaking the Cycle of Hatred: Memory, Law, and Repair.* Princeton, N.J.: Princeton University Press.

Moeller, Susan D. 1999. *Compassion Fatigue: How the Media Sell Disease, Famine, War, and Death.* New York: Routledge.

Narrain, Arvind. 2004. "Truth Telling, Gujarat, and the Law." *The Sarai Reader Crises/Media* 4: 217–25. http://preview.sarai.net/journal/04_pdf/26arvind.pdf.

Nasr, Salim. 2000. "The New Social Map." In *Lebanon in Limbo: Postwar Society and State in an Uncertain Regional Environment,* edited by Theodor Hanf and Nawaf Salem, 143–58. Baden-Baden, Germany: Nomos Verlagsgesellschaft.

Neyrat, Frederic. 2010. "The Birth of Immunopolitics." Translated by Arne De Boever. *Parrhesia* 10: 31–38.

Nussbaum, Martha. 2013. *Political Emotions.* Cambridge, Mass.: Belknap Press of Harvard University Press.

Nyayagrah. n.d. "Progress Report: The Fight for Justice." http://www.aman biradari.org/Progress_report_Gujarat_legal_justice_programme.pdf.

Pandey, Gyanendra. 1990a. "The Colonial Construction of 'Communalism': British Writings of Banaras in the Nineteenth Century." In *Mirrors of Violence: Communities, Riots, and Survivors in South Asia,* edited by Veena Das, 134–71. Delhi: Oxford University Press.

———. 1990b. *The Construction of Communalism in Colonial North India.* Delhi: Oxford University Press.

Parker, D., and C. Karner. 2010. "Reputational Geographies and Urban Social Cohesion." *Ethnic and Racial Studies* 33, no. 8: 1451–70.

Patton, Paul. 1997. "The World Seen from Within: Deleuze and the Philosophy of Events." *Theory and Event* 29, no. 3: 315–26.

Pearson, David E. 1995. "Community and Sociology." *Society* 32, no. 5: 44–50.

People's Campaign for Justice and Reconciliation in Gujarat India for Equal in Rights. 2010. "Transformative Learning for Human Rights: Case of Nyayagrah (TLHR)." Compiled by Prita Jha, Johanna Lokhande, Nitika Agarwal, and Sajjad Hassan. People's Campaign for Justice and Reconciliation in Gujarat India for Equal in Rights.

People's Union for Civil Liberties. 2002. *Violence in Vadodara: A Report.* Vadodara and Vadoddara Shanti Abhiyan.

People's Union for Democratic Rights. 2002a. "Maaro! Kaapo! Baalo! State, Society, and Communalism in Gujarat." http://www.onlinevolunteers.org/gujarat/reports/pudr/.

———. 2002b. "Gujarat Genocide: Act Two: Six Months Later."

People's Union for Democratic Rights and People's Union for Civil Liberties. 1984. *Who Are the Guilty? Report of a Joint Inquiry into the Causes and Impact of the Riots in Delhi from 31 October to 10 November.* http://www.unipune.ac.in/snc/cssh/HumanRights/04%20COMMUNAL%20RIOTS/B%20-%20ANTI%20-%20SIKH%20RIOTS/01%20-%20DELHI/a.pdf.

Petryna, Adriana. 2002. *Life Exposed: Biological Citizens after Chernobyl.* Princeton, N.J.: Princeton University Press.

Picard, Elizabeth. 1999. *The Demobilization of the Lebanese Militias.* Prospects for Lebanon 9. Beirut: Center for Lebanese Studies.

———. 2000. "The Political Economy of Civil War in Lebanon." In *War, Institutions, and Social Change in the Middle East,* edited by Steven Hydeman, 292–324. Berkeley: University of California Press.

Povinelli, Elizabeth A. 2011. *Economies of Abandonment.* Durham, N.C.: Duke University Press.

Protevi, John. 2009. *Political Affect: Connecting the Social and the Somatic.* Minneapolis: University of Minnesota Press.

Rabinow, Paul, and Nikolas Rose. 2006. "Biopower Today." *BioSocieties* 1: 197–217.

Rajchman, John. 2005. Introduction to *Pure Immanence: Essays on Life,* by Gilles Deleuze. Translated by Anne Boyman. New York: Zone Books.

Ramdas, Lalita. 2005. "Thoughts on 1984." *Economic and Political Weekly* 40, no. 38: 4108–11.

Redfield, Peter. 2005. "Doctors, Borders, and Life in Crisis." *Cultural Anthropology* 20, no. 3: 328–61.

Redfield, Peter, and Erica Bornstein, eds. 2011. *Forces of Compassion: Humanitarianism between Ethics and Politics.* Santa Fe, N.M.: School of Advanced Research Press.

Ricoeur, Paul. 1990. *Time and Narrative.* Translated by David Pellauer. Chicago: University of Chicago Press.

Rorty, Richard. 1993. "Oxford Amnesty Lecture." In *On Human Rights: The Oxford Amnesty Lectures,* edited by S. Shute and S. Hurley, 111–34. New York: Basic Books.

Rose, Nikolas. 2007. *The Politics of Life Itself: Biomedicine, Power, and Subjectivity in the Twenty-First Century.* Princeton, N.J.: Princeton University Press.

Rowe, Peter G., and Hashim Sarkis, eds. 1998. *Projecting Beirut: Episodes in the Construction and Reconstruction of a Modern City.* New York: Prestel.

Salibi, Kamal. 2003. *A House of Many Mansions: A History of Lebanon Reconsidered.* London: I. B. Tauris.

Schabas, William A. 2001. *An Introduction to the International Criminal Court.* Cambridge: Cambridge University Press.

———. 2003. "The Relationship between Truth Commissions and International Courts: The Case of Sierra Leone." *Human Rights Quarterly* 25, no. 4: 1035–66.

———. 2004. "Conjoined Twins of Transitional Justice? The Sierra Leone Truth and Reconciliation Commission and the Special Court." *Journal of International Criminal Justice* 2, no. 4: 1082–99.

———. 2006. *The UN International Criminal Tribunals: The Former Yugoslavia, Rwanda, and Sierra Leone.* Cambridge: Cambridge University Press.

Sennet, Richard. 1994. *Flesh and Stone.* London: W. W. Norton.

Shahabuddin, Mohamed. 2004. "Does the Principle of Legality Stand in the Way of Progressive Development of Law?" *Journal of International Criminal Justice* 2, no. 4: 1007–17.

Shklar, Judith. 1990. *The Faces of Injustice.* New Haven, Conn.: Yale University Press.

Sierra Leone Truth and Reconciliation Commission. n.d. *Final Report of the Truth and Reconciliation Commission for Sierra Leone.* http://www.sierra leonetrc.org/.

Sivakumaran, Sandesh. 2010. "War Crimes before the Special Court for Sierra Leone: Child Soldiers, Hostages, Peacekeepers, and Collective Punishments." *Journal of International Criminal Justice* 8, no. 4: 1009–34.

Skaria, Ajay. 2011. "Relinquishing Republican Democracy: Gandhi's Ramarajya." *Postcolonial Studies* 14, no. 2: 203–29.

Smith, Adam. (1865) 2000. *The Theory of Moral Sentiments.* New York: Prometheus Books.

Special Court for Sierra Leone. 2002–3. "First Annual Report of the President of the Special Court for Sierra Leone, 2 December 2002 to 1 December 2003," 9. http://www.rscsl.org/Documents/AnRpt1.pdf.

———. n.d. "Report of the Secretary-General on the Establishment of a Special Court for Sierra Leone." Report S/2000/915. http://www.rscsl.org/Documents/Establishment/S-2000-915.

Spelman, E. 1997. *Fruits of Sorrow: Framing Our Attention to Suffering.* Boston: Beacon Press.

Stevenson, Lisa. 2012. "The Psychic Life of Biopolitics: Survival, Cooperation, and Inuit Community." *American Ethnologist* 39, no. 3: 592–613.

———. 2014. *Life Beside Itself: Imagining Care in the Canadian Arctic.* Los Angeles: University of California Press.

Stewart, Susan. 1984. *On Longing: Narratives of the Miniature, the Gigantic, the Souvenir, the Collection.* Baltimore: Johns Hopkins University Press.

Ticktin, Miriam. 2006. "Where Ethics and Politics Meet: The Violence of Humanitarianism in France." *American Ethnologist* 33, no. 1: 33–49.

Tönnies, Ferdinand. 2001. *Community and Civil Society.* Cambridge: Cambridge University Press.

Tuan, Yi-Fu. 1977. *Space and Place: The Perspective on Experience.* Minneapolis: University of Minnesota Press.

Turner, Bryan S. 1987. "A Note on Nostalgia." *Theory, Culture, and Society* 4, no. 1: 147–56.

Vernon, Richard. 2002. "What Is Crime against Humanity?" *Journal of Political Philosophy* 10, no. 3: 231–49.

———. 2012. *Historical Redress: Must We Pay for the Past?* London: Continuum Books.

———. 2013. "Crime against Humanity: A Defence of the 'Subsidiarity' View." *Canadian Journal of Law and Jurisprudence* 26, no. 1: 229–42.

Vitellone, Nicole. 2011. "Contesting Compassion." *The Sociological Review* 59, no. 3: 579–96.

Weber, Max. (1919) 1946. "Politics as a Vocation." In *Max Weber: Essays in Sociology,* edited and translated by H. H. Gerth and C. Wright Mills, 77–128. New York: Oxford University Press.

Weil, Simone. (1986) 2005. "Human Personality." In *Simone Weil: An Anthology*, edited and introduced by Siân Miles, 69–98. New York: Penguin.

Weiss, Thomas, and Larry Minear, eds. 1993. *Humanitarianism across Borders: Sustaining Civilians in Times of War*. Boulder, Colo.: Lynne Rienner.

Wharton, Sara. 2011. "The Evolution of International Criminal Law: Prosecuting 'New' Crimes before the Special Court for Sierra Leone." *International Criminal Law Review* 11, no. 2: 217–39.

White, Hayden. 1996. "The Modernist Event." In *The Persistence of History: Cinema, Television, and the Modern Event*, edited by Vivian Sobchack, 18–38. New York: Routledge.

Wilson, Richard Ashby, and Richard D. Brown, eds. 2011. *Humanitarianism and Suffering: The Mobilization of Empathy*. Cambridge: Cambridge University Press.

Index

affect, 2–3, 19–22; empathy and, 74–90, 94; humanitarianism and 40–41, 57–59; Thomas Lacquer on, 58–59; life-itself and, 196–97; Brian Massumi, 19–20; passion and, 19–20; pathos and, 16–23; as reasoned empathy, 81, 85, 94–95; sentimentalist thesis, 58; social relationality and, 19–20, 187; theory, 18–19, 19–20. *See also* compassion; emotion; empathy; nostalgia; pathos; *ressentiment*

affirmative biopolitics, 13–14, 186–87. *See also* biopolitics; Hardt, Michael; Negri, Antonio

afterlife(s), 1–33, 169–85; citizenship and, 69–70; city and, 139–42; community, 106–9; as event, 3–4, 174–85; metonym, 26; pathos and, 21–22; space and, 101–3, 136, 138, 163. *See also* event–afterlife paradigm; life

Agamben, Giorgio: bare life, 13; *dispositif*, 176; *homo sacer*, 25; life, 1; method, 174; sovereignty, 95–98, 176; state of exception, 70; subjectification, 2, 95, 98

Anijdar, Gil: on life, 24–25

animal, 25, 58–59, 191–92; becoming-animal, 191, 197

apparatus, 2; as *dispositif*, 24, 63,

176, 177–79, 182–83. *See also* Agamben, Giorgio; *dispositif*; Foucault, Michel

Arendt, Hannah, 25

Aristotle, 16; on rhetoric, 18–19

bare life (concept), 13, 23, 32, 70–71, 95–96. *See also* Agamben, Giorgio

Baxi, Upendra, 72–73

Beirut, 6, 10, 135–68, 189; civil war, 143–46; Hamra, 145–52; Hezbollah, 136, 138, 158–59, 160, 163; Saifi 155–58. *See also* Lebanese civil war

Benjamin, Walter, 180

biopolitics, 11–16, 23; affirmative, 13–14, 186; as biocentricity, 23–24; mass crimes, 62; sacred, 25. *See also* Agamben, Giorgio; Esposito, Roberto; Foucault, Michel

bios, 23–33, 169–97; citizenship and, 70, 74; spatiality and, 167–68; transformation from pathos, 59–64. *See also* afterlife; Esposito, Roberto; pathos

body, 13, 27, 29, 39, 60, 62, 160, 173, 216n41; in biological sense, 15, 60

Brown, Wendy: on *ressentiment*, 121–22, 124

communitas, 103; immunization, 186, 194–95; impersonal 186, 191. *See also* Campbell, Timothy
event (concept): actualization of, 178, 183–84; Deleuze and Guatarri on, 183–84; Marx on, 185; pure event, 178–85, 230n12; representation of, 179–82, 230n13; Hayden White, 180–81. *See also* afterlife; catastrophe; event-afterlife paradigm
event-afterlife paradigm, 3–7, 174–85, 229n6

form of life, 6, 15, 57, 58, 61, 177, 191, 197, 206n39; affect and, 14, 23–33, 38; biopolitics and, 27, 62, 186; body and, 62; death as a, 171, 219n27; individuation and, 27, 188, 206n39; as life itself, 13, 14, 22, 23, 101, 192, 195, 207n43; as metaphor, 63; metonymic, 26, 29; in reference to afterlife, 120, 130, 169–70, 172, 187, 192–93; in the social, 14, 191–92
Foucault, Michel: biopolitics, 11–14, 62; Deleuze on, 177–78, 182; *dispositif*, 176; governmentality, 95–96

Gandhi, 67–103; dayadharma, 93–93, 100; *Hind Swaraj,* 67; ramrajya, 93; satyagraha, 77–78, 90–94; Ajay Skaria and, 92, 93
Geras, Norman, 53–54. *See also* humanity
governmentality, 96, 170; affective 14, 58, 60; majoritarian, 93, 101
Gujarat, Indian state of, 67–103

Hardt, Michael, and Antonio Negri, 13–14
Hindus, 91, 93
humanitarianism, 4–6; affect and 20, 45–46, 57–58; law, 38–65; sentimentalist thesis, 58; sovereignty, 55–56. *See also* humanity
humanitarian law, 40–41, 55, 59, 189. *See also* international law
humanity (concept): afterlife, 38; Robert Buch, 21, 205n29; crimes against, 38–41, 43–65, 53–59, 72–73; Norman Geras on, 53–54; law, 35–65; metonymy, 54–57
human rights, 41–42, 58; Esposito on, 195–96; Human Rights Commission, 73, 79–80; Lacquer on 58–59
Hume, David, 27–28, 30, 206n41

ICC (International Criminal Court), 8, 31; Susan Lamb on, 45; Rome Statute and, 35
ICL (international criminal law), 37, 43–45, 63–65
identity: ascriptive, 70, 79, 88, 99–100, 108, 189, 193–96; citizenship, 14, 69, 88, 95, 98, 100–101, 123, 189; community, 85, 103, 107, 108, 112, 123–33, 193–94; faith-based, 10, 69, 106, 136–41, 185, 197; identity-in-space, 193; justice, 98; life, 101, 188, 190, 193–94, 196; mourning, 126; *ressentiment,* 115–16, 127, 131; sectarian, 69, 129, 138–39, 144, 159, 162; Sikhs, 107, 108, 116 126, 130; survivor, 127; violence, 107, 108, 114, 115, 141, 167

identity, 106, 129, 147, 149–51,
162–64; Sikhs and, 103–4; space,
162–63; spatiality of, 162–64,
227n37
representation, 63, 112, 143, 108,
179, 180–83. *See also* event
ressentiment, 113–14; Wendy Brown,
121–22; community of, 125–26;
mourning and, 119–20, 126–27;
temporality and, 116
rhetoric (concept), 18–19, 172
Rome Statute, 35, 39, 44, 52, 53,
209n17

sacralization: John Rajchman,
206–7n41; life, 24–25, 62–63
SCSL (Special Court for Sierra
Leone), 36–43
Sennet, Richard, 168
Sierra Leone, 6, 8, 14–15, 189;
AFRC case, 43, 46; Armed
Forces Revolutionary Council,
35–36; CDF case, 43; Civil
Defense Forces, 35–36; civil war,
31, 35–65; Lomé Peace Accord,
41–42; Revolutionary United
Front, 35–36; Revolutionary
United Front case, 43, 46. *See also*
child conscription; TRC
Sierra Leonean civil war, 6, 8, 14–15,
189
Sikhs, 9, 103–33, 189–90; violence
against, 103–5, 109–11
singularity, 11, 106, 180, 185,
187–88, 230n12. *See also* event
social, 1–33; affect and, 16–23, 187;
afterlife and, 170–71; citizenship
and, 88–90; communitas and,
123–33; distinction with society,
15–16, empathy and, 94–95;

international social, 35–65; justice
and, 80–81; pathos and, 76;
potentialities of, 6–7; rhetoric
and, 18–19; social outside
governmentality, 14–16; spatiality
of, 160, 163, 166–68; violence and,
69–70. *See also* life; violence
SOLIDERE (real estate company),
153–58, 225n23
sovereignty: contract, 70, 71;
Gandhian satyagraha, 92, 93;
humanity, 39–41, 55–56; pathos,
61–62; state of exception, 95–98.
See also Agamben, Giorgio
space: confessional space, 101–3,
163; emotion and, 10, 135–68; as
emplacement, 10, 21, 131, 141,
142, 160, 163; Henri Lefebvre,
141–42; nostalgia and, 142–59,
227n34; as spatiality, 16, 141–42,
163, 167; violence and, 10,
136, 139–42, 173. *See also* city;
SOLIDERE
subjectification, 2, 22, 30 108–9,
120, 125; pathos and, 172, 177;
place and, 31. *See also* identity
subjectivities, 2, 17, 20–22, 30–31,
172, 177, 190
suffering, 3, 140; affect and, 16–20;
community, 131, 133, 174–85;
individuation, 29; law and, 8,
31, 59–60; representation of, 4,
20–21, 107, 128; rhetoric, 172;
therapeutic governance and,
17–18
surrogate power, 70–74, 81, 97–98.
See also sovereignty

thanatopolitics, 12–14, 23–24, 27, 32,
170, 186–87. *See also* biopolitics

Yasmeen Arif is associate professor of sociology, Delhi School of Economics, University of Delhi, India. She has held teaching and research positions at the Graduate Institute, Geneva; the University of Minnesota–Twin Cities; the Center for the Study of Developing Societies (CSDS), Delhi; and the American University of Beirut, Lebanon.